BUREAUCRATIC REFORM IN PROVINCIAL CHINA
Ting Jih-ch'ang in Restoration Kiangsu, 1867–1870

Jonathan K. Ocko

Published by COUNCIL ON EAST ASIAN STUDIES, HARVARD UNIVERSITY *and distributed by* HARVARD UNIVERSITY PRESS, *Cambridge (Massachusetts) and London* 1983

The Council on East Asian Studies at Harvard University publishes a monograph series and, through the Fairbank Center for East Asian Research and the Japan Institute, administers research projects designed to further scholarly understanding of China, Japan, Korea, Vietnam, Inner Asia, and adjacent areas. Publication of this volume has been assisted by a grant from the Shell Companies Foundation.

Library of Congress Cataloging in Publication Data

Ocko, Jonathan K., 1946–
Bureaucratic reform in Provincial China.

(Harvard East Asian monographs; 103)
Includes index.
Bibliography: p.
1. Kiangsu Province (China)–Politics and government.
2. Bureaucracy–China–Kiangsu Province. 3. Ting, Jih-Ch'ang, 1823–1882. I. Title. II. Series.
JQ1519.K542024 1982 354.51'13'000924 82–15595
ISBN 0–674–08617–1

To the memory of Mary Wright
and with love and thanks to my wife, Aggie

Acknowledgments

Without the late Mary Wright, this study would have been impossible. She acquired for Yale the unique political papers of Ting Jih-ch'ang, upon which I have relied heavily, and she suggested to me that an examination of his career would test her view of the T'ung-chih Restoration. It is a mark of Professor Wright's rare distinction as a scholar and teacher that, in the interests of knowledge, she set her own work before her students as ideas to be challenged rather than as truths to be revered.

Jonathan Spence was a superb adviser. Patiently instructive and intellectually stimulating, he also taught by the example of his own unique, thought-provoking work. I have benefited from three additional "lao-shih": K. C. Liu and Paul Cohen, whose encouragement, support, and advice have been invaluable; and Parker Huang, whose excellence as a language teacher made my research possible. Critical readings of various versions of the entire manuscript by John Schrecker, Mary Rankin, Susan Jones, and Philip Kuhn, and numerous conversations with James Polachek and Andrew Hsieh sharpened my understanding of nineteenth-century China. My colleague at North Carolina State, Tony La Vopa, also made valuable suggestions. A special thanks is due Susan Naquin, who not only repeatedly incisively read the manuscript, but also prodded me to finish by asking that dread question only good friends have the temerity to ask: "When are you going to get done and move on to something else?" In Taiwan, Lü Shih-ch'iang generously shared with me his own research on Ting.

Librarians at Yale's East Asian Collection, Harvard Yenching, UNC-Chapel Hill, Academia Sinica, and the Library of Congress have helped bring this work to fruition by assisting my search for sources. For their editorial polishing, I would like to thank Mary Ann Flood and Florence Trefethen.

To my wife, Aggie, to whom this book is in part dedicated, I acknowledge a special debt, for, even when I woke her in the middle of the night to read a section on taxes or yamen underlings, she managed to respond "enthusiastically," and with editorial acumen. Finally, to my children, Matthew and Peter, for both of whom this work has for too long been too much a part of their lives. And to Sue Naquin, I can say, "I'm done and moving on to something else."

Contents

Tables

Note: In order to keep clear the distinction between various official ranks and those persons who hold them, capital letters will be used whenever persons are meant, lower-case letters whenever the rank or office is intended (e.g. magistrate, as a generic term, Magistrate for a particular holder of that office).

ONE

Introduction

The Ch'ing dynasty was ailing—so concluded a number of late eighteenth- and early nineteenth-century Chinese scholar-officials. They wrote with concern about what they perceived to be vitally threatening problems: rapidly increasing population exerting inflationary pressure on prices of land and services and limiting opportunities for upward social mobility; the beginning of a downward slide in the standard of living (the social critic, Kung Tzu-chen, commented that the rich were becoming poor and the poor hungry); commercialization of all aspects of life; and military and bureaucratic decay.[1] Although these phenomena did not undermine the fundamental stability of the dynasty until perhaps the 1820s, by 1800 it is already clear that in the minds of these writers something was amiss. Their growing anxiety occasioned around this time a significant shift in political thinking.

In the relative tranquillity of the mid-eighteenth century, the epitome of good governance had been the detached magistrate who "avoided trouble":

> The [good] official does not investigate matters too deeply. Rather, he finishes those that can be finished and involve fewer documents. Those who are without talent press their investigation, thoroughly checking it and piling up troublesome documents. . . . The magistrate ought not to stir up trouble over small matters.[2]

Peace and prosperity demanded little of the magistrate in the way of leadership; moral charisma was unnecessary. But, in the midst of a heightened sense of crisis, the insipid governance characterized by "avoidance of trouble" was intolerable to the aroused scholar-officials who castigated it as "perfunctory" (*yin-hsun*) and pernicious, and descried it as an abnegation of the Confucian ideal of activist sage-statesmen.[3] The chasm between their ideal and the status quo induced a transformative tension (recently discussed by Thomas Metzger) in these critics, who consequently "felt urgently obliged to re-examine every institution and practice in order to recreate a working balance and harmony among them" and thereby close what was acknowledged to be a growing gap between state and society.[4]

Influenced by the lesson of the Classic *The Great Learning* that the individual who wishes to bring order to the state must first cultivate himself, these officials turned inward. They concluded that they, in the aggregate as the bureaucracy, were the source of the trouble. Bureaucratic decay in this view was not one among many symptoms of social change, but itself the cause. Heterodox groups, such as the White Lotus, the Triads, and the Taiping, sought to close the gap by eliminating the existing state. Officials, however, looked at the world through a bureaucratic lens. For them, the state and the elite that staffed it were the touchstone. A consensus arose that the Confucian scholar-official once again had to put his learning to use, to manage the world (*ching-shih*).

Those who saw the need for change were, nevertheless, not agreed on how it should be undertaken. Thomas Metzger has suggested that we analyze the issue of governmental approach in antipodal terms of "radical" and "moderate."[5] While I would allow more overlap between the categories than he (Lin Tse-hsu, for instance, could be included in both), the categories are still analytically useful. "Radicals" tended toward the "euphoric" view that order derived from an exemplary center created by the moral leadership of men of spirit who believed in the ability of scholarship to affect action.[6] Their political programs were built on a concern with "right principles" and were couched in macroscopic terms. Hostile to the perfunctory and ambitious careerist official, "radicals" emphasized internal motivation and esprit in the selection and promotion of officials and showed little interest in or knowledge of the realities of daily governance. Given such a definition, the sobriquet "radical" could fairly be applied to the Ch'ing-i (Righteous Party) within the metropolitan (central government) bureaucracy and to Tseng Kuo-fan.

"Moderates," though not devoid of spirit or moral fervor, were inclined to attack problems of order through the use of coercive and managerial institutions. They were utilitarians, interested in results, not in general principles. To them Teng Hsiao-p'ing's comment that the color of the cat is irrelevant as long as it catches mice would have made eminent sense. Moral cultivation for "moderates" such as Wei Yuan, one of the compilers of the *Huang-ch'ao ching-shih wen-pien* (Collected essays on statecraft, published in 1826), was, observed Hao Chang, "not in itself adequate to attain practical statesmanship; it had to be supplemented by institutional arrangements."[7] Still, the orientation of the "moderates" was inward-looking, for the reform they sought was implemented more often than not on the basis of how it would affect internal bureaucratic discipline rather than in terms of the ultimate needs of the people. Wei Yuan's *Essays on Statecraft,* the culmination of the scholar-officials' re-examination of institutions and practices, tells us more about how to *manage* socioeconomic problems than about their sources or long-term solutions. Indeed, for most of the nineteenth century, scholar-officials confidently presumed that China's difficulties were ones of administration, that, once the proper men were selected as officials and appropriately disciplined, societal harmony would be restored. Rarely did any scholar-official get at the root of China's problems, its social inequities.

At least into the 1860s, these disparate modes constituted a matrix of political thought that was unadulterated by Western elements. "Radicals" reacted to the West with what Benjamin Schwartz has called "muscular Confucianism," while "moderates" conjured ways to employ the West's "Faustian energy" for Chinese purposes without compromising Chinese values.[8] Some scholar-officials had departed sufficiently from core political beliefs to be able to abandon the concept of world empire and to commit themselves to the ideal of "collective power and achievement."[9] But, like the wayward members of a netted school of fish which detach themselves from the core group to explore the periphery, these men could go no farther. It is not until the 1880s and 1890s that one encounters within the intellectual mainstream discussion of alternative legitimizing principles for China's political system.

The debate between "radical" and "moderate" over political approach was neither arcane nor arid; it colored, if subliminally at times, an ongoing struggle for control of bureaucratic reform among the imperial institution and metropolitan bureaucracy, senior provincial officials, and non-bureaucratic elites. In the initial three decades of the nineteenth century, the imperial institution, represented by the Emperors Chia-ch'ing (1796–1824) and Tao-kuang (1826–1850), took the initiative in reinvigorating the bureaucracy.

Almost immediately upon his assumption of power, Chia-ch'ing moved to identify the administrative deficiencies and abuses that bribery and mutual face-saving had previously concealed. Impeachments by censors were welcomed, and capital appeals (*ching-k'ung*) from alleged victims of injustice were facilitated. As the revelations, particularly of tax surcharges and manipulations, accumulated, the provincial officials were stimulated to attack the sources of trouble. (Since the responsibility for handling the increasingly numerous appeals had been placed upon the governors, however, it seems reasonable to suggest that they acted as much to relieve themselves of that burden in order to forestall being disciplined as to redress the people's grievances.)[10] To ensure that initiative would not be stifled and to prevent vigorous officials from being consigned to backwater posts, Chia-ch'ing also ordered changes in the disciplinary regulations. Disciplinary measures for petty infractions were eliminated, and the minor demerits that previously had undermined the careers of capable men were not allowed to be considered in the evaluation of officials for transfer or promotion to important posts.[11] Complementing these actions was the cooperative support that Chia-ch'ing and Tao-kuang lent to the effort of some provincial officials such as Chiang Yu-hsien, Governor-

General of Liang-kiang, to create from among outstanding censors and Hanlin scholars a cadre of able intendants and prefects who could serve as crisis managers. Frequently selected outside of normative procedures, these men were appointed in a manner designed to break established bureaucratic relationships, and were, in today's parlance, both "red" (spirited men of impeccable academic backgrounds) and "expert" (skilled administrators).

As James Polachek has shown, however, imperial activism waned by 1840 and thereafter resurfaced only rarely. Within a decade, a critical scholar would conclude that the imperial institution was "frail" and unaware of its own best interests.[12] Even before this gloomy assessment was made, provincial governors, particularly such officials as Chiang Yu-hsien, Liang Chang-chü, T'ao Chu, and Lin Tse-hsu, had already begun to reassert their moral leadership vis-à-vis the Emperor. Like a good cadre in contemporary China, these Ch'ing governors claimed (credibly) to be seeking power not for self-aggrandizement but to serve better the general interest. Specifically, they sought to improve local government by strengthening their ties to and tightening their discipline of the magistrate. To be effective in this enterprise, the governor needed to influence the appointment of the key intermediate supervisory officials, the intendants and prefects.[13] We have seen how, with imperial support, Chiang Yu-hsien achieved this by breaking routinized appointment patterns. Yet, without sustenance from the Emperor, any reformist impetus was susceptible to the animus of inertia emanating from a status-quo-oriented metropolitan bureaucracy.

Indeed, the experience of Chiang Yu-hsien was not to be repeated. In the 1840s, routinization set in under the influence of the Grand Secretary Mu-ch'ang-a. Mediocrity and sychophancy prevailed until the Hsien-feng Emperor, buoyed by his ascension in 1850 and pressured by the Taiping Rebellion, turned again to "men of spirit" like Tseng Kuo-fan.[14] Through the personal staffs (*mu-fu*) of Tseng, Hu Lin-i, and Li Hung-chang, soldiers and men with only lowly degrees but ample governmental abilities also entered officialdom. However, although Tseng eventually secured appointments for many of his staff (*mu-yu*), the latter were not united by either the tight personal linkages or singleness of purpose that characterized the officials around Chiang Yu-hsien. Li Hung-chang's alleged network was interested in increasing revenues rather than improving local government, while later provincial officials possessed neither the political connections nor "moral" clout to influence provincial appointments. Furthermore, at the outset of the T'ung-chih reign in 1860, the pendulum swung away from relatively open selection and promotion procedures. The officials in the metropolitan bureaucracy and, for that matter, Tseng Kuo-fan had never been completely comfortable with the idea of allowing ambitious men whose only credentials were exceptional abilities to serve as local officials, not to mention high ones. The Board of Civil Appointments ordered that preference be given to successful examination candidates.[15] For the next forty years, until the last decade of the dynasty, "outsiders," with the exception of those qualified solely by wealth, were largely excluded from the bureaucracy.

It was precisely this lack of access to office that created among the scholar-official local elite (qua gentry) the constituency for non-bureaucratic reformism.[16] Increased population, tight examination quotas, and competition from purchasers of official ranks combined to make it increasingly difficult in the nineteenth century for the educated man to win positions in government. A candidate for the lowest degree had only a one in six thousand chance of ever obtaining an official post. Even if one became upwardly mobile on the national scene, land scarcity precluded consolidating family status and security through estate-building.[17] Competition for income and power at the local level was consequently intense and often clashed with the interests of the local official. Anger at the latter fueled the old frustration at being excluded from officialdom in favor of lesser men and induced a jaundiced view of the bureaucracy. There was, however, no antipathy toward officials per se, for the local elite's vision of change was structured on the premise of their employment as a new type of sub-county official. Having frequently gained experience as directors of local waterworks projects, foundling homes, and schools, the local elite could argue that they were not only closer to the people than were the officials; they were also equally capable administrators . By eliminating levels of bureaucracy between them and the Emperor, reasoned the local elite, above and below would be united and a working balance restored to society.

There were, then, many elements of nineteenth-century society that acknowledged the need for change. At issue was who should control the pace and style of that change. In 1850 the question was dramatically "called" when the Taiping rebels forcefully advanced their case for a cataclysmically transformed China. Though the concurrent Second Opium War with foreigners and Moslem and Nien Rebellions were not as individually threatening to Ch'ing sovereignty as was the Taiping, the concatenation of these events confronted the Ch'ing with the feared dyadic harbinger of dynastic catastrophe–internal chaos and external calamity (*nei-luan wai-huan*). To avert collapse, the Ch'ing *de minimō* had to meet the immediate imperatives of suppressing the rebellions and stabilizing foreign relations–feats it accomplished successfully. But the dynasty that survived and embarked on the arduous task of reconstruction was qualitatively different from before.

In the 1860s, imperial power, which, while previously not activist, had at least been clearly delineated, was amorphous in shape. With a boy Emperor, T'ung-chih, on the throne, the regent Prince Kung was putatively in charge, but in fact there was rule by committee, in which Prince Kung and the boy's mother, the Empress Dowager Tz'u-hsi (later to develop autocratic power), were first among equals. In the absence of a strong figure on the throne, the metropolitan bureaucracy assumed the role of conservator, defining and sustaining the interests of the center. Nevertheless, conservators are agents of others, by nature cautious and predisposed toward stabilization rather than change. Without a vibrant imperial institution, there could be neither clear-cut direction for the dynasty nor support for innovation from below.

Other troubling residua from the Rebellion were a latent anti-Manchuism and an emboldened local elite. Chinese scholar-officials had sided with the dynasty against the Taiping, yet it is precipitate to assume that elite Chinese could have been unaffected by the anti-Manchu slogans of the rebels. Indeed, the inherent tension between the local elite and the center not only was not attenuated by the Rebellion but also was increasingly tinged with ethnicity.[18]

Composed of the more truculent rural gentry directors as well as scholar-official types, the local elite was hardly a homogeneous group with uniform interests; but its disparate elements shared a formidable capacity to affect official policies that even in the best of times elicited from officials caution rather than arbitrariness. The relationship between the government and elites was constantly in flux, oscillating between cooperation and antagonism, shifting in its balance of power. In the 1860s, the local elites, confident that an insecure dynasty was reluctant to challenge them, undermined its rehabilitation by concealing from taxation much of the land newly recultivated and infringed upon its monopoly on justice and public order. Political centrifugalism was a problem, not at the provincial level, but within the provinces, at the county and sub-county level. In the second half of the nineteenth century, the duel for political dominance in the countryside between governors and their ostensible agents, local government, on the one hand and the local elite on the other, was continuous.

Unhappily for a governor, another legacy of the post-bellum period was a diminution in the efficacy of his arsenal, particularly of local government. The county magistrate's yamen (or office) was for most Chinese a symbol of imperial power and their only point of contact with the state. Weak, ineffectual magistrates who could control neither their own underlings nor influential members of the community ineluctably undermined the majesty and reach of the dynasty. Yet, not only was the pool of potential local officials diluted in quality in the 1860s, but structural problems also impeded governors' ability to eliminate the incompetent from service. Yamen underlings (clerks and runners), the magistrates' "teeth and claws," all too often dominated an official and became the de facto administration of a county. For the dynasty to re-establish local control, the underlings had either to be by-passed, replaced, or transformed.

The last element of the new post-Rebellion situation was the permanent and more intrusive presence of the Western powers which had obtained major concessions through humiliating treaties in 1858 and 1860. Fortunately for the Ch'ing, the Western powers determined that a cohesive China was preferable to a fragmented one and refrained from taking excessive advantage of her weakness. The Cooperative Policy (1860–1870) that they adopted tempered the imperialist competition among them and afforded the Chinese a respite from significant Western incursions.[19] Within this context, the Ch'ing pursued a mildly adventurist policy by allowing its diplomatic agents, especially in places such as Shanghai, to test the limits of the Cooperative Policy by attempting to retrieve old concessions and to resist new demands without arousing the ire of the Western powers. The external task was merely to *manage* the foreigner while the primary endeavor of domestic reconstruction proceeded; yet, the work of foreign affairs, insulated to a degree from entrenched bureaucratic and conservative opponents, afforded a relative freedom of action, and, abetted by the Cooperative Policy, had achieved institutional breakthroughs—the Tsungli Yamen, armories, and schools—and had stemmed in places the tide of foreign expansion.

Foreign affairs, however, will not be considered within this study. Rather, our attention will be devoted to the more vital domestic arena where there was no version of the Cooperative Policy, where there was less freedom of action, and where the modest successes of foreign affairs were not replicated.

To understand why the Ch'ing failed to re-establish perhaps even ante-bellum levels of governance, I will focus in the following pages on the tenure of Ting Jih-ch'ang as Kiangsu Financial Commissioner and Governor during the years 1867 to 1870. This study does not purport to be a biography. It is instead a detailed examination of three basic aspects of provincial administration—law and society, fiscal affairs, and personnel—in which Ting is merely a device that affords us a singular insight into the processes of the Ch'ing bureaucratic machine.

But why Ting Jih-ch'ang and why this particular province?

Unquestionably, as G. William Skinner says, "Kiangnan is not China," but Kiangsu, especially its southern portion, Kiangnan, was the site of the Taiping capital and the area most devastated by the Rebellion and its suppression.[20] Hence the province was the cynosure of the dynasty's recovery efforts. Similarly, although Ting Jih-ch'ang was not the archetypal Confucian official (in fact he was somewhat idiosyncratic), by the consensus of his colleagues he was one of the ablest provincial officials of his time.[21] His was one of the best and strongest efforts the dynasty mounted in the wake of the Rebellion. Of use to us not because he was an original thinker or a policy-maker, but because he was a diligent and, at times, creative administrator, Ting was an amalgam of the fervent moralism of the "radical" and the pragmatic managerial orientation of the "moderate." He was, moreover, a transitional figure, a man of avant-garde ideas in foreign policy, but alternative domestic political models were as yet beyond his ken.

Precisely as a function of his atypicality, of his lack of the high degree and the political power and influence of some of his contemporaries (Hu Lin-i, Tseng Kuo-fan, Shen Pao-chen, and Li Hung-chang), Ting had a peculiar perspective. He was an "outsider" on the "inside." As an "outsider," Ting was able to set himself apart from the established way, stand back, and critically examine it, while, unlike other "outsiders," he was also a part of the establishment, an official, and later a Governor with direct access to the throne. As Governor, moreover, Ting occupied a Janus-like position in that he dealt with both the broader national issues and the daily concerns of local government. Indeed, his unique political papers include not simply memorials, but also orders and directives to subordinates, replies and reports from them, and comments on their performances. We are consequently able to move beyond administrative guidelines and exhortations and obtain a grasp of their impact at the local level, where lay the "center of political gravity."[22]

Inevitably, in the course of this study, there arose the question of whether the Ch'ing had achieved in the 1860s a dynastic "restoration," that exceptional case of a renewed lease on life after the suppression of a major rebellion. In her pivotal study, *The Last Stand of Chinese Conservatism: The T'ung-chih Restoration,* the late Mary Wright described the key elements of the Restoration's domestic program as the re-establishment of the network of local control, the rehabilitation of the economy, the reform of local government (the inadequacy of which officials considered at fault for the Rebellion), and the restoration of a system of government by superior civil officials. There is no doubt that the Ch'ing dynasty *survived* the Rebellions, but the issue of its *revival,* of its restoration of vitality, must be examined more critically; for the major structural change that the dynasty needed was in late-nineteenth-century China still an impossibility. Too many people were attuned to or profited from (or at least believed they benefited from) dynastic dysfunctions.

TWO

The Man and the Province

Institutional history has the unfortunate characteristic of being written too often *in absentia hominis*. Obviously, it is essential to understand the ideal structures of institutions, but institutions, after all, come to life only when manipulated by people; and these heterogeneous people, together with the environments in which institutions are situated, inevitably transmogrify ideal forms. Therefore, before beginning our substantive discussion, it is necessary to say something about the complex character of the man through whose eyes we shall see and of the province in which he served.

THE MAN

Born in 1823 in the backward northeast corner of Kwangtung, Ting Jih-ch'ang epitomized the people of his native Feng-shun county—tough, fractious, and argumentative. Relentlessly ambitious, Ting determinedly sought to excel, much like Canton's *hung-mien* tree, whose branches in their search for sunlight will always reach higher than those of the surrounding trees. Though desirous of his superiors' approbation, if forced to choose, the prickly and abrasive Ting preferred their recognition and attention to their perfunctory approval.

Convinced that old dilemmas could be resolved in a day by determined men, Ting tended to approach problems with an impetuous certitude that not infrequently offended his colleagues. Yet, without his conviction and his ambition, both derided by Tseng Kuo-fan, the Restoration's leading provincial official, Ting would have lacked the drive that made him, in the words of Feng Kuei-fen, a leading Soochow literatus and erstwhile secretary of Lin Tse-hsu, Kiangsu's best Governor since Lin Tse-hsu.[1]

Ting's origins were modest. His father was a pharmacist, who, though reputed to be something of a local philanthropist, on his death bequeathed his family "just enough to help with bread and water." Ting was nonetheless able to attend school at a local temple; and, just before his twentieth birthday, he became a licentiate, thereby acquiring privileged status in society. Subsequent distinction in the annual examination (*sui-k'ao*) required of all licentiates earned Ting the rank of stipendiary student (*ling-sheng*).[2] Unlike the common man, he could throw away his hoe and plough, abandon his unfertile fields, and rely upon his quick mind and deft brush for a livelihood.

Ting's essays were noticed not only by the educational officials but also by others: Feng-shun's able and popular Magistrate, Chang Na-t'ai, accepted Ting as a protégé; an unidentified patron underwrote Ting's expenses for the provincial examination in Canton and may have purchased for him the rank of student of the Imperial Academy; and the Hui-ch'ao-chia Taotai, Li Chang-yü, impressed by Ting's writing, invited him to join his staff as a Secretary (*mu-yu*).[3] As a Secretary, Ting's forte was cogent analysis of current affairs and political problems.

While the Feng-shun gazetteer's praise of the clarity and depth of Ting's writing is merited, it exaggerated in suggesting that Ting's contemporaries considered his papers the near equal of such great stylists as Chia I, Lu Chih, Ou-yang Hsiu, and Su Shih.[4] Unfortunately, Ting never was able to master either the refined eight-legged style (*pa-ku*) or the arcane themes demanded in the provincial examinations which he twice failed. Embittered by the format of the examinations and skeptical of the abilities of those who passed them, a chagrined Ting Jih-ch'ang asserted to a friend that he should have passed, that he would not forever be obscured, and that someday he would have power and the last laugh on those who had mocked him for his shortcomings.[5] Denied the *chu-jen* degree, and painfully aware of its value in terms of prestige, influence, and social mobility, Ting retained throughout his career an antinomic mixture of awe and disdain for higher degrees.

Like so many others of his generation, Ting was a victim of the genuine difficulty of passing the examinations. Some, such as Hung Hsiu-ch'uan, who were frustrated at the first level became rebels. But Ting had survived the initial test and had been drawn into the establishment. Moreover, the examination system provided, in a sense, two alternatives for its repeaters and failures: they could become either teachers of prospective candidates or secretaries to the successful but frequently administratively incompetent products of the examinations. As a teacher, one's ironic task was to instruct students in the tricks of writing a successful examination essay. A secretary, or *mu-yu,* was an expert either in law, taxation, general administration, or document drafting.[6] Since the examination demanded stylized rote answers to questions on the Classics, officials who had obtained higher degrees and then were dispatched directly to their first appointments as local officials rarely had a working knowledge of statecraft and thus required a *mu-yu* to handle the daily administration of their offices. Even for experienced officials, *mu-yu* were a necessity in busy districts.[7]

Ting followed both these courses—each, with rare exceptions, a dead end for an ambitious man. For three years after his initial failure in the provincial examinations in 1845, he taught in a small two-room school house he had built himself, and then served two years as a Magistrate's Secretary in neighboring Chieh-yang hsien. Unsuccessful again in 1850, Ting remained an itinerant Secretary until success in 1855 as the leader of a local militia against bandit allies of the Taiping rebels in the Ch'ao-chou area earned him appointment to a minor educational post in Hainan and concurrent elevation to the rank of Magistrate. (An official's nominal rank often exceeded his actual office.)[8]

In 1858, just short of thirty-six (about the same age at which a *chin-shih* might expect a magistracy), Ting was promoted to the magistracy of Wan-an in Kiangsi. He was at last on the threshold of a successful career. Fashioned after those of his old teacher, the former Feng-shun Magistrate Chang Na-t'ai, Ting's swift, sure actions and policies were praised by the Wan-an gazetteer and were later used by Ting as an example to which new magistrates should aspire. Within a month of his arrival in Wan-an, it is said, he reduced the number of backlogged legal cases from over a hundred to only three or four and quickly settled all subsequent litigation; by strict supervision he controlled the corruption of yamen underlings; he lectured the students twice monthly on the need for learning and proper behavior, and paid the traveling expenses of students taking the provincial examinations; and he began the reconstruction of the local academy (*shu-yuan*) and the temple of the city god, both of which had been previously destroyed by the Taiping rebels.[9]

Ting had departed Wan-an for Kwangtung in late 1859, little expecting that a year and a half later he would, under less happy circumstances, again relinquish a Kiangsi magistracy. He had been sent to Kwangtung at the behest of its provincial officials to work on foreign affairs (*yang-wu*), the nature of which remains obscure.[10] In any case, Ting was soon reassigned to Kiangsi, not, however, to Wan-an, whose people had petitioned for his return, but to its neighboring hsien, Lu-ling. There the Taiping Rebellion impinged upon Ting's career for a second time, and dismissal rather than promotion was the result. Called from Lu-ling by the Prefect to assist in the recovery of the prefectural city of Chi-an, Ting saw his very success become his downfall, for, as the Taiping forces evacuated Chi-an, they marched through Lu-ling, taking the county seat. In May 1861, Ting was cited for failing to prepare his defenses in advance, removed from office, and deprived of his rank.[11]

After a short hiatus, Tseng Kuo-fan, at the suggestion of Li Hung-chang, rescued Ting from oblivion by inviting him to join his secretariat (*mu-fu*) at Anking. So began Ting's close relationship with Li and Tseng. Ting had probably come to Li's attention in 1859 while he was Wan-an Magistrate and Li was in Tseng's secretariat, serving as liaison between Tseng and the Governor of Kiangsi.[12] Apparently attracted by Ting's administrative talents,

Li in subsequent years relied upon Ting's abilities and promoted his career. Nonetheless, although Li was his patron, Ting was never Li Hung-chang's creature. For Ting had an independent mind and, unlike Li, a genuine concern for "the basic questions of administrative and political reform."[13] It was this commitment that tenuously cemented Ting's ties with Tseng Kuo-fan, who never quite overcame his hesitancies about Ting's character. Tseng both acknowledged and used Ting's considerable skills and was instrumental in having Ting's rank restored, but he also once blocked a promotion for Ting. Tseng, who tended to withdraw from advocacy of positions rather than risk conflict, was repeatedly repelled by Ting's harshness toward his subordinates, his brash assertiveness, and his aggressive espousal of change.[14] Indeed, it is probable that both Li and Tseng regarded Ting as a "loose cannon" whose activities and interests did not always serve theirs. Thus, while Ting owed the resuscitation of his career to Li and Tseng, in later years whatever success his policies achieved was largely his own, for he did not tailor his views to cultivate their patronage, and they rarely lent support to his initiatives.

In 1861, however, Ting was still just one of Tseng's two hundred secretaries, drafting policy suggestions and seeking a way to catch Tseng's eye. Although Ting succeeded in doing this with memoranda on land-tax reduction and on the likin, a value-added transit and *in situ* tax, it was to be an expertise in foreign ordnance that catapulted him upward.[15] It seems unlikely that his earlier foreign-affairs work in Kwangtung had involved armaments; otherwise Tseng would not have wasted Ting's talents on taxation problems. Ting probably began his study of foreign arms in Anking, where Tseng had commenced his experiments in the manufacture of guns and shells before Ting joined his staff in late 1861; and, just over six months later, Ting was assisting Li Han-chang, older brother of Li Hung-chang and then Tseng's principal adviser on likin problems, to purchase weapons in Hong Kong for shipment to Hung-chang's Huai Army in Kiangsu.[16] Indeed, Ting, ostensibly sent to Kwangtung to raise likin revenues for Tseng (and rewarded with return of his rank for his skill at it), spent most of his time preparing earthworks and manufacturing arms for the Kwangtung provincial officials.[17]

These officials were reluctant to release Ting for duty elsewhere. By arguing that Ting's services were still essential to the success of the imperial forces, Yen Tuan-shu, the Governor-General of Liang-kwang, was twice able to resist Li Hung-chang's efforts to have Ting transferred to Shanghai. Li, however, having been rebuffed in January and April 1863, in November finally persuaded the court that the need for Ting's skills was more urgent in Kiangsu than in Kwangtung. Thus it was that, in December 1863, Ting joined Li's staff as supervisor of an arsenal staffed by foreign craftsmen.[18] Later that month and again in April 1864, Li Hung-chang praised Ting's work and, stressing his role in the capture of Soochow and Ch'ang-chou, recommended him for promotion to the ranks first of Magistrate of an independent department (*chih-li chou chih-chou*) and then to Prefect.[19]

This interest in him shown by high officials and his rapid advancement–both results of his newly acquired abilities–surely would have encouraged Ting to develop his knowledge further, however he first came by it. Ting was apparently undeterred by the fact that foreign affairs (*yang-wu*) in the Ch'ing were a shoal upon which official reputations and careers foundered, and by the possibility that he could therefore just as easily dig his own grave as lay the foundation for a meteoric rise. Yet, for the most part, although Ting himself may have felt defensive about his association with *yang-wu,* he managed to avoid being stigmatized by it, and at the end of his career had become one of the best informed and most perceptive of China's "Westerner watchers."[20]

While in Kwangtung, Ting had demonstrated another talent that attracted the attention of his superiors and drew him into foreign affairs–an ability to negotiate shrewdly. Mao Hung-pin, Yen Tuan-shu's successor as Liang-kwang Governor-General, considered Ting's reconciliation of two feuding generals the key to the recapture of a Taiping-held city, and described him as a talented, perceptive man, outstanding among his contemporaries.[21] And in May 1864, Li Hung-chang, with great faith in Ting's skill, entrusted to him the difficult and delicate task of arranging the disbanding of Charles "Chinese" Gordon's Ever Victorious Army (EVA).[22]

Ting handled this assignment like a consummate diplomat. Aware that Gordon was under pressure from Harry Parkes, the British Consul in Shanghai, and Robert Hart, Inspector-General of the Customs Service, to retain the force, Ting played upon Gordon's pride, encouraging him to adhere to his original decision to disperse the EVA; eventually they achieved a satisfactory compromise.[23] The Chinese probably overestimated Parkes's and Hart's influence over Gordon, thereby making Ting's achievement even more notable.[24] From the Chinese viewpoint, not only had Ting successfully managed the prickly Gordon, but he also had indirectly handled the infamous Harry Parkes, the most insistently belligerent of the British diplomats. His reputation as a negotiator proven, Ting was promoted to the post of Shanghai Taotai, a position that entailed constant dealing with the aggressive foreign community.[25]

Over the next four years, Ting became more deeply involved in domestic affairs as he was appointed to successively higher positions in Kiangsu: Liang-huai Salt Controller, Soochow Financial Commissioner in 1867, and finally Governor in 1868. (He retired from this last post in 1870 in order to mourn his mother's death.) Having arrived at the top of the provincial bureaucracy, Ting turned his early struggles into a source of pride and political advantage. Humbly describing himself in a memorial to the Emperor as "a man up from the fields" (*ch'i tzu t'ien-jen*), Ting also told subordinate officials in letters of reprimand that, had they, as he, shared the sufferings of the common people and served as a secretary, they would be neither so insensitive to the plight of the commoners nor so incompetent in administration.[26] Conversely, though, Ting felt a certain vulnerability about his humble origins and "irregular" rise that manifested itself in defensiveness about his stodgy moralism, and, combined with institutional constraints, in periodic uncertainty in his use of authority. Thus Ting, the tough, innovative administrator, could also be a lax supervisor whose bark was worse than his bite.

Ting's status-consciousness and need to be accepted by the "right" people also superficially influenced his relationship to Kiangsu's local elites. As Governor, probably through the aid of introductions from Li Hung-chang and Tseng Kuo-fan, through his avowed fervent commitment to reform, and through a disingenuous policy of book-lending from his spectacular rare-book library, Ting made and cultivated the acquaintance of such Soochow scholar-official luminaries as Ho Shao-ch'i, Weng T'ung-ho, and Feng Kuei-fen.[27] To seek social acceptance is not, however, ipso facto to seek identity of political views. Consequently, although in subsequent years these ties may have cushioned him against political attacks, they never compromised Ting, who throughout his career remained very much his own man, profoundly bureaucratic in his approach to reform and consistently opposed to government roles for any sort of elites.[28]

Not a priori constructs but practical experience underlay Ting's attitudes and policies. Although I have posited an interpretive framework for nineteenth-century bureaucratic politics and have limned Ting as an amalgam of moderate and radical tendencies, Ting himself rarely evinced an opinion on where he stood in the spectrum of Confucian bureaucratic ideologies. (Ironically, one of his few self-assessments was at odds with the facts.) Unlike the eighteenth-century Japanese "charismatic bureaucrat," Matsudaira Sadanobu, he engaged in no philosophizing about whether the key to reform was men or institutions.[29] Ting was fundamentally indifferent to theorizing; he simply wanted to make government work. Thus, while Ting would concur with those who regarded men of quality as the *sine qua non* of a reinvigorated bureaucracy, the standard of quality for him was administrative ability, not status as a scholar. Moreover, experience appears to have convinced Ting that to find and properly employ such men, and to allow their skills fully to affect the people, institutions had to be reformed. One can infer, then, that for Ting the "loyal servitor" (to paraphrase Tetsuo Najita's assessment of Ogyu Sorai's views) went beyond seeking "goodness or spiritual power in the self . . . to make structures responsive to changing social patterns."[30]

The governorship of Kiangsu had a certain cachet, for, although the province must have had its share of mediocre governors, it also had had as its chief administrator some exceptionally able "loyal servitors": T'ang Pin in K'ang-hsi's reign; Ch'en Hung-mou in Ch'ien-lung's reign; T'ao Chu, Lin Tse-hsu, Li Hsing-yuan, and Liang Chang-chü in Tao-kuang's reign. All were tough, honest officials who diligently attended to the details of fiscal, moral, and judicial administration. T'ao, Lin, Li, and Liang were, furthermore, part of the "Tao-kuang reform movement," which was characterized by major fiscal reforms and conducted under the intellectual aegis of Kung Tzu-chen and Wei Yuan. However, with the outbreak of the Taiping Rebellion in 1850, the efforts of the Tao-kuang Kiangsu officials to construct long-term administrative reforms were supplanted by the drive to crush the Rebellion. Until Ting's selection, the Governors of Kiangsu, with one brief exception, were chosen not for their administrative competence but for their military skills. Thus, when the rebellions were essentially pacified by 1868, the province, as manifested in excerpts from a poem of Ting's, was sorely in need of reform:

> *. . . distress prevailed . . .*
> *Streets brimming with voracious hirelings*
> *The land lay bleeding.*[31]

THE PROVINCE

Kiangsu was a difficult province to govern: riven not simply by residual hostilities from the Rebellion but also by an enduring geographical and psychological cleavage between its northern (Kiangpei) and southern (Kiangnan) sections. The division was more than the obvious one of the Yangtze River. Much of the immediately adjacent north bank can be considered part of the south; and, as G. William Skinner has recently shown, the Huai River

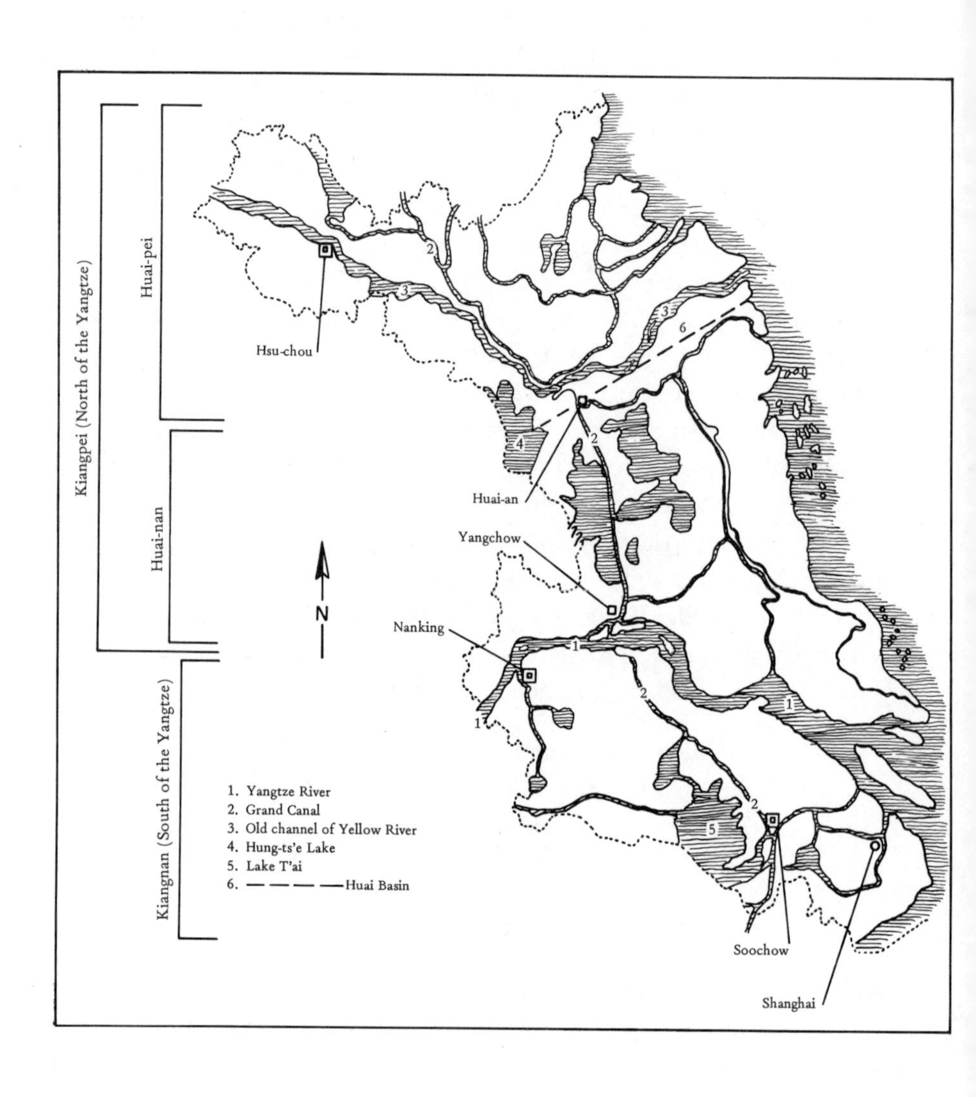

Map of Kiangsu, from Chu K'o-Pao Chiang-su ch'üan-sheng i-t'u, *1895.*

Valley (to the north of the Yangtze) is the truly important internal boundary in Kiangsu.[32] Rather, it is that Kiangnan and much of Kiangpei were parts of discrete physiographic regions. Kiangpei was evenly divided between the core and periphery of what Skinner has described as North China, while Kiangnan constituted the bulk of the lower Yangtze core, and portions of both of these core regions were in provinces other than Kiangsu. This incongruity of provincial and regional boundaries was intentional on the part of the Chinese state, argues Skinner, for it impeded the concentration of regional power that would have arisen had there been a precise coincidence between the political networks of the provinces and the economic networks of the core regions. Yet, when one province encompassed two regions, there were negative side effects, for interregional communication, even in Kiangsu with the North-South Grand Canal, was, in Skinner's words, depressed.[33] Hence, in Kiangsu, the very policy designed to prevent challenges to official control weakened it. At times in the late Ch'ing, Kiangnan and Kiangpei seemed to be almost two separate provinces.

Indeed, early in the dynasty, the Ch'ing had formalized the natural division between North and South by establishing separate financial commissioners and literary chancellors for each region.[34] After 1860, this normal separation was intensified when the Taiping rebels took the provincial capital of Soochow, thereby forcing the provincial authorities to flee to Shanghai where they were cut off from easy access to the North.[35] To ensure continued central control of the North, the court assigned responsibility for Kiangpei affairs to the Director-General of grain transport (*ts'ao-yun tsung-tu*) who was stationed at Huai-nan and, to facilitate his task, approved new bureaucratic routines, especially in the administration of justice.[36] Unfortunately, with the Director-General too involved in military affairs to supervise the local officials adequately, and, without the restraint of the provincial "great reckoning" (*ta-chi*) at which a magistrate's competence was assessed, the quality of local government sharply deteriorated.[37] Magistrates closed old cases by falsely accusing totally innocent people and then punishing them, often with summary execution; suspects and witnesses were left unremembered in gaols and prisons for four to five years; the official post system was allowed to collapse.[38]

In 1867, three years after it had returned to Soochow, the provincial government reassumed direct control over Kiangpei and attempted to redress this dismal situation. As Governor, Ting Jih-ch'ang found that the northern officials only very slowly abandoned their old habits in favor of new procedures. By using their distance from Soochow, they delayed action on or even ignored his directives. Ting could have made a personal inspection tour; curiously enough, he never took this step.[39] Instead, he carried on his struggle with Kiangpei officials by correspondence, a frustrating endeavor in view of the poor condition of the post system. But Ting did have an extensive system of secret agents; and, to the surprise and sorrow of a number of magistrates, he was remarkably well informed about local conditions in the North.

From reading his agents' reports, Ting also formed an opinion of the character of the Kiangpei people: they were without exception incorrigible. Throughout China, officials considered the peasant population to comprise an obedient majority (*liang-min,* lit. "good people") and a recalcitrant minority (*yu-min,* lit. "weed people").[40] Conditions in Kiangpei lent themselves to a reversal of these proportions. The endemic poverty of the region produced a class of tough, rootless unemployed who engaged in salt-smuggling, banditry, protection rackets, extortionary litigation, and pettifoggery. Furthermore, as Ting repeatedly stressed, the problem of control was compounded by the practice of recruiting *yu-min* to serve as police officers and yamen underlings.[41]

Economically, Kiangpei's two most notable characteristics were its enormously productive salt fields, running from the mouth of the Yangtze to the Shantung border, and its fragile agriculture. All aspects involved in production and distribution of the salt were overseen by a government monopoly. This monopoly provided only a living for the actual producers; but it generated sizable revenues for the government and enormous profits for the Yangchow transport merchants, who used their wealth to patronize the arts and to educate their sons.[42] Because of the salt trade's profitability, illicit production and smuggling also flourished, especially in times of bad harvests. Such times were common in Kiangpei, for her agriculture, hampered in Huai-pei by poor soil and light rainfall and in Huai-nan by periodic floods and dense population, was generally unproductive. Poverty was common, and the indigent migrated to Kiangnan in search of alternative or supplementary livelihoods.[43]

In summation, from the viewpoint of senior provincial officials, Kiangpei had the attributes of a classical border area: distance from the administrative center, administration by local officials unresponsive to the provincial authorities, troubles generated by evasion and overlapping of official responsibility, a marginal economy, and a refractory population. The region was seen this way despite, or perhaps because of, the fact that much of Kiangpei was part of the core region of North China.

Kiangnan was the reverse image of Kiangpei. Not only Kiangsu's political center, Kiangnan was also the province's, and to some extent the empire's, cultural and economic heartland. Its economy was prosperous and diversified: blessed with good harbors at Shanghai and Woosung, astride both the Grand Canal and the Yangtze, crosshatched by an intricate system of waterways, Kiangnan was the base of an extensive, lucrative internal and coastal commerce; silk was produced in the southeast corner; in the Yangtze Delta widespread cotton production sustained an important handicraft industry in cotton-spinning; Kiangnan's extraordinarily rich, intensively irrigated and cultivated alluvial soil yielded renowned harvests of rice; and numerous major cities and market towns (many of the latter larger than county and prefectural seats in the North) dotted the countryside. Finally, Kiangnan was an importer of population; among its immigrants were not only the poor and unskilled of the North but also the wealthy and talented from other provinces.[44]

Indeed, as befitted what was probably the most important single source of tax revenue in the empire, Kiangnan abounded in wealthy gentry and merchants.[45] Patronized by these men, Kiangnan's cultural life was rich and varied; Soochow, Nanking, Ch'ang-chou, and Yangchow produced and attracted scholars, bibliophiles, painters, and actors.[46] Kiangnan men took more first-class *chin-shih* degrees than any other provincial group; the libraries of Soochow contained the three greatest collections of Sung and Yuan books in the empire, and the actors of Yangchow dominated the theater scene in Peking as well as in the South.[47] The ability to move in this sophisticated milieu could make a newly arrived official's public and private life immeasurably more pleasant.

Imperative, however, was an official's acceptance by Kiangnan's politically powerful gentry, many of whom were also members of the cultural elite. By virtue of their examination successes, Kiangsu's native sons constituted the largest number of senior officials and innumerable junior ones.[48] Though they did not act as a clearly defined clique at court, Kiangsu officials serving in Peking coalesced around issues of concern to their native place. Moreover, when home on leave or in retirement, they were active on the local and provincial levels where they continued to have influence with senior metropolitan and regional officials through political, familial, and social ties.[49] By supplying censorial officials with apparently damaging information or even by memorializing directly themselves, influential gentry could put a governor on the defensive. And, while lower-ranking gentry, such as the numerous holders of purchased degrees, did not have direct access to the levers of power, they could harass officials by generating doubts about their competence through repeated litigation.[50] When even a governor (rank 2b), who generally had his own powerful connections, had to be circumspect in his dealings with important gentry figures, one can imagine the overwhelmed feeling of a mere local magistrate (rank 7b) if confronted by the group described by Ting Jih-ch'ang as "some Ch'ang-chou gentry": a Hanlin compiler (7a), a retired judicial commissioner (3a), a former salt controller (3a), a department director, and a section head in the Board of Punishments (both 5b), and an assistant reader in the Grand Secretariat (6a).[51]

Our hypothetical magistrate's sense of inferiority would have been heightened after 1864 when the Restoration's leaders in Peking sought to restore and buttress the gentry's function as the keystone in local control, as the interlocutor between the magistrate and the people. In the words of Mary Wright, "The state scrupulously respected all the gentry's traditional legal and economic privileges": tax reduction benefited large landholders; the gentry's right to appeal officials' decisions to the court was reconfirmed, and gentry opinion was sought on all manner of questions.[52] But there also arose an important new institution—the bursary. This was a rent-collecting organization run by gentry with official ties, which for a fee collected rents for absentee landlords and paid their taxes. Not only did most Kiangnan officials overlook this supposed violation of the law against *pao-lan* (intervening between the government and the taxpayer); they also lent their support by ordering government runners to assist in collection of rents. Gradually, in a process described by Yuji Muramatsu, the gentry built up their authority over their tenants until their bursaries became "states within the state."[53]

Although the Taiping Rebellion left intact and may have even increased the political power of the gentry, it ravaged Kiangnan's population and fields. Wherever the struggle was severe, the aftermath was the same: desolated villages, abandoned fields torn by trenches, destroyed waterworks, emaciated survivors, and death—nearly six million people died in Kiangnan as a consequence of the rebellion.[54] Essential, then, to the post-Taiping reconstruction of Kiangnan was the resettlement and reclamation of the land.

These tasks were especially critical in western Kiangnan (Ch'ang-chou, Chen-chiang, and Kiangning prefectures), whose population had been decimated by the constant conflict which raged from 1853, when the Taiping leaders made Nanking their capital, until 1864, when the Ch'ing recaptured the city and ended the Rebellion. To entice immigrants, the government established special bureaus which offered potential settlers free tools and seeds, three-year tax exemptions, and after three years (if there were no legitimate counter-claims) title to their reclaimed land. Unfortunately, many of the immigrants, especially those from Kiangpei, did not stay beyond the expiration of the tax exemptions. Having worked their land for maximum profit, they returned home, often to tenancy, rather than assume the tax obligations that came with land ownership.[55] This failure to resettle the land permanently led to some basic changes in the countryside: large tracts of land remained uncultivated (as late as 1882, 50 percent of Nanking prefecture); land productivity and land rents decreased sharply; and land formerly used for rice was shifted to cultivation of mulberry trees, which required less capital and labor.[56]

In the east, with the major exception of the bursaries which were an indirect result of the Rebellion, the nature of the countryside remained unaltered. The Taiping forces did not attack in the east until 1860, and after a relatively tranquil occupation were pushed out by a furious but short (1862–1864) Ch'ing counter-offensive.[57] The affected areas in Soochow and Sung-chiang prefectures were quickly reinhabited by their former residents, who flooded back from their coastal refuges in Shanghai and Ch'ung-ming. Unhindered by severe labor shortages, the people gradually reclaimed their land, reducing, between 1865 and 1868, the amount of waste and abandoned land from two-thirds to one-fifth.[58] Then, as harvests and taxes were again gathered, public and private capital were invested in the rebuilding and improvement of canal and irrigation systems. The cities and the public buildings within them, however, were repaired more slowly.[59] Three years after the Rebellion's end, many of Soochow's streets and canals were still clogged with debris; and a district Magistrate in Soochow, unable even to find a suitable house to rent while his official residence still lay in ruins, was forced to receive his seals of office in a common hostel.[60]

The laggard recovery of the public sector was due largely to the Nien Rebellion. The actual physical damage inflicted by the Nien on Kiangsu was limited to several hsien in the far north of the province, but the Nien suppression campaign was an enormous drain on Kiangsu's provincial treasury. On the one hand, Li Hung-chang and Tseng Kuo-fan used their tight control of Kiangsu's tax revenues (attained by Li while he was Governor of Kiangsu) to channel large sums of cash to Li's Huai Army fighting in Honan, Shantung, Anhwei, and Chihli; and, with court support, the

Governor-General of Chihli also obtained a share of Kiangsu's revenues. This situation led Ting Jih-ch'ang to comment that Kiangsu alone was supporting the campaign against the Nien.[61] On the other hand, as a result of large monthly payments to provincial forces in Shensi and Kansu, where the Moslem Rebellion was in progress, Kiangsu was instrumental in Ch'ing successes in the northwest.[62] But, as Ting complained, Kiangsu's income was not unlimited. The province had still not completely recovered from the Taiping Rebellion and had its own needs for tax monies: pay for its disbanded soldiers, repair of waterworks, modernization of the provincial armies, and relief payments to destitute refugees.[63] That Kiangsu twice had to borrow from its neighboring province, Chekiang, to meet the extra-provincial demands demonstrated the straightened circumstances of the once wealthiest province in the empire.[64]

THREE

Rectifying Society

> *Lead the people with governmental measures and regulate them by law and punishment, and they will obey but will have no sense of honor and shame.*
> *Lead the people with virtue and regulate them by the rules of propriety* (li), *and they will have a sense of shame and, moreover, set themselves right.*
>
> Confucius, *The Analects,* 2.3

In the wake of the Taiping Rebellion, one of the primary tasks confronting Kiangsu officials was the mending of the province's frayed social fabric. Sensitized by the Rebellion's challenge to existing (that is, Confucian) values and by the implicit ideological threat from the West, Ting Jih-ch'ang and his colleagues determined not only to repair the gaping holes—brigandry by ex-soldiers in the countryside and piracy along the rivers—but also to expunge patterns and textures they considered structurally debilitating. Thus, the gambling, the plays, the local burial and marriage customs, and the popular religious observances that had long been officially (albeit tacitly) tolerated integral parts of daily life and that flourished as people expressed their relief at war's end were subjected to attack.

From the classical Confucian viewpoint adopted by Ting, these defects in Kiangsu's society were a manifestation of malignant moral decay. Social and political order in this view could not be restored simply by repressing the symptoms of that decay—rebellion, outlawry, and decadent customs. Restoration of order by repression was simply the stage of arrest and containment, the first step of long-term therapy. Ultimately, society's health could be redeemed only by fostering correct values, by stressing proper order in human relations through the teachings of Confucian morality. This strengthening of social ties was the key to the prevention of future rebellions. Only after the structure and content of education were re-established could the people be taught and transformed and society rectified.

This chapter examines the institutional aspects of that two-stage process of restoring order and re-education. A recurrent but not ubiquitous thread in our discussion is the dialectic between institutional (bureaucratic/official) and informal (non-bureaucratic/local elite) approaches. In some areas, the opposition is absent. For instance, local elites neither volunteered nor were recruited for campaigns against opium cultivation, forced remarriage of widows, theaters, gambling, or religious processions, probably because many of them were implicated in these activities. And in the instance of the revival of traditional Confucian cultural institutions, local elites and officials cooperated. Elsewhere, however, the dialectic is inescapable. Scholar-official local elites, for example, concentrated their energies on schools and charitable institutions, not only because they fostered correct values, but also because they were remunerative and, perhaps most important, served the elite as a public base independent of bureaucratic/official authority. Indeed, non-bureaucratic autonomous political presences were the crux of the issue, especially in the policing of local society. For, although scholar-official local elites, unlike rural gentry-director types, were rarely themselves instigators of turmoil, Ting Jih-ch'ang regarded involvement of elites of any sort in maintenance of local order as a cure nearly worse than the disease.

RESTORATION OF ORDER

As Philip Kuhn has shown, the Chinese countryside, once armed and militarized during the course of the Taiping Rebellion, remained so.[1] Many groups in Kiangsu, including the local-elite-led and locally funded local militia networks (*t'uan-lien*) which had been so vital to the defense of the Ch'ing, were potential threats to the fragile post-bellum peace.[2] Of most pressing concern, however, to the Kiangsu officials were the former soldiers of Tseng Kuo-fan's Hsiang Army, which he had begun to disband upon the fall of the Taiping capital at Nanking. In a few instances, disbanded soldiers, joined at times by disguised former Taiping officials, organized into secret societies and engaged in overtly rebellious acts. While Ting reacted forcefully, ordering summary execution of the leaders, he also cautioned his subordinates against provoking nonrebellious groups with undue displays of force. "When one man seeks military merit, ten thousand dried bones result."[3] Indeed, most of the societies were quiescent, and the ex-soldiers' more usual activities were brigandage—both where they were dismissed and at home—and battening off reconstruction efforts. In the Nanking area, the soldiers' interference in the allocation of deeds and their malfeasant operation of likin stations discouraged settlers and financially eviscerated reconstruction bureaus to such an extent that the court blamed its erstwhile defenders for the failure to reconstruct Nanking.[4]

Tseng Kuo-fan, who had disbanded his army as a sign of loyalty, had not anticipated that the dismissed soldiers would precipitate such difficulties. At the time, Tseng optimistically reported to the court that most of his men were anxious to return to waiting homes and jobs.[5] Clearly, he knew his men less well than he thought. Four years later, in 1868, Ting, then Governor of Kiangsu, found that many of the ex-soldiers had kept their weapons and remained to fight in the province—for themselves rather than for the state.[6] He considered even those soldiers retained to receive modern training potential brigands and prohibited their retirement until ten years after completing training.[7] But Ting, who as Shanghai Taotai had cleared that city of Cantonese gangsters by what the *North China Herald* called "an almost indiscriminate exercise of the power of life and death," granted that many of the soldiers were financially unable to reach the bureau that Tseng had established in Nanking to aid their return home.[8] To assist the soldiers Ting established a "reception and forwarding" office (*shou-liu tzu-sung hui-chi chü*) in Soochow, which, like the Nanking bureau, promised the soldiers money for their weapons, free transport home, and a daily food allowance for themselves and any accompanying family.[9] Ting set a one-month time limit to this offer and suggested in his proclamation that it was an offer best not refused:

> *If you return home early, you will be able to be reunited with your family and till your fields. Nobody will bother you. What honor this is! What freedom this is!*
> But if you do not listen to me and stay in this place, in a while your expense money will be gone, thus forcing you into banditry or suicide. While you are away from home, your family is anxiously awaiting you. How will they know that you have already fallen—executed—in a strange place. Think it over a little and decide which measures up best: returning home soon, or loitering about and not returning at all.[10]

These forceful words had a negligible impact. *Yu-yung* persisted in their brigandage, organization of secret societies, and disturbances; they reportedly once even seized a district town.[11] Two of the most influential Soochow gentry, Feng Kuei-fen and P'an Tseng-wei, supported by Ting, petitioned the throne to stay Tseng Kuo-fan's departure from the governor-generalship of Liang-kiang so that he could cope with the soldiers, all of whom were his former subordinates. For, according to the petitioners, "Tseng blocked the road like an old bear with a face that forbade trespass."[12]

Tseng was transferred, however, and the *yu-yung* remained. As official and popular frustration increased, both criminal and law abiding ex-soldiers became primary suspects in any crime; and since criminal ex-soldiers could be summarily executed (*chiu-ti cheng-fa*), even common criminals were accused of being *yu-yung.* The false charges against commoners were a device to close difficult cases; charges were trumped up against *yu-yung* to seize their booty as well as to close difficult cases. (Summary executions became an entrenched "legal" practice, an affront to many late Ch'ing judicial officials who considered it a violation of Chinese concepts of justice and who disdained its deterrent effect.)[13] Ting warned local officials that rapacious runners could turn the peaceable into bandits. He instructed them to distinguish between commoners and soldiers, and to examine carefully all charges against soldiers to ensure that the innocent were not executed. Ting's compassion was limited, however, to the innocent, for, when *yu-yung* were indeed guilty of banditry, Ting fulfilled his warnings and ordered the accused summarily executed.[14] As in times of famine or flood, once relief was made available, hard times could no longer mitigate guilt.[15]

Like the problem of the soldiers, piracy in Kiangsu was a function of the increased local militarization that had occurred during the Rebellion. The armed boats (*ch'iang-ch'uan*), which plagued Lake T'ai and the Chekiang border counties, first appeared when the boat people armed themselves for protection against the Taiping. Plunder, however, soon became their primary activity.[16] In early 1868, Ting's immediate predecessor as Governor, Kuo Po-yin, reported to the throne that he had successfully enforced his prohibition against the boats by capturing and executing the pirates' ringleaders; but he warned that official laxness would lead to an immediate revival.[17] Most of the boats were disarmed in observance of the ban on either official or civilian use of *ch'iang-ch'uan,* but both the salt patrol and salt smugglers continued to use them. Ting blamed insufficiently detailed regulations for this lapse. Although weapons were forbidden, the people had no idea of how to turn them in; and, while the "simple were confused, the cunning took advantage of the confusion to hide their guns."[18]

Relying on suggestions forwarded from the Financial Commissioner, Tu Wen-lan, in late 1868, Ting formulated a set of regulations which focused on the problem of the collection of weapons. Before examining these, however, it is worthwhile seeing what ideas Ting rejected. While acknowledging the tremendous speed advantage of the *ch'iang-ch'uan,* he steadfastly opposed their use for either official post or police business.[19] He was equally firm in his opposition to Tu's proposals that gentry and publicly selected village directors (*kung-chü ts'un-tung*) have the sole responsibility for checking on adherence to the rules, and that they be allowed to make secret accusations against violators.[20] Yet, in contrast to his distrust of the gentry, Ting placed faith in the advice of an ex-pirate leader. If, Ting promised, the man could devise a verifiably effective way of eliminating the *ch'iang-ch'uan,* he would not only be released but even rewarded. "To hoe," Ting counseled the concerned local officials, "one ought to ask a slave (*nu*); to weave one ought to ask a maidservant (*pei*). Just because he was once a bandit does not mean we can abruptly dismiss his words as unworthy of adoption."[21]

The pirate's response and ultimate fate are unkown, but Ting eventually issued his regulatory proclamation, which seems to have reduced the problem, and which received court approval.[22] Promised immunity, the boat people were to turn in their weapons and ammunition within two months and be reimbursed at a fixed price.[23] The gentry of each precinct (*t'u*), while denied police power, were nonetheless entrusted with the heavy responsibility of collecting, storing, and issuing receipts for the weapons. The magistrate would then personally visit each *t'u* to redeem the receipts and to obtain from the village leader a bond against future illicit manufacture of armaments.[24] The boats themselves, however, would have to be disarmed within a month. Violators of this deadline, though unengaged in piracy, would still be punished and their boats destroyed, while recalcitrant pirates would be more severely punished and their homes converted into charitable schools. Ting's proclamation also forbade further construction of even *ch'iang-ch'uan* hull types,[25] reiterated the ban on official use of the boats—particularly by salt patrols and warrant-servers—and recalled all outstanding warrants issued to boat owners.[26] To force these people into peaceful professions, gambling, which had financed the pirates, was outlawed. And, finally, to eliminate piracy "root and branch," all boat owners and boat people were ordered registered in *pao-chia,* a system of houshold registration.

Implementation of the *pao-chia* and encouragement of agriculture were the warp and woof of bandit suppression.[27] As Mary Wright wrote, "Whenever bandits appeared, the state ordered the enforcement of the *pao-chia* regulations as a means of detaching the bandits from the common people and thus depriving them of food and shelter."[28] Had the rules been properly observed, commented one Censor, there would have been no Rebellion,[29] while another suggested that the decimated post-Rebellion population "would make surveillance easier and public business less troublesome"![30]

Although Ting made no effort to ease the transition of the boat people from pirate to farmer, his vehement campaign for *pao-chia* registration drew the attention of even the foreign press.[31] As Governor, he edited and published Hsu Tung's *Pao-chia shu* as a guide to *pao-chia* procedures and seems to have based the boat people's *pao-chia* on models in this work.[32] Moreover, together with Ma Hsin-i, Ting repeatedly urged the court to instruct that all *yu-yung* be strictly enrolled in their native places' *pao-chia* as a guard against brigandage.[33] Ting was flexible, however, in the organization of the *pao-chia,* allowing his magistrates to depart from the strict gradations of the system.[34] But he adamantly opposed supplementing the *pao-chia* with Chou-style village leaders as an invitation to gentry abuse of authority.[35]

"Ignorance of proper behavior," to which Ting attributed the piracy and Kiangsu's other social ills, had long characterized the province, otherwise renowned for its scholars.[36] Ch'en Hung-mou, an able mid-Ch'ing Governor, deprecatingly characterized the paradoxical nature of Kiangsu's residents:

> Kiangsu is the richest, most literary area in the empire. Yet its people think only of the present, not at all of the future. Their marriages and burials exceed regulations. Men and women mix freely together. Adepts and monks deceive the people, while bullies foment trouble.[37]

Clearly, many of the practices that so affronted reform-minded Restoration officials and attracted their full attention were deeply ingrained in the people. Some, such as opium cultivation, delayed burials, and forced remarriage of widows, were directly exacerbated by the Rebellion's devastation of the land and decimation of the population. The flourishing theaters, religious festivals, and gambling (none of them new to Kiangsu) were not physically impacted by the Rebellion; rather they were nourished by the powerful psychological forces generated by it. As in Europe after the Black Death and World War I, so too, in post-bellum Kiangsu, people sublimated whatever guilt they may have felt as survivors and frenetically celebrated the joys of being alive. Clashing head on with this *joie de vivre* was the stern determination of officials that a restoration could not be achieved until all hedonistic sprouts were extirpated.

As Ting pursued his campaign, an embarrassing incident occurred which publicly tested his rectitude. In November 1869, the *Peking Gazette* printed a memorial from Ting who reported that, while he was out in the countryside inspecting flood damage, Ting Pin, a distant clansman, had passed through Soochow and, together with some of his (Ting Jih-ch'ang's) family servants, had gone to a brothel where they had brawled with some marines. In response, the court ordered Ma Hsin-i, the Liang Kiang Governor-General, to conduct a trial, and, while it approved Ting's request for the dismissal of Ting's clansman from his minor office, the court seemed to exempt Ting from discipline.[38] In the second of two subsequent published memorials, Ting then produced the stunning revelation that his nephew had definitely participated in the brawl and that he suspected the involvement of his son.[39] Ma's trial absolved Ting's son of any guilt and praised Ting's handling of the whole matter, but, since this memorial was never published in the *Peking Gazette*, foreigners and Chinese were left to speculate on the final resolution of the case.[40] The *North China Herald* suggested that Ting had bribed Ma, while Ting's vituperative enemy, the Sub-Director of the Court of Sacrificial Worship, Wang Chia-pi, futilely tried to tie Ting to Ma's later assassination.[41]

Doubts about this case coalesced with rumors about Ting's alleged coercive acquisition of his rare-book collection and with knowledge of his irregular background to feed suspicion that Ting's outraged Confucian moralism was specious. Although Ting's prudishness and sense of rectitude were genuine rather than postured, Ting was not a "let-them-eat-cake" moralist, for he recognized that only when competent governance elevated people's lives above a daily struggle to survive would they respond to the value lessons of Confucian orthodoxy.[42] Yet Ting never publicly voiced this view. It too pointedly blamed officials for heterodoxy, and it was often obscured by Ting's distress at the imperviousness of popular customs to regulation from above. He vented his frustration by attending to even the most mundane customs and by accompanying the obligatory exhortations in his public pronouncements with harsh threats against the unrepentants in a rhetoric of impotence.

Not insensitive to the doubts about his motivation and sincerity, Ting, in defense of a ban on religious processions and pilgrimages, explained to his judicial commissioner: "I am doing this for the sake of ridding the people of this evil and not to look for a place in the ranks of the Confucian temple's good officials (*fei wei liang-wu t'e-tung chi*)."[43] Certainly it was highly unusual for a governor to justify his motives to his subordinates, but Ting had already been identified as a foreign-affairs expert and must have been on the defensive in matters concerning the rites. Moreover, he had been mocked before Tseng Kuo-fan as a "fame-seeker" (*ch'iu chin-kung*).[44]

Whether he sought it or not, Ting achieved fame, at least in the eyes of the eminent Soochow literatus Feng Kuei-fen, as the best governor since Lin Tse-Hsu.[45] But Ting's drive against opium was even less successful than Lin's had been. In Kiangpei the destruction of the already inadequate waterworks had led to several years of bad harvests and the spread of opium cultivation, for the poppy "feared neither drought nor flood."[46] Ting pressed the officials of Hsu-chou and Huai-an prefectures to "repair waterworks and plan a livelihood for the people" and asked them to investigate the extent of the opium-growing;[47] but he complained that his instructions went unanswered "like a rock thrown into the sea."[48] Ting's urgency was fed by the fear of opium's spread:

> It is like leprosy, able to spread its infection in an instant. Its residual evil is like that of locusts. . . . Opium land will increase as farm land decreases. In ten years the houses will be like empty vessels and there will be no green grass.[49]

Increased planting led to increased addiction; and Ting vowed that any magistrate successful at eliminating opium would be treated not simply as a colleague but "as if he were an older brother who irrigated so that he [Ting], the younger brother, could gain the benefit."[50] Although Ting temporarily succeeded in closing urban opium dens and completed some of the waterworks projects, none of the Kiangpei Magistrates ever achieved the distinction of being treated by the Governor as his older brother.[51]

The thousands of coffins awaiting burial which lined the river banks and covered the fields of Soochow and other districts were an even more immediate health hazard than opium, as well as a major offense against the rites. The punishment of eighty blows with the heavy bamboo had never deterred people from committing what one official dubbed "the greatest crime" of delaying burial, so Ting's proclamation sought to dissuade people by explaining why each of their reasons for delay was invalid.[52] To postpone burial for fear of embarrassing oneself with a simple one was understandable; but reverence, said Ting, could not be equated with opulence. Simply piling dirt into a mound, sweeping the grave, and making sacrifices fulfilled the rites. Similarly misguided and improperly selfish were prolonged searches for grave sites with good *feng-shui.* Striking a well-worn Confucian theme, Ting warned the people that their grandfathers' bones were not a tool for seeking good luck or glory. Auspicious influences, should there be any, derived from the ancestors' merit and virtue, not from the land itself. "If virtue had accumulated, how could the land control what happened?"[53] Finally, one should not await a propitious combination of stems and branches. It was intolerable, said Ting, for the living's discordant horoscopes to deprive the dead of their peace. Even Lao-tzu upon his sudden death had his house burned and his body buried immediately.[54]

The heart of Ting's proclamation was his program of action.

Those with means were to bury their own relatives. The indigent were to seek assistance from charitable institutions (*shan-t'ang*), of which a number were recently organized (largely by the gentry) for just this task.[55] The *shan-t'ang* were also to bury unclaimed coffins, set up inscribed headstones for identifiable ones, and compile a location register for the unknowns. Should their own resources prove insufficient, the *shan-t'ang* were to be assisted with public funds.[56] As Ting reminded the Magistrates, "the burying of stray bones will build good fortune" (*fu*). A few officials cleared their hsiens of coffins; and, while elsewhere the numbers were reduced, the custom itself proved ineradicable, persisting well into the twentieth century.[57]

While not posing a health hazard, still more shocking to Ting on moral and religious grounds were the practices of poor people's cremation of their encoffined relatives on the very day (Ch'ing-ming festival) that they should have been sweeping their graves, and the removal of one's parent's bones from their coffin to a jar to await a second and more favorable burial.[58] Prevalent in Kiangnan since the Sung, cremation was once denounced by a Ming Magistrate of Wu hsien as an abominable practice, unused as punishment even by the tyrannical Sui Wen-ti and Yuan Emperors. It was moreover, he said, the practice of a foreign teaching–Buddhism.[59] To deter those "who feared the law" and "to move those with feelings," Ting instructed his magistrates to make widely known that sons or grandsons who destroyed their parents' or grandparents' corpses, or disinterred them to examine them for omens, were by law to be decapitated. Constables and neighbors were warned that failure to report such crimes would make them accomplices.[60] But, in spite of the pervasiveness of these customs and the strong Confucian moral opposition to them, I have been unable to find an instance of Ting's applying these provisions.[61] This does not mean that he relaxed his vigilance, but rather that the very prevalence of the customs had made them normative behavior. (Indeed, as Barbara Ward has shown, in the eyes of the people, orthodoxy was frequently "the way things are done" in a given community.)[62] And, despite the importance of ancestors in the Confucian scheme, these "crimes," unlike the equally reprehensible ones of murder and rape, were essentially victimless ones and, as such, less likely to be punished.

By contrast, another old Kiangsu (and, as the work of Spence and Wolf suggest, widespread Chinese) practice aggravated by the Rebellion, the forced remarriages of widows, clearly victimized someone, yet, as we shall see, proved equally resistant to official opposition. As early as the mid-eighteenth century the problem had become endemic as families throughout the province forced their widows to remarry in order to increase their landholdings.[63] And, though family pressure on widows is the chief concern of the Penal Code, in the post-Taiping period the pressure for remarriage was generally extra-familial. It came from clerks and small-time bullies known generically as "ant sticks" (*i-kun*) or "white ants" (*pai ma-i*).[64]

This problem first came to Ting's attention when as Shanghai Taotai he noticed how many Su-Sung-T'ai widows had remarried. Subsequently, as Financial Commissioner, Ting issued a proclamation forbidding forced remarriages.[65] His decision was based on two assumptions: that "the relationship between husband and wife is the most basic of human relationships" (*jen-lun*), and that proper women would not remarry of their own volition.[66] (That such documents had to be issued suggests that the social norms they, and the supportive sections of the Penal Code, sought to uphold had long been considered inoperative by most of the people.)[67] Ting made no effort to explore or explain the cause of this phenomenon; although others blamed it on tax precinct directors (*t'u-tung*) and the influence of "lewd" plays, he did suggest a way beyond strict punishment of the culprits to deal with it—the establishment in each hsien of halls for honoring the pure (*ch'ing-chieh t'ang*) and of associations for assisting widows (*hsu-li hui*).[68] Like his other cures for social ills, Ting's program was in a thoroughly traditional vein; but, unlike them, it was not distinguished either by its detail or rigor. Subsequent provincial officials offered more elaborate solutions, but neither they nor Ting eliminated the problem.[69] It continued unabated throughout Ting's tenure and into the 1880s in Chia-ting, Nan-hui, Tan-yang, and Ch'ung-ming hsiens. Tan-yang's Magistrate, who Ting charged was "the clerks' puppet (*k'uei-lei*)," jailed a man who had accused the clerks of coercing widows. But, even in Nan-hui, a strict Magistrate failed to end the practice.[70] For widows, like orphans and girls, were an unrewarding burden to a family; and when the associations' assistance proved insufficient, the honorary arches and banners could not be eaten.[71]

Since some social ills were closely related, Restoration officials hoped the purging of one would lead to the demise of the others. Such was the case with religious fairs and their attendant gambling and theaters. The religious activities were a communal undertaking, which C. K. Yang described as an opportunity "to bring individuals, out of their family-centered routine activities, to enable relatives and friends to meet and renew their social ties, and to break the simple monotony of the peasants' life which followed the fixed organic cycle of nature."[72] Designed to invigorate the peasants for the imminent spring planting, the fairs and processions were sanctioned by the Penal Code so long as they only asked assistance from or paid thanks to the gods of the soil.[73] But the people of Kiangsu, long known for their belief in spirits (*k'uei-shen*) and fondness for "lewd ceremonies" (*yin-chu*), were not so restrained and had religious associations for nearly every spirit.[74] And what is temporary liberation to a modern sociologist like C. K. Yang was, to a Restoration official, libertinism.

Religious processions (*ying-shen sai-hui*) were basically celebrations of a local deity (legally only that of the communal spirit of the soil), in which young people would dress as the spirit and as they ran through the streets on the appointed day, would be greeted with drums and cymbals by their fellow villagers. But the processions honored myriad deities, were very elaborate—at times even grotesque—expensive and, lasting three to five days, attracted undesirables at whose stands (*chieh-ch'ang*) plays and games of chance could be enjoyed.[75] Despite the legal penalties for both instigators and responsible local officials, each locality in turn celebrated its own deities, thereby disrupting spring planting.[76] Unless forbidden, Ting determined, such processions would cause "incalculable damage to the people's customs and livelihoods" in a Kiangsu still struggling to recover from the Rebellion. His ban instructed the people to redirect their energy to the basic tasks of planting and sericulture.[77]

Ting's proclamation against the processions was one of those rare instances when the Confucian viewpoint, so often derided by treaty port observers, and the Western one coincided. Ting's reasoning, the *North China Daily News* smugly wrote, was worthy of Western philosophy; he had told his people that one's happiness and the gods' blessings depended on one's own fulfillment of filial and fraternal duties and on attendance to vocation, not on godforsaken, frivolous participation in religious festivals. "Whatever may be Ting Futai's individual defects," the paper condescendingly concluded, "he must be allowed credit for expressing broad and just views."[78]

Still more threatening to the recently restored order than the processions were the incense-burning associations (*shao-hsiang hui*). For, unlike the resident religious processions, the incense-burners' pilgrimages often crossed county and provincial boundaries, thus potentially concealing rebel movements and facilitating the spread of heterodoxy.[79] Moreover, the pilgrims traveled in sexually mixed company, and the associations were often confidence operations or covers under which pirates, disguised as pilgrims, could prey upon their fellow travelers.[80] Ting had already reduced piracy, and used his order against the pilgrimages to reiterate his theme that the ultimate solution to such problems was moral education and dedication to work:

> If everyone were well-to-do or at least had every thing he needed, there would be peace and no banditry. Then, if the people wanted to thank the spirits, there would be no objection to acceding to popular feelings. But since the Rebellion, probably not even one percent of the commoners have more than enough food or clothing. The Financial Commissioner shall issue a proclamation asking upright gentry to lecture on the need for frugality and to see to it that every family knows not to follow the rotten ways.[81]

From our perspective, Ting seems overly strict, but his actions must be understood in the context of his concern that an atrophying Confucianism was losing its central place in society to flourishing Buddhism and popular religions. It was not a baseless fear, for, while some Magistrates earnestly but unsuccessfully tried to end the religious processions, one had the temerity to request official sanction of yet another spirit's temple, for the Kiangtu water fairies. Ting denied this request on the ground that there was little evidence that they, like the main deities, had actually protected the region against flood or calamity.[82] In any case, Ting desired magistrates instead to concentrate on the rebuilding of Confucian temples and the training of sacrificers. Not to make the sacrifices would be an insult, and to allow "rabble" to ride the coattails of the officials into the temples and create a "hubbub" would cause the sacrifices to lose their propriety. Ting's insistence that magistrates alone were responsible for preparing the temple rites and were never to delegate that task to their subordinates notwithstanding, the Magistrates of the three head hsien–Yuan-ho, Ch'ang-chou, and Wu–were particularly evasive of this responsibility.[83]

Ting was highly conscious of the people's belief in the supernatural, abjuring extremism in favor of caution, unlike the contemporary Censor who requested that all temples other than those of the deities of the soil be forbidden and that all icons, particularly Buddhist ones, be destroyed. Recognizing the danger in such radical gestures, the court had responded with reserve. In place of any general prohibition, it banned reconstruction of only those temples which had not been previously in local histories.[84] Ting, too, was not opposed to Buddhism per se, just to its distortion and to its potential for misuse. Explaining his order to close some twenty nunneries for allegedly having become brothels, Ting said he had acted to save the people "from drowning in a sea of iniquity and to let Buddhism again shine brightly." While it is impossible to substantiate Ting's charges (though they were valid in the case of the nunneries in the same locale in K'ang-hsi's reign), it is clear that the nunneries seemed little affected by Ting's order.[85]

Clearly, although Ting's writings on religious fairs, unlike those of other Ch'ing officials and emperors, were curiously devoid of apprehension about the mixing of sexes, he was not unconcerned about such socializing.[86] Indeed, in 1867 he had imposed a ban on women in Wu hsien's tea shops. In his order Ting had been careful not to accuse all involved of base motives: "Not all women are prostitutes; not all men are in search of them. But though they try to avoid the appearance of evil, they are still playing footsie *(lü-hsi chiao-ts'o)* under the table." Denouncing such impropriety as "destructive of morals," Ting forbade tea shop owners from inviting women to drink in their shops, and threatened violators with the heavy bamboo and two months in the cangue (a stock carried on the shoulders). The ban was directed against Wu hsien only, but the custom probably pervaded all Kiangnan's wine and tea shops, which, claimed Ch'ien-lung, were located even in the midst of the fields.[87]

Although relaxed sexual barriers were an attraction of the religious fairs, the opportunity to gamble was an even greater one. Indeed, in some places the gambling financed the fair itself (as well as supporting pirates and serving as a recruiting tool for rebels).[88] Dissipation of character as well as of finances was the basis for official opposition. From gambling winnings the lucky drank and whored, while the unlucky fell from robbery to brigandry, eventually to rebellion.[89] Yet, local officials rarely caught or punished the big-time gamblers—the gentry in their protected exclusive dens[90]—and generally avoided a direct attack on gambling, despite the powerful punitive weapons at their disposal (applied also by analogy to opium dens).[91] Instead, they enjoined the religious and theatrical activities to which professional gamblers flocked, or severely punished particularly arrogant professionals.[92]

Indeed, only twice did Ting specifically prohibit gambling.[93] The case of Shanghai is interesting because to eradicate gambling throughout the city he had to obtain foreign cooperation. As a new Taotai, Ting had opposed the foreign Consuls' suggestions to control gaming through taxation, rather than to attempt to eradicate it.[94] Though the Chinese knew well from their dealings with merchants that "the power to tax is the power to destroy," in such "moral" matters as opium and gambling they showed a distinct preference for straightforward suppression.[95] Taxation suggested toleration. Eventually, Ting persuaded the foreign Consuls to support his ban, although they, as well as he, had expressed doubts about the ability and probity of the Chinese police. Ting consequently urged the Shanghai Magistrate personally and secretly to check on the enforcement and announced his intention to do the same.[96] The *North China Herald* expressed the hope that fear of detection at any moment by the incognito Ting would restrain the gamblers; but the chief result of Ting's snooping was not the demise of gambling, which successfully resisted all efforts to control it.[97] As the *Hong Kong Daily Press* reported in November 1864:

> The Chinese are now occupied with a story to the effect that . . . Ting made his appearance in a gambling house, and got into a dispute with some one or another whom he detected cheating. A row ensued, but one of the party, recognizing the Taotai, gave the alarm and the house was quickly emptied.[98]

Unlike the gambling, the dramas performed at the religious fairs were ideally an integral religious component presented to thank the spirits for a good harvest and to encourage good behavior and works among the people. In one part of Kiangsu, voluntary rotational tax-urging groups (*i-t'u*) used fines collected from laggard or delinquent ratepayers to underwrite theatrical performances for the group upon full payment of its taxes.[99] Drama at the fairs or regular theaters, moreover, was not in itself antithetical to the Confucian ethos.[100] But, because plays were equally fine vehicles for heterodoxy and bawdiness, and theaters excellent covers for illegal activities, the Ch'ing state attempted to regulate both the content of drama and the establishment of theaters.[101] Nonetheless, over time, romance and adventure supplanted moral didacticism, much to the horror of literati, who denounced theatrical versions of *Hsi-hsiang chi* (Western chamber) and *Hung-lou meng* (Dream of the red chamber) as "lewd destroyers of youths' souls and women's morals." Allowing one's children to see such plays, one writer charged, was no better than buying opium for them.[102] Even the Shanghai-based Chinese language newspaper *Shen Pao,* which rarely concurred with "establishment" views, complained in 1881 that "lewd plays" were causing widows to remarry and asked for their prohibition.[103]

In Kiangsu, both the theater and its literati detractors were well established before Ting's service in the province. In the wake of the Rebellion, however, literati and officials took advantage of the fortuitous destruction and decay of many of the theaters. In 1867, the Shanghai Taotai, Ying Pao-shih, apparently acting on his own initiative, outlawed theatrical performances; and in 1868, Ting issued a similar proscription for the entire province.[104] Though the "vicissitudes of luck" were certainly responsible for the state of the theaters, admitted Ting, to an extent they had brought their ill fortune upon themselves "through their extravagance and wasteful customs." (Indeed, some years later a Shansi Magistrate observed that the 300 to 400 cash per *mou* levy assessed to sponsor plays was so heavy that only wealthy market towns could truly afford theater.)[105] Impelling Ting to issue his ban was the damage a few resurrected theaters had caused by enticing sexually mixed audiences away from their work to hear stories about "heavenly retribution." Dismayed that the people, only just returned to the "simple and true," might again fall away, Ting ordered a halt to all construction of theaters, the confiscation of their land and buildings, and strict punishment for resisters or violators. Yet, if the record of such endeavors in Peking (or in even more tightly controlled Tokugawa Japan) is any indication, over the long run Ting's efforts proved futile, for even in the Imperial City itself officials were unable to exert control over actors and their theaters.[106]

As Financial Commissioner, Ting had presaged his gubernatorial ban on drama when he proscribed "lewd" stories and novels.[107] The following year, as Governor, he reaffirmed and elaborated his proscription in conjunction with his orders to establish the Kiangsu Printing Office (Kiangsu shu-chü)[108] The printing, sale, and ownership of such literature were all strictly forbidden by the Penal Code, and a number of the works had already been attacked during Ch'ien-lung's Literary Inquisition.[109] But the great popularity of these novels prompted one mid-Ch'ing official to contend that they had become another teaching (*chiao*) alongside Confucianism, Buddhism, and Taoism.[110] Indeed, Ting somewhat exaggeratedly claimed that rapacious publishers had printed so many copies of *Shui-hu chuan* (Water margin) and *Hsi-hsiang chi* (Western chamber) that "almost every house and person had one."[111] As Ting and others ruefully admitted, the novels were simply more appealing than the Classics and, far worse, made a deeper impression upon their readers:

> Though thousands have labored to teach filiality and frugality, none have met with success; while only a few need show the way to false, evil books, and calamity immediately ensues. . . . Reading *Shui hu* and *Hsi-hsiang* makes naive youths fall prey to their passions and emboldens village toughs.[112]

While acknowledging that the Rebellion was "not necessarily a calamity secretly fomented by the transgressing words," Ting wondered where "the poison would stop if the books were not destroyed."[113]

Ting answered himself. The poison of these "evil words" would infect everyone, for even "innoculation" of the people with lectures on the *Sheng yü kuang hsun* (Expanded sacred edicts) and Chu Hsi's *Hsiao-hsueh* (Primer) could not guarantee permanent protection. Only extermination of the virus could do that. (The metaphor is Ting's.) To accomplish this, Ting established an annex to the printing office to collect and burn the proscribed books. Long and varied, the list included famous novels like *Shui-hu chuan* (Water margin), *Hung-lou meng* (Dream of the red chamber), and *Hsi-hsiang chi* (Western chamber), as well as frankly pornographic material with suggestive titles like *Hu-ch'un pai-shih* (Women in heat) and *Pa-mei t'u* (Eight soft spots).[114] Each hsien established a branch office where local book dealers and collectors could turn in and be compensated for (though not necessarily at full market value) their plates and books with no questions asked. All Magistrates were given the standard warning not to allow their yamen underlings to use this order as a pretext for harassing the people; and, with the exception of cases in Ch'ung-ming and Lou hsiens, at least this part of the directive seems to have been fulfilled.[115]

Impressed by Ting's actions, the court instructed other provinces to ban "lewd" literature.[116] Like an earlier effort of Tao-kuang Kiangsu officials, however, the success of the proscription was only temporary.[117] During the height of the campaign, two Magistrates received merits for their work; but three years later, in 1871, a Censor reported that book dealers throughout the empire were again openly flouting the law, and asked for the prohibition and destruction of novels.[118] Thus Ting was tilting at windmills; even Tseng Kuo-fan's library contained a copy of *Hung-lou meng.*[119] The *North China Herald,* moreover, reported "murmurings" among the Chinese to the effect that many of the proscribed books were "of the most harmless character," unlikely to offend "even the severest puritan."[120]

Yet, hindsight does not permit us to mock either Ting's intent or his methodology. The impact of the Literary Inquisition suggests that, pursued with rigor as a coordinated national policy over several decades, his program might well have succeeded.[121] Moreover, as Lu Shih-ch'iang has pointed out, Ting was acting within the scope of traditional concepts which connected attitude to social order, and, in turn, to political order.[122] Eschewing the more rabid literati opposition's concentration on cases of personal disasters induced by novel reading—the official whose dismissal and subsequent death were caused by accidentally copying portions of his beloved *Jou-pu t'uan* (Pillow of flesh) into his official reports; the youth who so immersed himself in *Hsi-hsiang chi* that he forgot to eat or sleep for a week and died—Ting concerned himself with the broader social effects that the popularity of such characters as *Hung-lou meng*'s Pao Yü and *Shui-hu chuan*'s Sung Chiang might have upon a still unsettled populace.[123]

Paradoxically, while Ting systematically attacked the small pleasures of the people, he sought to reduce the harshness of their lives and increase their income by controlling yamen underlings' depredations, eliminating illicit tax surcharges, reducing pawnshop rates, and encouraging the opening of better financed and regulated pawnshops.[124] In place of the proscribed plays and novels (unlike the People's Republic which has had the sense to retain the dramatic and literary forms while altering the didactic content), Ting simply closed the theaters and offered the people weekly moral exhortation. He tried, however, to ensure that they could afford their few leisure moments by fixing the price of a cup of tea at 5 cash. Though Tseng Kuo-fan's *mu-yu,* Chao Lieh-wen, ridiculed this action as beneath the attention of a governor and unfair to the small shopkeepers, it was characteristic of Ting's attention to the small problems of daily living, and was a significant act, for a cup of tea was about the only form of relaxation Ting had left to the people.[125]

STRUCTURE AND CONTENT OF EDUCATION

Ting had once characterized his craving for books as "sick." The decadent customs of Kiangsu, in his view, were also an illness. We have examined how he ministered to its symptoms and have alluded to what he considered its cause: a fundamental breakdown in education—that is, a failure to instruct and sustain the people in the knowledge of proper behavior (*li*). This educational process literally had to begin in the cradle, and the Chinese assumed it naturally to include appreciable behavioral regression.[126] For the elite, it was an education that was their birthright. For the poor, it was an education provided in foundling homes and charitable schools. For both, it was an education putatively reinforced by constant reiteration in temple ceremonies and lectures on the *Expanded Sacred Edicts.*

The social welfare institutions (*shan-t'ang*) which cared for the poor were a focus of elite-official tension. The majority were elite-organized, financed (largely by rents from varying amounts of land), and directed, while the state took an active supervisory interest. Its aim was twofold: to ensure that they were well enough funded to fulfill their obligations—public funds were sometimes provided to equalize differences between rich and poor hsiens' *shan-t'ang*, and to ensure that the funds were not mishandled.[127] Local officials were also required by law to establish public relief homes (*yang-ch'i yuan*) for the feeding and housing of those in need without close family: the ill, the aged, the widowed, the orphaned, and the abandoned.[128] The Rebellion, however, had destroyed most of both the public and private welfare institutions; and it was the state which, through the initiative of energetic magistrates, took the exemplary lead in re-establishing them.[129] Because the number of indigent adults seems to have been relatively small, Ting and other Restoration officials devoted their attention to caring for abandoned children and to stopping the practice of female infanticide, which was particularly acute in the hard times following the Rebellion.[130]

Infanticide, contrary to most generalizations, though far more prevalent among the rural poor, was also practiced by the rich and literate, and sometimes claimed boys as well as girls.[131] In the pre-Taiping period, seven to eight infanticides in a single family and more than ten per year in a village were reported, and one would expect the figures to have been higher in the more difficult post-bellum period.[132] A prohibitory proclamation had been issued in 1866 by Ting's predecessor as Financial Commissioner, Wang Ta-ching; but more substantive action was needed to stop the practice.[133] The law was not particularly severe, considering infanticide to be less serious than printing or selling novels, and containing no legal constraints against abandonment.[134] Exhortations against both customs were an integral part of the bimonthly lectures in the villages, but the most effective deterrents were financial support for the family and/or the establishment of foundling homes.[135] Ting took the latter approach.

Before examining Ting's actions, however, a brief digression into terminology is necessary. The *yang-ch'i yuan* generally did not include orphaned or abandoned children, but children accompanying their widowed mothers seem to have been accepted.[136] More commonly, foundling homes were called *yü-ying t'ang* or *ch'ih-t'ang;* and, though they accepted all children, most of their residents were girls.[137] Moreover, the foundling homes excluded children over the age of eight. These youths, until age fourteen, were placed in homes for the winter only and were expected to make their own way by begging in the warmer months, or were placed year round in manual training schools. In other sources, children over ten were considered capable of supporting themselves; and indeed the law, for purposes of defining murder, regarded anyone over ten as an adult.[138] Finally, there were organizations known as *pao-ying hui* which financed the care of children in their own homes and also supported the foundling homes.[139] When considered *in toto,* China's public and private relief homes, foundling homes, charitable granaries, soup kitchens, free schools, and burial societies suggest that, when functioning perfectly, Chinese society could provide the cradle-to-grave support generally associated only with the modern welfare state.

Ting was particularly concerned about two aspects in establishing foundling homes: that there be adequate financial support to maintain the homes and the children; that adequate and proper staff be hired. Depositing interest-bearing principal in a pawnshop, exacting surcharges on pawnshop licenses, and owning income-producing land were all acceptable to Ting as means of generating monies for the homes;[140] but he cautioned magistrates on the handling of the principal and seemed to prefer landed income.[141] Fortunately for the homes of Kiangsu, the court had recently approved a Censor's request to forbid the reconstruction of destroyed Buddhist temples and monasteries. Acting upon this decision, Ting ordered the closure of two decimated Yangchow monasteries, the confiscation of their 10,000 *mou* of land, and its deeding over to various welfare institutions. In another case, Ting explained that, unlike Han Yü, he did not oppose Buddhism itself, but rather the occupation of so much land by so few monks. He feared that bogus monks might take it over to finance the spread of heterodox ideas.[142]

Ting's organizational instructions for the foundling homes seem to be based on Tao-kuang precedents in Wu-hsi and Chin-kuei.[143] The two key posts, he wrote, were the directors and the wet nurses. Unless the directors were carefully chosen men who would "look upon the orphans as they would their own children," they would exclude the poor in preference to those who could pay, would select incompetent or immoral wet nurses, would feign to hire a pediatrician (*ying-i*), and might even sell the girls into prostitution. Ting feared that poor wet nurses would either play favorites, allowing some children to go unfed, or would stupidly try to nurse too many at a time. Still worse, they might simply be unconcerned whether the child was wet or dry, warm or cold.[144]

Financially enabling families to keep their children at home could, however, save the cost of maintaining the foundling homes and avoid the administrative problems of operating them. Indeed, this home-care approach seems to have been favored in Kiangsu. Gentry-funded "save-the-children associations" (*pao-ying hui*) supported an infant for its first six months with monthly payments of 200 cash to its family. Only if the family was still unable to care for the child properly was it to be placed in the *pao-ying hui*'s foundling home, but one *hui* reported that this happened with fewer than 20 percent of the children.[145] As Wang Ta-ching, Ting's predecessor as Financial Commissioner, phrased it, "The help will cause the parents to think about keeping the child; because they keep it, love will develop; because they love it, they will save it." The first six months were especially critical, for, by their end, the child would be laughing and personable, and it would be far more wrenching for the parent to kill a little person than a mewling newborn.[146] This view manifests a shrewd assessment of human character, an understanding of the family's excellence as a nurturing environment, and a strong anti-institutional bias. That Ting and other officials preferred a centralized, closely regulated, institutional solution does not mean that he was any less concerned for the children's welfare. Rather, it suggests that he was leery of the decentralized, independent style characteristic of all gentry undertakings.

Charitable schools (*i-hsueh*) were often attached to foundling homes and *ch'ing-chieh t'ang,* and Ting ordered the Yangchow *yang-ch'i yuan* to establish an *i-hsueh;*[147] but more important, in 1867, he instructed every hsien to establish at least four such schools, one for each *hsiang.*[148] Before this, few hsien had more than one, and some had none at all.[149] Yet the schools were supposedly an integral part of the Ch'ing's system of ideological control. Accepting students—preferably the poor or orphaned—between the ages of seven and fourteen, the schools instructed them in the *Hsiao-ching* (Classic of filial piety), Chu Hsi's *Primer,* the *Four Books,* and the *Expanded Sacred Edicts.* T'ang Pin, an early Ch'ing Governor, suggested that students should begin with the *Primer,* Chu Hsi's distillation of his basic teachings on the "fundamentals of self-cultivation"; but he considered that *au fond* nothing was more basic than the *Classic of Filial Piety,* a work of highly authoritarian teachings.[150] Although there were lively debates on teaching technique, on the relevance and vitality of instruction, on prospects for the poor's education, on the difficulty of the readings, and on the length of the school year, this basic Confucian curriculum was never challenged. Perhaps that is why peasant youths allegedly could perform capably on the stage a hundred days after they joined a theater troup but learned nothing after two years in the schools,[151] for, as Evelyn Rawski has noted, classical texts were "inappropriate" for transmitting "Confucian values to the general populace in clear and easily understood terms within a relatively short time."[152]

To "change the customs and strengthen the minds of the people" through Confucianism was indeed the aim of these schools.[153] In particular, said Ting, the schools should seek out and indoctrinate the brightest among the poor; otherwise "the people's alertness and cleverness become cunning":

> The obstacle [for the talented among the poor] is poor social position. Books are beyond their power. *Yet there is not a father or older brother who does not love his sons or younger brothers. There are none who do not hope for their success. But to want to encourage the youth to become good men and not give them a measure of understanding of the principle of righteousness would be like setting aside the five grains and seeking elsewhere a means to sustain life, like throwing away a measure and seeking to level a thing!*[154]

In Ting's view, then, the schools had multilevel but coordinate tasks to accomplish: "on high to store men of ability for the nation; below to change the bad customs of the villages."[155] In practice, however, the latter was the primary concern, and the former, at best, a secondary one. But for the few who climbed the examination ladder to the *chu-jen* degree, Ting ordered the re-institution of provincial government travel stipends, so that the "poor scholars' desire to travel to the capital [Peking, for the metropolitan examinations] would not be impeded by a lack of funds."[156]

Ting's proposed school regulations followed well-established patterns.[157] The schools would come under the general supervision of the district director of schools (*chiao-yü*), who was to check each school regularly. Together with two gentry directors, who were to act as school heads, the *chiao-yü* was to compile and file with the magistrate a monthly register which reported on the students' biographical data and educational progress and on the teachers' competence. For every ten students there was to be one teacher selected from first-degree holders of "excellent character and conduct." Literary excellence could not be substituted for this criterion. Teachers' salaries were to be fixed at 6,000 cash a month, but Ting subsequently urged adoption of the Hsiao hsien model where stipendiary students at the local *shu-yuan* taught for nothing at the *i-hsueh*.[158]

The test of a teacher's diligence was the quality of his students' conduct and knowledge. The students themselves were rewarded or punished according to their rankings:

1. Exemplary conduct and thorough knowledge of assignments: rewarded.
2. Good conduct but unprepared assignments: neither rewarded nor punished.
3. Poor conduct but fine student: additional moral instruction.
4. Wild behavior and poor preparation of assignments: beating and reproval with expulsion after three beatings.

Teachers unable to exercise control over their students were to be dismissed (as were opium smokers).[159] Equally critical was the teacher's ability to explain readings clearly enough for the students to understand how to apply their lessons to their personal conduct, "for," said Ting, "the natural disposition of a youth is to be ripe for change."

Ting did not offer guidelines, however, on the financing of the *i-hsueh.* He announced that the provincial government would pay the salaries of teachers in the first four schools established in each hsien, but did not specify the length of this support.[160] He clearly expected that the additional schools he ordered for every market town (*chen*) and village (*ts'un*) would be supported by their localities through methods devised by their respective directors. Even the initial schools do not seem to have been fully financed by the provincial government, and income was variously derived from donations put out to pawnshops for interest, confiscation of clerks' illegal exactions, and land taken from monasteries.[161]

Again, Ting preferred landed income; and in T'ai-hu, T'ai-ts'ang, Yangchow, and Chiang-yin, expropriated temple lands provided a ready source. Not only did this approach endow the *i-hsueh* with operating revenues; it also buttressed Confucianism at the expense of Buddhism. As a Tao-kuang Magistrate observed, the more land used for charitable schools, the less incense, the less superstition.[162] This policy was, nevertheless, not without its problems. In Yangchow, the Prefect, probably to save time, asked the monks themselves to report the amount of arable land they controlled, whereupon Ting commented that this was like "asking the fox to plan its own skinning." And he warned the Chiang-yin Magistrate to expect slander and organized mob opposition under the leadership of the monks and the litigation tricksters (*sung-kun*).[163] Although, in the last decade of the Ch'ing, the clash between the financial imperatives of the state's new educational programs and the clergy's interest in temple property erupted into violence, there is no evidence that Ting's fears of trouble ever materialized during his office.[164]

Only a fortunate few schools, however, had sufficient landed income to support themselves; and this fiscal uncertainty was one of the basic flaws in the Ch'ing's social-welfare institutions which were in some cases legal obligations of the state, and in all instances moral and social responsibilities of the elite. Yet the schools, key elements of social control, were only grudgingly supported by the state and erratically by the elite, some of whom, validly fearing harassment from the yamen, paid to avoid its directorial obligations.[165] Even when the elite accepted their responsibilities, Ting expressed doubts about their management, commenting that too often an acquaintanceship with the director rather than an ability to pay determined who was admitted to the free schools.[166]

To check on the performance of magistrates, educational officials, and gentry directors, Ting relied on informers to supplement the monthly reports which he considered not wholly reliable. Ting found that he had to prod the Magistrate of Yuan-ho (one of the three head hsien) who had been noticeably laggard in establishing the schools.[167] In Wu-chiang, the excellent work of Shen Hsi-hua had not been sustained by his successor, while in Tan-yang the schools outnumbered the students, and only four students attended I-hsing's schools.[168] Ting warned the Magistrate of Nan-hui, who fabricated reports on the numbers of students and schools, that he would not allow him to compensate for his long impoverished wait for office at the expense of the people. "Better to have one family crying," Ting wrote, "than to make everyone cry."[169] "He laughed with joy," he said, after reading the Hsiao hsien Magistrate's report, for the Magistrate's diligent establishment of schools had reintroduced after a long hiatus "the sound of music and poetry" to Hsu-hai.[170] Finally, evidence in local histories suggests that, overall, Ting's establishment of free community schools was one of his more notable and durable successes. In the wake of his order, there was a surge in the construction of the schools; and after a period of rationalization, in which the less viable ones were eliminated or consolidated, many of them survived well into the Kuang-hsu period. Whether the schools fully accomplished the task Ting had set out for them is, unfortunately, too broad a question to be answered here, although it seems unlikely that Confucian values were as deeply inculcated as he desired. But many of the youths who attended the schools attained a measure of functional literacy, a skill that enabled them on their own to achieve another goal desired by Ting, to make them less vulnerable to yamen underlings, shysters, and landlords.[171]

Complementing and extending the free community schools was the *hsiang-yueh* lecture system, which sought to indoctrinate the broad unschooled masses in the principles of proper conduct. Throughout the dynasty, officials or locally selected lecturers had delivered at the county seat and in the countryside bimonthly lectures on the *Hsiao-hsueh* and the *Expanded Sacred Edicts.*[172] But, said Ting, just as in the Han and T'ang, a general decline in teaching had allowed religious rebels to arise. Since the people no longer knew the *li,* their reinstruction was critical. Therefore Ting reprinted the *Expanded Sacred Edicts* at the Kiangsu Printing Office and issued them to all Magistrates together with a circular order instructing them to reestablish the lecture system in their jurisdictions.[173] Tseng Kuo-fan, according to Chao Lieh-wen, considered it absurd for a man of Ting's limited scholarly background to undertake this educational task;[174] but Ting's regulations were innovative, if only in minor ways, and were marked by the seriousness and insistence that characterized all his actions.

Of all the various elements in Ting's regulations, K. C. Hsiao regards the increased frequency of lectures, the salaried lecturers, the supervision by education officials, and the monthly reports as the most significant.[175] Apparently, Ting felt that a subject to be taught effectively had to be taught often, for he ordered the lectures to be given in every *hsiang* once every five days instead of once every ten or fifteen. To alleviate any additional burden this frequency might have placed on the magistrate, he assigned supervisory and primary lecturing responsibility to the district director and assistant director of schools. (Although this might seem an impractical piece of window dressing, at least one hsien followed this system well into the next reign.)[176] Selected and paid to assist them, were to be local men whose only qualifications had to be literacy and good conduct. (Ting explicitly excluded degree-holding as a criterion.)[177] These men, together with the local constables, were to designate schools or temples as regular sites for the lectures; and the constables were to prepare adequate seating "so that there would be no overcrowding causing the people to tire of standing and think of leaving." Finally, the lecturers and education officials were to submit to Ting, through the magistrate, a monthly report on the operation of the system.

Traditionally, lecturers had always filed reports on local customs and conditions.[178] Ting asked them also to incorporate information on men of unusual skills or abilities in astronomy, mathematics, or medicine. But more important, he further required them to submit copies of the lectures themselves, a discussion of which ones were most effective, and an estimation of the size of the audience and its percentage of possibly enlightened. Ting reminded the potential evaders and prevaricators among the magistrates and teaching officals that, regardless of their reports, local conditions would reflect their success or failure, and warned all of them that their performance of these tasks would determine official merits.[179] And, for one lecturer in Li-yang whose "clear voice and persuasive style kept the people from fidgeting and thinking of leaving," success did, indeed, bring a reward.[180]

Strengthening the morale of the people was essential, in Ting's opinion, not only to combat domestic heterodoxy but also "to remove the foreign calamity."[181] He made this connection explicit by accompanying a memorial on the importance of rewards for diligent magistrates and teaching officials with another on the positive impact of the lecturers in Chiang-yin, an area of extensive foreign presence. Where Chinese came in close contact with the "foreigners' detrimental teachings," wrote Ting, the heterodoxy, still common in Kiangsu after the Rebellion, was exacerbated. In the face of this dangerous situation, officials were "as lax as 'our party' when Wang An-shih established his new laws."[182] But, said Ting, in Chiang-yin, where administration was able, where the taxes were fair, where the Chinese local officials provided the poor with foundling homes, burial costs, medicine, and gruel, and where the lectures were diligently delivered and charitable schools established, not only were there merely no converts to Christianity, but apostates numbered in the thousands. There was, concluded Ting, no more reason "to fly from the tall trees [of Confucianism] down into the valley [of heterodoxy]."[183]

Ting had purposively and straightforwardly pinpointed the cause of the state's failure to teach Confucian principles to the people. When the people's lives were unbearable and when they were treated poorly or with "benign neglect" by the elite and by the state, there was little or no reason for them to accept—much less to put faith in—the "imperial Confucianism" of the state and of the elite. Economic pressures could also subvert the elite's adherence to Confucian principles, and officials themselves were in a parallel situation.[184] As Huang Liu-hung had asked two centuries before, how could the local official be expected to teach the people when he, himself, was governed so harshly and was so preoccupied with avoiding the slightest error?[185] Yet an age-old view, reiterated here by Ting, held:

> The order of chaos of the empire is based on the magistrates, whose effectual administration is nothing more than the two principles of instruction and nourishing (*chiao-yang*).[186]

Herein lies the irony, for such a central element of administration, indeed in the Ch'ien-lung Emperor's own words, "The very way of governance," was omitted from the evaluation (*k'ao-ch'eng*) of local officials. Little wonder then, as Ting phrased it in his request for rewards for the diligent ones, that most officials dismissed the lectures (and we may infer the rest of *chiao-yang*) as "irrelevant."[187]

FOUR

Judicial Administration and Reform

Biting through has success
It is favorable to let
justice be administered
I Ching, No. 21

Ch'ing officials recognized that social order could neither be restored nor sustained by moral education alone. When education's transformative powers proved deficient, the supplementary instructional force of law had to be invoked—that is, one had to punish in order not to have to punish again. Although in this schema law was subordinate to education (one had to teach before punishing), in another sense the law was literally of cosmic importance. Deeply imbedded in Chinese thought by the nineteenth century was the syncretic belief that man and nature were organic elements in a seamless cosmic web. Injustice of any kind rent the web, not simply at one point, but placed tension on the entire structure as well. For officials to ignore the injury was to court catastrophe—cosmic disequilibrium and the withdrawal by heaven of a dynasty's mandate to rule. It was for the law to restore equilibrium by perfectly redressing, or at least requiting, the injustice. Although Restoration officials, who had just rebuffed a challenge to the Ch'ing's mandate, appear not to have explicitly addressed these sublime issues, their ostensibly mundane concerns were still

The God of Walls and Moats Judging a Wrongdoer, *popular print, from "The Mythology of Modern China," by Henry Maspero, in* Asiatic Mythology, *ed. J. Hackin and others (New York, Crowell, 1932), p. 287.*

correlative to the mandate of heaven; for, together with tax collection, the administration of justice was the most conspicuous public function of the state. Performed well, it induced cooperation from the people. Performed poorly, it alienated them. To cope properly with the criminality and litigiousness that even the most idealistic Restoration officials accepted as immutable elements of human society, the judicial system had to be cleansed of its accumulated abuses.

In ordinary times, a court of law was a last resort; as in many societies, it was potentially a nexus of hazardous entanglements resulting in loss of time and money, physical abuse, and social alienation. (Not surprisingly, to involve an enemy in litigation was a traditional form of vengeance.)[1] Officials, both to save themselves from the additional responsibility and to spare the people from dangers, discouraged civil suits. Avoidance of them was a central theme in everyone's socialization and in lectures on the *Expanded Sacred Edicts.* From plays and religious practices people became familiar with court procedure and its pitfalls, and, for many, the popular saying "rather to die of indignation than to be involved in litigation" took on concrete form.[2] Indeed, Ting Jih-ch'ang's concern for compassionate and efficient justice probably stems from his recollections of just such an incident which he witnessed as a youth:

> When I was a poor commoner, a woman who lived nearby committed suicide after a quarrel with her in-laws. Soon after, several tens of her relatives gathered; then a bit later, several tens each of constables, clerks, and runners arrived, followed in turn by a collection of more than one hundred sedan-chair carriers and beggars, all making such a racket that they drowned out the chickens and dogs. The next day the mother-in-law committed suicide; and the father-in-law took this opportunity to flee, leaving their land, house, and utensils to be divided up without a trace by the mob. *In an instant a reasonably well-to-do family had collapsed and died. Even today I still think it heartbreaking. If we only expend a little more effort, the commoners will receive immeasurable blessings.*[3]

Still, fear of the courts may not have been either so pervasive or so dissuasive of litigation as we are wont to think. Conditions were hardly uniform throughout China. The quality of justice, and hence the attitude of people toward the law, depended upon a number of variables: the press of judicial business; the ability of the magistrate; and the socioeconomic context—in particular, the power of vested interests and the strength of village or clan dispute-settlement institutions. Moreover, the very plays and stories that horrified people with riveting accounts of torture, inequity, and aggrieved ghosts often enthralled them at the climax with ultimate triumphs of justice. Perhaps the message to people was not an unequivocal caveat to avoid the courts, but a more measured admonition that, though justice would be done, only a genuine and significant grievance warranted the risks. Yet the alacrity with which people brought minor disputes to court and the heavy use of the appellate system suggest that, regardless of the magnitude of the complaint and the potential dangers of having it heard, courts were nonetheless for many an attractive dispute-resolution mechanism.[4]

In examining Ting's efforts to improve justice in Kiangsu, we must rely on evidence that provides us with a skewed sampling of cases. For, as Financial Commissioner and then as Governor, the cases that came before him were either criminal ones, or civil ones which had escalated into criminal ones, had been appealed, or had been marred by serious procedural errors. Regardless of the case, however, the basic judicial process was essentially the same. A petition or accusation would be submitted to the magistrate, who decided solely on the basis of the presentation in the plaint whether or not to accept the case for judgment. In cases accepted for adjudication, summonses or warrants would be issued for the plaintiff, the defendant, and relevant witnesses to appear in court; and in capital cases (those involving death or armed robbery) the magistrate personally conducted an on-the-spot inquest or investigation.

After trying the case in open court, the magistrate rendered his decision, and, in minor cases (*tzu-li tz'u-sung*) involving punishments no greater than the cangue, immediately executed the sentence. More serious cases were subject to a process of obligatory review through a retrial at each level up to the governor, and, in instances of capital crimes, to the Board of Punishments and the Emperor in Peking. Any case, moreover, regardless of its seriousness, could be appealed to higher levels.

The judicial process was, of course, not as streamlined as this outline suggests. Indeed, the most common problem was the intentional delaying of cases in order to implicate additional people and exact bribes from those involved. As Wang Hui-tsu, the famous late-eighteenth-century Magistrate, observed, too frequently, "once a paper goes into the yamen, even nine oxen cannot drag it out again."[5] And, though there were myriad other difficulties, Ting, as had others before him, reasonably argued that there was a simple key to the proper operation of the system: "Cases should not be lightly accepted [for trial]. Once accepted, they should be quickly tried; once tried, quickly concluded. Then all abuses will be eliminated."[6]

Ting spoke from experience, for from his magistracy in Kiangsi to the governorship in Kiangsu, he himself dealt swiftly with cases and developed procedures designed both to hasten the judicial process and to uncover its abuses. Yet this ostensibly praiseworthy advance in social justice may well have produced the blameworthy social phenomenon of encouraging litigation, because it facilitated the bringing of suits over even the most minor matters. Handbooks and edicts all urged magistrates to handle cases with despatch, and, though magistrates at times fancied themselves a Judge Ti or a Judge Pao (renowned judges of the T'ang and Sung who were canonized in popular dramas) to whom the aggrieved flocked, in the real world a crowded docket was seen by superiors not as a sign of skillful and honest justice, but as a failure to maintain social harmony. Caught in this "Catch-22," good magistrates were often forced to discourage plaintiffs. As one admonished a persistent petitioner, "You have mistaken my diligence at hearing litigation for pleasure."[7]

PETITIONS

Unless the authorities themselves caught a criminal in the act or discovered a corpse, the Ch'ing legal machinery remained inoperative until it was triggered by either a written or oral complaint. Not every petition, however, was successful in initiating the process, for the magistrate, functioning as the system's gatekeeper, was authorized to accept (*chun*) or reject (*po*) any petition for a hearing.

While a criminal complaint could be pressed at any time, the bringing of civil charges was literally not a daily occurrence, since such petitions could usually be submitted only on six specific days a month.[8] To critics who complained that such restricted access was suitable for the high provincial officials but not for the magistrate, who should not delay people with pressing grievances, the early Ch'ing writer Huang Liu-hung replied that, to the contrary, this was a reasonable procedure which allowed people time to calm down and settle a dispute amicably out of court.[9] Even civil complaints that were submitted on the appropriate day were frequently refused by magistrates on the same grounds—they could just as well be resolved out of court. Criminal cases, however, because of the penalties involved in unfairly rejecting them, were almost always heard.

Inevitably, petitioners sought to influence the discretionary power of magistrates, which often had become de facto invested in the hands of yamen underlings. For a fee these clerks and runners, frequently without the cognizance of the magistrate, could guarantee acceptance of special written and shouted petitions (*ch'uan-ch'eng, han ch'eng*). A petition submitted in the morning, accompanied by the not insignificant amount of 10,000 cash (less for a shouted petition), would result in a favorable judgment by afternoon. The defendant meanwhile was not only losing the case but also being menaced by the bribed underlings, who had at the plaintiff's behest arranged in advance to be the runner on duty (*tso-ch'ai*) the day the petition was submitted. These warrant-servers would confront the defendant with a choice: a bribe to squash the warrant or arrest and illicit confinement (*niu-chiao chih-chiao*) with little chance of redress. Of course, noted Ting, were a gentry director (*shen-tung*) to forward the complaint under cover of his calling card, these ruses would be unnecessary, since local officials were reluctant to reject petitions from gentry. Angered by this distorted justice that "provided certain victory for the strong and endless trouble for the weak," Ting ordered the elimination of all such practices in a general notice that reiterated an 1866 ban on special petition fees.[10]

As Governor, Ting subsequently reaffirmed these prohibitions, but with two interesting deletions. He removed the ban on shouted petitions, not only because it duplicated the proscription on written special ones, but also in order not to discourage the legal shouted petitions through which hard-pressed commoners frequently expressed their grievances. Ting, moreover, seems to have felt that the ban would discourage commoners from stopping his sedan chair to make an accusation. Although such accusations were technically illegal, Ting thought they should be allowed and be given a sympathetic private hearing.[11] Second, probably under gentry pressure, he excised the references to gentry involvement for they failed to differentiate between the well-intentioned activities of upright gentry who might have been acting in an amicus curiae role and the litigation mongering of *sheng-chien* "litigation tricksters" (*sung-kun*). To distinguish between the two became the responsibility of the magistrates, whose duty, Ting reminded them, was also to save the people's livelihood from the danger of litigation. In a characteristically double-toned notice, Ting threatened and cajoled the magistrates:

> Any magistrates who continue in their old ways will be impeached as soon as I have proof. I know well that litigation is a great threat to the people's livelihood. Certainly this is crystal clear to everyone. *I want you to attend to it [the people's litigation] with the heart of a boddhisattva and create blessings for posterity's children.*[12]

As Ting himself undoubtedly knew, his rhetoric was unrealistic. Within months he seems to have accepted the inevitability of special petitions, and focused upon eliminating the fees. He again forbade them and also fixed the price a scribe could charge for making up a petition; but both problems were ineradicable, for a short time later Ting received reports of scribes' fees ten times too large and special petition charges ranging between 10,000 and 20,000 cash.[13] Even simply to present a petition or to press charges, a plaintiff had to meet yamen underlings' demands.[14] Probably in Kiangsu, as in late Ch'ing Hunan, both the special petition and its fee gradually became accepted as legitimate.[15]

For those interested in expediting their legal affairs but unable to afford the special petition, a less expensive alternative was the pettifogger or litigation trickster. Described in a Penal Code commentary as anyone who "taught the unknowing to make a plaint and induced the reluctant to submit a plaint," the tricksters included scribes who falsified petitions, exacerbators of nearly mediated minor suits, and appeals specialists who took advantage of magistrates' carelessly worded decisions. (Although the social composition of litigation tricksters is not wholly clear, it seems that many were otherwise unemployed *sheng-yuan* and *chien-sheng.*)[16] The trickster's basic function was to enhance a simply worded petition by inflating the seriousness of the charge or adding colorful detail in order to entice the magistrate's interest and induce him to accept the plaint. Since the trickster could not accompany the plaintiff into court, the outcome of the suit ultimately depended upon the plaintiff's performance in the courtroom. Hence, regardless of the result, the trickster could assert that he had done his part. If the case was lost, it was the plaintiff's bad testimony. If the case was won, it was the quality of the petition.[17]

The trickster, moreover, was profiting not simply from the plaintiff. In his petition he had implicated innocent people and listed wholly irrelevant but well-to-do individuals as witnesses, for the purpose of eliciting bribes to have their names deleted and thus escape the issuance of summonses.[18] For, though magistrates were supposed to call to court only the most important witnesses, it was not at all uncommon for everyone from the protagonists to the most minor witnesses (save generally very wealthy or influential) to be held in custody until the case came to trial and then afterwards throughout any appeals.[19]

Because the legal process was a minefield of regulations in which a careless error could be career-threatening, magistrates abhorred the tricksters for fomenting and then complicating litigation. Owing to the extraordinary specificity and particularism of the Chinese Penal Code, the magistrate had to be especially cautious in adjudicating a case. Failure to establish the basic facts resulted not only in discipline for that transgression itself, but also in consequent errors in judgment or sentencing for which the magistrate could also be punished. Magistrates, engaged in an ongoing combat with the pettifoggers, had to be alert to effective tactics.

The linchpin of the magistrate's defense was the trickster's own weapon, the petition. By constricting the scope of the trickster's pen, the magistrate limited his chances of success. Thus, in Kiangsu and Taiwan, preprinted simplified complaint forms with space for a limited number of characters were issued, and petitions that exceeded this length were not accepted.[20] If a complaint met this standard, a magistrate was, upon its receipt, to "weigh the circumstances and distinguish the treacherous falsehoods [from the truth]" by looking for the recommended indicators of falsification: multiple defendants, an extensive list of witnesses, inconsistency between the petition and the plaintiff's oral presentation, and an inability of the plaintiff to explain the brief's language.[21] Should a discrepancy be discerned, the magistrate was expected to discover the instigator (not always an easy task) and bring him to justice.[22] Finally, in commenting on the petition, the magistrate "should use a good simple style so that every word of his comment is to the point. Then the conniving will submit, and pettifoggers will not dare to try their tricks."[23] In Ting's view, magistrates who could not prevent the tricksters from "grubbing off" the common people (*ma-shih pai-hsing*) were of no use at all.[24]

To reinforce the impact of the established restrictions on "litigation tricksters," Ting issued a proclamation in July 1867, forbidding the instigation of litigation. Noting that the Penal Code called for habitual tricksters to be sentenced to military servitude in malarial border regions, he emphasized that "it did not say not to be strict"; and he warned that there would indeed be no leniency: "When I speak, the law follows."[25] Yet here, as in other cases, Ting's behavior proved more moderate than his rhetoric. In one case a *sheng-yuan* was permanently deprived of his present title and button, but was not additionally punished, and then was granted permission by Ting to retake the examinations to get a new start in life. Should he ever again, however, "use his pen as a knife," Ting promised to mete out full merciless retribution. Other tricksters were arrested and punished by Ting's order, but never in their cases did he urge severity.[26]

Ting also initiated a measure which appears further to have subverted his efforts to control the tricksters' fomenting of litigation: he suspended the requirement that the officially designated scribes seal their copies of petitions.[27] This action is significant for two reasons. First, it shows that, as inclined as Ting was toward detailed control of clerks, he was willing to chance the resurgence of abuses and to deregulate if he perceived (as he did in this case) potential substantial advantages for the commoner. Instituted originally to bind the scribe to the veracity of his petition, these sealing procedures were soon turned by the scribes to their own advantage. Should a plaintiff implicate a clerk or refuse to pay additional illicit fees, the scribe would simply decline to seal the petition, thereby dooming it to rejection. By removing this impediment, Ting hoped to ensure that the people's grievances against yamen underlings would get a hearing. Second, Ting's action indicates that the Penal Code, which clearly required the scribes to sign and seal petitions, could be modified by provincial officials without prior or even subsequent approval from the central authorities.[28]

INQUESTS

Cases involving death were almost as hazardous for the deceased's family and officials as for the defendant. Only tricksters and the yamen staff welcomed them, for they promised the greatest illicit rewards. Ting described, without exaggeration, the joy such cases caused in the office of one Kiangpei Magistrate:

> The clerks in that office all sent congratulations to the clerks and runners on duty that day, together with presents of wine and flowers. Then, after the clerk of the day had gotten his profit [out of the inquest], he thanked the others tenfold. Such blatant gall which took the people's lives as a source of profit was heart-rending and hateful.[29]

The sums involved were substantial, for, despite the laws to the contrary, large yamen retinues always "assisted" in inquests. People implicated in the case, correctly or not, paid as much as 9,000 cash, while the surrounding neighborhoods might be dunned for another 10,000 cash. Even the deceased's family was not immune from such depredations.[30]

Officials approached inquests with trepidation, because they were conducted in public, and particularly dreaded those in which the issue was whether a death was homicide or suicide, since friends and family of the deceased gathered, ostensibly to await the results. Actually, they were there to superintend and in some instances to dispute the magistrate at every step, to intimidate the official into a certain conclusion.[31] Moreover, any error of fact made by the magistrate might directly result in an aggravation or diminution of the nature of a crime and lay the grounds for an appeal.

Ting once commented that a carefully conducted inquest not only would persuade people to accept its conclusions and close tricksters' loopholes, but also would allow the magistrate to "face the spirits with a peaceful heart."[32] Too often, though, sloppily rendered inquests stimulated further litigation which troubled the people's peace of mind, if not that of the magistrate. By law, a magistrate assisted by a coroner was personally to examine a corpse before it decayed, interrogate witnesses, and file an accurate report in accord with accepted terminology.[33] But, except in major cities, coroners were few and trained either poorly or not at all.[34] Rarely familiar with the *Hsi-yuan lu*

(Coroners' handbook), the coroners wrote reports that were vague and inaccurate. Magistrates were even more unfamiliar with correct procedures and terminology. They were, moreover, prone to entrust such business to unauthorized subordinates and were thoroughly reluctant to examine fresh, much less decomposing, corpses. One Magistrate explained his muddled report to an irate Ting by claiming that he had no guide upon which to rely in conducting the autopsy.[35] And the problem became so serious that Ting was moved to complain to a Prefect that "Kiangpei Magistrates constantly coin their own words to replace the proper ones, and I never know what they mean to say. If they keep it up, the Board of Punishments will have to hire interpreters!"[36]

Ting's reform of the inquests was not extraordinary. The basic elements can be found in the Penal Code and in earlier administrative writings: inquest fees should be fixed and paid for by the magistrate, who should bring only a few assistants and resist suggestions that he needed a large retinue for protection against local toughs; he should personally examine the corpse on the basis of the *Hsi-yuan lu* regardless of the stench and make a quick initial judgment before tricksters could muddle the case; finally, he should interrogate only a few witnesses, for, especially in suicide cases, the deceased's family, "seeking someone fat to bite," might make all sorts of accusations.[37]

Here again, Ting did not adduce the precedents which in this instance stipulated the magistrate's personal performance of the autopsy, the limited size of the retinue, and the magistrate's provision of all administrative costs and fees.[38] Granted, these were elementary and obvious points, yet Ting flatly stated that his program was a personal spontaneous response to the present situation.[39] Thomas Metzger, moreover, has argued that the reiteration of such basic information was considered by officials to be necessary for a "full presentation of a subject," and that, even when an official chose an administrative policy on practical grounds, he subsequently "found the precedents to back it, or at least part of it."[40] Ting's slightly defensive phrasing suggests he might very well have known the precedents, or perhaps he was genuinely unaware of them. Whatever the case, he appears to have been seeking to embellish his reputation for administrative innovation.

WARRANTS AND JAILS

An enduring problem in the Ch'ing judicial system was the dangerous misuse of warrants—both civil summonses (*ch'uan-piao*) and arrest warrants (*chü-piao*).[41] Abuses of arrest warrants were less widespread but had more dire consequences. In these instances, because there were strictly enforced deadlines for both runners and magistrates, and because the warrants often referred only to unknown perpetrators, there were both the opportunity and the motive for runners and magistrates to conclude troublesome cases by falsely accusing (or suborning to confess), arresting, and quickly trying innocent people. Examining one of these cases, Ting deduced:

> If we measure it with reason, it was certainly a case of the policeman getting a beating [from the magistrate] he could not bear. Because [he feared another beating], he enticed Mr. Ch'en with an offer of money and duped him with the rule about avoiding punishment by turning oneself in (*tzu-shou mien-tsui chih-li*). At first Mr. Ch'en was fooled into confessing, but when he found he would still be punished he changed his testimony.[42]

Ting noticed this case because of the gross discrepancies between the victim's and accused's descriptions of the events; and, though the charge was a serious one of robbery, there was no danger of capital punishment. In other instances, however, such as those when magistrates were allowed to request summary execution for disbanded soldiers suspected of brigandage, the consequences of false accusation for both accused and accuser were far more grave.[43] In a one-year period, Ting reversed forty such cases in Kiangpei, and in at least two of them saved the defendants at the last minute. But for others he was too late, and he labeled the involved Magistrates "butchers."[44]

Ting repeatedly urged Magistrates to put themselves in the people's place. *Shu,* reciprocity, was a basic tenet of Confucian ethics;

yet few Magistrates, the "officials close to the people" (*ch'in-min kuan*), seemed to practice it.[45] "For every drop of red ink in the yamen," Ting reminded the Magistrates, "the people shed a drop of red blood."

> Think how you would feel when you received the warrant, of how much money you would have to spend [in bribes], of how you would have to send the old and weak to the neighbors [to escape the runners' depredations], of how you would entrust your wealth to powerful households to speak for you. Close your eyes and think for a minute. Certainly you'll be sympathetic and unable to put pen to paper, much less to sign a single warrant. . . . We are all up from the fields and know well that the commoners have barely skin and bones after the Rebellion. We certainly know we cannot disturb and trouble them.[46]

Of course, had the Magistrates been able to switch roles, they might have shown more concern; but many of them had enough trouble coping with the demands and responsibilities of their own roles. They were expected to regulate the content of warrants by weeding out unimportant witnesses inserted into the petitions by tricksters, and to reduce the impact of the warrants on people by issuing few of them and by restricting the number of runners who served them. One runner per warrant or, still better, one per case was the ideal; but Ting discovered instances when seven served a single warrant, and fifty to sixty runners per warrant were not uncommon.[47]

Regardless of their number, runners could still manipulate the judicial process through procrastination. By delaying first in serving a warrant and then in delivering the parties to the magistrate, runners could prevent the disputants and the magistrate from ever seeing each other.[48] Officials traditionally responded to these dilatory tactics by setting strict time limits. Similarly, Ting, as Financial Commissioner, instructed Magistrates, on the basis of the distance and the numbers of people involved, to set and record deadlines for the delivery of people to the yamen. Subsequently, as Governor, he further refined the regulations at the suggestion of the Wu-hsi Magistrate. Runners were to report directly to the magistrate upon their arrival regardless of the hour, and were forbidden to lock up anyone on their own authority. Merits and rewards were to be awarded for meeting the deadline; reproval and fines inflicted for exceeding it. Interestingly, the aid of the subject of the warrants was enlisted by attaching the time-limit sheet to the warrant itself, and by interrogating the subject upon his arrival as to its observance.[49]

The agonizing threat of arrest was prolonged for anyone involved in a case, even after its conclusion, since warrants had a tendency to remain in circulation. The collection and destruction of warrants from closed cases was an old problem and one of particular concern to Ting. He constantly had to remind Magistrates of his earlier orders to close after two months all cases the plaintiffs had not pressed, and to destroy all outstanding warrants in open court; and he further instructed them to post throughout their hsiens a list of closed cases so that runners could not use old warrants for extortion.[50] To invigorate the Magistrates, Ting returned to the theme of reciprocity:

> When you were *hsiu-ts'ai,* you probably borrowed money. If the creditor had retained the receipt even after you had repaid in full, he could have demanded money and harassed you forever. *This is what an undestroyed warrant is like for the people.*[51]

But the Magistrates proved responsive only intermittently.

Ironically, responsiveness to his Magistrates' suggestions was a hallmark of Ting's career as Governor. Discussing the Wu-hsi Magistrate's proposals, Ting noted that, other than the time-limit sheet, the ideas were established ones, many of which he had already implemented. But, said Ting, it was good that the Magistrate had made known his thoughts.[52] Ting regularly sought out his Magistrates' ideas and used them whenever and wherever possible. In this sense, he was a good administrator, for by not only using his subordinates' ideas but also by giving them credit instead of taking it for himself, Ting encouraged Magistrates to continue to respond actively to his requests for comments and also to initiate new methods on their own. The problem in the long run was that many yamen underlings were more creative in their chicanery than most officials were in administration.

Although it was established policy, especially in minor cases, that, whenever possible, defendants and witnesses should be released on bail, receipt of a warrant, even in civil cases, generally led to detention, often without the magistrate's knowledge. For many Magistrates, a basic difficulty was that there was no officially fixed place where witnesses and disputants were held. Sometimes parties to a case (especially those of means) were detained in runners' unauthorized lockups (*ssu-she pan-kuan, ch'ai-kuan, ya-so*) before a trial and held even after they had been ordered released in order to generate bribes.[53] The lockups were often nothing more than an open stockade or even a room in the runner's house, although some runners made arrangements with small hostels to keep their charges. At other times witnesses and disputants were either kept in special litigants' hostels or left with serious convicted criminals in the yamen's regular prisons. Plaintiffs were held for months without ever being questioned, and deaths in jail of unindicted suspects and convicts in transit were not uncommon.[54]

The situation, however, was neither new nor limited to Kiangsu. Even at the Board of Punishments prisons in Peking, hardened criminals and innocent witnesses were randomly mixed.[55] In seventeenth-century Shantung, powerful gentry (*shen-chin*) rather than runners controlled the hostels for litigants and witnesses; Huang Liu-hung recommended that, instead, the magistrate, at his own expense, erect officially controlled hostels immediately adjacent to the yamen.[56] A few hsiens in nineteenth-century Kiangsu had such establishments, and Ting ordered (without immediate results) that the rest of the province follow suit: detainees should be listed on a public notice board, and the hostels should be kept rigorously clean, for it was unconscionable, Ting felt, that innocent people be felled by filth and disease.[57]

Derk Bodde has suggested that the propensity to imprison anyone remotely involved with a case "reflects the official point of view that legal involvement is ipso facto a culpable matter, to be avoided whenever possible."[58] Administrative writings indicate, to the contrary, that such hostility was directed against only the perpetrator of unnecessary litigation, and demonstrate that officials encouraged efforts to reduce the number of people who had to be held in custody through the course of a trial.[59] Bodde further argues, by quoting a jailer, that the mistreatment of prisoners had a logical basis in the mind of the yamen staff: "Law (*fa*) has been established to warn others by punishing criminals and to caution posterity. If we didn't act like this, people would get the idea that they deserve to have it easy."[60] This seems reasonable and suggests, moreover, that mistreatment had a basis in class differences. It was a way for the legally "mean" runners and jailers to tilt the social scales against people of regular status, who perhaps totally inadvertently had become involved in the legal process. And, though officials never condoned such behavior, they cited the risks of imprisonment and maltreatment at the hands of jailers to forestall unnecessary litigation.[61]

PROCEDURAL CONTROLS

Since neither litigation nor criminal activity could be eliminated, however, Ting (as had others before him) attended to creating mechanisms that would protect anyone unfortunate enough to be detained, speed up the flow of cases, and reveal any abuses.[62] In an early 1867 circular order, Ting instructed Magistrates to prepare prison and litigation registers in which all prison and all civil and appellate court activity was to be recorded.[63] Public notice boards were also to be set up so that the people themselves could check the progress of a case and the accuracy of the jail rolls. (Evelyn Rawski's work demonstrates that most poeple were literate enough to recognize the characters in the names of their family and friends.) The first registers revealed that Ting's desire for the public boards was warranted, but their quality was a sharp disappointment to him. Nine-tenths of them were unsatisfactory in terms of their form, yet from their contents he discovered improperly incarcerated prisoners, hsiens with over one hundred unconcluded cases, and all too many Magistrates who omitted awkward or difficult cases (such as a *mu-yu*'s opium addiction). To ensure improved compliance in the future, Ting reissued his circular order with a detailed form sheet appended (Table 1) and new controls included. Secretly deputed special agents in each hsien were to check the registers against the public notices of litigation and prisoners, and personally visit the prisons. Omissions and noncompliance with the form would be punished with demerits, and false reports with impeachment.[64] Indeed, despite subsequent erratic enforcement by Ting, when the system was first extended to litigious Kiangpei in 1868, it soon caused the impeachment of three Magistrates for failure to submit registers and for serious discrepancies in those that they did prepare.[65] (For Magistrates' compliance, see Appendix D.)

Measures to regulate the flow of litigation through the legal process had been established at the outset of the dynasty.[66] Magistrates naturally gave precedence to handling more serious cases (*an-chien*), that is, those requiring automatic review by senior provincial and metropolitan officials, for the Magistrates' disposition of these cases, in particular, any involving robberies and murders, was one of the key elements in their annual evaluation of performance in office (*k'ao-ch'eng*). Moreover, their judicial performance was monitored through the course of the case by an ongoing series of reports they were required to make and, after their initial judgment, by the obligatory review.[67] In contrast, civil and minor criminal cases (*tzu-li tz'u-sung*) were to be summarized in monthly abstracts (listing concluded and unconcluded cases) for the magistrate's superiors, but the procedure was never intended to constitute a substantive review. Moreover, by the 1830s, preparation of the registers had become so burdensome that it was ignored. Deprived of this tool with which to prod dilatory local officials who were already predisposed to put aside civil cases "on a high shelf," senior provincial officials were also without the means to check claims about magisterial justice when disgruntled appellants came to their yamens.[68] And the morass of unsettled civil litigation which impinged upon numerous lives indeed frequently boiled up into violence and appeals.[69]

TABLE 1 Form Sheet for Prison and Litigation Registers

PRISON REGISTERS[a]

A) In Custody for Long Time	B) Newly Received Prisoners	C) Prisoners Released	D) Total
1. Name a. date of admission	1. Name a. date of admission	1. Name	1. Names of all held
2. Name of case a. brief description	2. Name of case a. brief description	2. Reasons for release	

LITIGATION REGISTERS[b]

A) Old Cases	B) New Cases (since last register)	C) Concluded Cases	D) Total
1. Title 2. Background 3. Date begun 4. Progress report	1. Title 2. Summary 3. Date accepted a. Summary of comment	1. Title 2. How concluded a. adjudication b. mediation 3. Appeal a. progress report	1. Titles of old and new cases

Sources: FWKT, 2: 8–11; *Kiangsu Sheng-li,* "Fan," TC 6, pp. 20–24.

Notes: [a]There was one register for each of the following: inner prison (*nei-chien*) for serious criminals; outer prison (*wai-chien*) for less serious criminals; gaol (*pan-fang*) for persons being held in custody as witnesses.

[b]There were two separate litigation registers: for civil cases concluded by the magistrate on his own authority; for appellate cases that had been remanded back to the lower court for rehearing.

Litigation, observed Ting, could throw a family or village into a parlous condition:

> One person in custody meant one family could get no peace. One warrant served in a village meant ten families could get no peace. It had gotten to the point that, when a person was arrested, the officials did not know when the case was completed; that, even when completed, the warrant was undestroyed and served as a source of pleasure and sustenance for the yamen for some time.[70]

But, reported Ting, officials responding energetically to his orders on registers had changed these conditions. Between June 1867 and August 1868, more than 7,700 cases in Kiangnan had been tried, mediated, or dismissed; between May and September 1869 more than 5,000 cases had been completed in Kiangpei; and by January 1870, another 5,000 throughout the province had been concluded.[71] The key to the proper operation of the system ostensibly had been found. The court happily noted that, as a consequence, "new cases could be judged as soon as they arrived, and concluded as soon as they had been tried," and awarded merits and hereditary rank (*feng-tien*) to the recommended magistrates.[72]

Astonishing as the size of the backlog might seem, it included cases only from after 1864; and Ting was faced with the additional problem of clearing up old capital cases in Kiangpei that antedated 1864. The backlog had occurred because provincial officials, isolated in Shanghai during the Taiping Rebellion, had been unable to retry the cases; and efforts to handle the 120 of them through regular procedures after 1864 had completed only 10 percent of the cases. The continuing delays were caused by the constant transfer of prisoners back and forth between the north and south as their cases wended their way through the legal process. The cost, however, was not only temporal and monetary, but also human, as aged and ill suspects and witnesses frequently died on their peregrinations.

To save lives and expense, Ting proposed to the court a compromise method which required only the most troublesome cases to undergo full-dress retrial in Soochow. The judicial commissioner would make up a register of all pre-1864 cases from Kiangpei and place them in three categories. In the first would be cases, ostensibly properly handled, which were to be checked and forwarded to the Board of Punishments. In the second would be those in which the fact and nature of the crime were unambiguous, but in which the surrounding circumstances were confusingly reported. In these, the judicial commissioner was to depute officials from his office to re-examine each case in conjunction with the magistrate at local level and send a report, but not witnesses or suspects, to Soochow. In the third category would be those cases with anomalies in the confessions, doubts about the nature of the crime, or discrepancies between original and subsequent investigations. Only in these should all the involved parties be sent to Soochow. Cases that had never been checked by the prefect and unconcluded cases postdating 1865 whould be handled in the regular manner.[73] The court (which had a Tao-kuang precedent to rely on) readily approved these regulations, and one hundred of the cases were quickly concluded. But the compromise procedures soon had to be extended to a wholly unexpected flood of previously unreported pre-1864 cases.[74]

When this deluge of cases descended, Ting immediately applied pressure on the Magistrates by informing them that he intended to discern men of talent on the basis of their responsiveness to his orders. He both increased the pressure and buttressed his own authority by forcefully pointing out to them that, since he had memorialized on the method of handling old cases, that method "had to be carried out."[75] Whenever the opportunity arose, Ting reminded the Magistrates that his willingness to make this extraordinary compromise had relieved them of the financial burden of transporting prisoners to Soochow, and that remissness in acting conscientiously would be punished severely both by law and the spirits. Nonetheless, Magistrates, fearing discipline, continued to procrastinate concluding the previously unforwarded or unreported cases.[76] In order to clear the backlog, Ting again partially relaxed regulations, while warning that there could be no carte blanche exemption from discipline in these old cases. Magistrates who could conclude them within three months, however, would receive dispensations, even if they had intentionally covered them up before![77]

Little, if any, news about these continuing problems with Kiangpei and the registers ever reached the court, although Ting had acknowledged to the court at the outset that he anticipated backsliding among the Magistrates as time went on. Ting exercised his control over the Magistrates' registers by checking them for accuracy in three different ways: whenever he received a deposition, a shouted petition, or a chair petition, he personally questioned the plaintiff on the handling of his petition at the local level and then examined that hsien's registers to see if the case had been listed; he also used informers; and he simply compared successive months' registers.[78] Ting's cross-checking often revealed woeful incompetence and malfeasance in legal matters.

Ingenuous Magistrates' reports indicated that as a matter of routine they permitted or engaged in practices specifically forbidden by Ting: acceptance of litigation by petty officials, and the use of highly literary language in commenting on commoners' cases.[79] Ting described the latter practice as "talking without communicating," and warned that the parties to a case would reopen it if they did not understand a decision.[80] Some ingenious Magistrates concocted easily solvable spurious cases to build their percentage of closed ones, but their forgery was readily spotted by Ting, since the older, more difficult cases remained in the registers.[81] But worst of all, said Ting, were the temporizers who always hid behind the reply (taught them by evil *mu-yu*) that they were "just now" checking.[82] While litigation in Ch'ung-ming backlogged, its Magistrate scuttled about "stroking" his superiors; in Tung-t'ai only 24 out of 100 outstanding cases were concluded, and most by dismissal rather than by examination; and still another Magistrate, "delaying like an old man," had disposed of merely 39 out of 176 cases; and of these only 7 were actually tried.[83] Nonetheless, Ting complained that he was being buried under a mountain of papers, most of which, moreover, were insufficiently detailed for him to act upon.[84]

Ting accorded such Magistrates demerits only reluctantly and saved impeachment for the incorrigible, since he was, he said, beginning to despair about the potency of punishment as a preventive against backsliding. Once again we find Ting prodding officials with ironic cajolery. Even if they did not care about right and wrong, he coaxed, surely they must care about their careers. How could they allow their diligence to dissipate into neglect under pressure from clerks, or, still worse, how could they behave like common clerks?[85] Even more distressing to Ting was the Magistrates' confusion about whom they were supposed to be protecting and nourishing. Indeed, he said, they misdirected their sternness against the people instead of directing it against the clerks, who one Magistrate claimed were blameless "saints" unreasonably accused by the people. Quoting an old saying that, "when the water is weak the people play, and when fire is hot the people are afraid," Ting urged a Magistrate to use both fire and water to govern his district. Correct application, however, said Ting, was essential: "Taoism (water) to rule the people and Legalism (fire) to rule the clerks."[86] Yet, despite his certitude on this matter, Ting himself seemed uncertain whether to apply fire or water to his subordinate officials.

Rot had certainly permeated the prison administration in Kiangpei. Upon becoming Governor in 1868, Ting learned of a Shantung man who, in 1853, had been detained in Kiangpei on his way to do transport service in Fukien, and then had been forgotten until he was discovered starved to death in 1868.[87] When Ting extended his orders on registers to the province as a whole that year, he clearly hoped that such incidents would never be repeated. In a sternly worded warning to Magistrates, he noted that, while of no benefit to clerks and runners, the new regulations were of great advantage to the people. "After all," he observed, "the clerks are only your slaves (*nu-p'u*), while the people are your children. How can [I allow you] to treat your children contemptuously and your slaves richly?" Urging the Magistrates to "take care," Ting reminded them of his intention to check the registers closely against the boards.[88]

Still, when improprieties recurred, Ting's discipline was neither so strict as he had threatened, nor so severe as the Penal Code and *Ch'u-fen tse-li* (Administrative regulations for officials), both of which called for the use of prisoner registers, required.[89] The case of the Magistrate of Wu hsien, one of the three head Magistrates and a supposed exemplar for other officials, illustrates Ting's lack of severity. A sub-district Magistrate's son, who had been accused in a land dispute, was put under custody, extorted, and not listed in either the register or on the board. For allowing his clerks to do this, Ting recorded one major demerit against the Wu hsien Magistrate and admonished him to punish the clerks strictly.[90] By comparison, depending on which provision of the codes one selected, the runners could have been dismissed and the Magistrate fined three months of his salary or reduced in rank one degree and transferred.[91] In almost all other cases, too, Ting's disciplinary measures fell far short of his rhetoric; and, at least in one instance, the court approved these lenient measures without comment.[92] Is it possible that Ting's behavior was not the result of leniency but rather of ignorance of legal precedents? In Ting's case the answer is partially yes, as it surprisingly seems to be for the court too. For never did Ting, the metropolitan officials, or the throne adduce these precedents in their discussion of Ting's initial proposals and subsequent enforcement.[93]

Yet, there is also evidence in Ting's behavior, if not exactly of leniency, at least of a definite predilection to change behavior by arousing shame through mockery. He did not discipline the Shu-yang Magistrate who first had failed to control warrants and then for two months omitted the names of two prisoners from his registers. Instead, Ting offered him a wry assessment of his performance: "I would be truly surprised if you knowingly did not report, for if you were in fact ignorant [as you claim to have been] of the runners' illicit lockups, you couldn't differ from a wooden puppet."[94] Ting himself, in another case in which there was conclusive evidence of the Magistrate's collusion in illegal detentions, explained the rationale behind this approach:

> I procrastinate in impeaching him [the Magistrate of Hsing-hua] because I know it is not easy to attain his status (*kung-ming*) [of *kung-sheng*]. I want to see what he can do, so I have asked you [the Taotai] to speak with him again. If he continues consciously to ignore the clerks' and runners' detention of good people, *then I shall put aside the jade and cloth and pick up my weapons. For then I cannot simply use empty words alone to persuade him.*[95]

The question is, would Ting's blunted weapons have had any effect either? That even Ting's personal intervention in a case could neither expedite its hearing nor free the suspect before his death suggests that this question must be answered negatively.[96] Clearly, local officials took sanctuary in their knowledge that constraints on gubernatorial control of personnel made their removal almost more trouble than it was worth (see Chapter 6).

The throne was nonetheless sufficiently impressed with the efficacy of Ting's system of registers to order in 1868 all other provinces to emulate the model.[97] Tseng Kuo-fan instituted identical procedures (without according credit to Ting) when he was transferred to Chihli that year, and Shansi both established official hostels and implemented use of the registers.[98] The litigation registers, moreover, worked well enough for subsequent Kiangsu provincial officials to propose expanding them to encompass capital cases as well.[99] Yet, as we have seen, Ting's system was not without shortcomings. It was not a panacea. Illicit lockups persisted as did manipulation of prisoner rolls (fifty to sixty detainees were reported as one). And the system was undermined by the failure to apply it to the judicial commissioner's auxiliary court (*fa-shen chü*) and to allocate funds for hostels.[100] Finally, if we judge by the objective standard of frequency of provincial (*shang-k'ung*) and capital (*ching-k'ung*) appeals, Ting's registers and other control measures appear less successful to us than they did to his contemporaries.

APPEALS

Parallel to but independent of the obligatory review, appeals were perceived by all concerned, from appellant and magistrate to Emperor, as symptomatic of breakdowns in the lower levels of the judicial system as well as of defects in the general quality of governance. Such appeals were made because of a magistrate's refusal to hear a case, because a plaintiff wished to prod into action officials who had rendered no decision in a case, and because of dissatisfaction with a judgment, either at the court of first instance or in the course of review (a move often instigated by litigation tricksters). From the trivial to the sublime, from rent and property-line disputes, through charges of unfair taxation and police oppression, to homicide, appeals encompassed nearly every imaginable legal, social, political, and economic issue. To prevent chaos and to discourage the frivolous or baseless appeal, the law stipulated two prerequisites for lodging either a provincial or a capital one: it had to be submitted at an immediately superior court, and it could not be lodged unless a case already had been either rejected or concluded. In practice, however, these barriers were highly permeable. The by-passing of intermediate courts (*yueh-su*) was undeterred by the rarely enforced penalties, and complaints of bias during trials and reviews seem to have constituted grounds for an appeal before the final adjudication of a case. Needless to say, there were litigation tricksters who specialized in appeals.[101]

The capital appeal was intended to be an avenue for those who had exhausted all the judicial remedies at the provincial level without gaining justice. Appellants (or enlisted proxies) endured the fiscal and physical rigors of the journey to Peking in the hope of obtaining an imperial imprimatur that would stimulate officials to resolve their grievance both quickly and justly. Since, by the mid-nineteenth century, few, if any, capital appeals were rejected, it was not a far-fetched hope. After submitting their charges to either the censorate or capital gendarmerie (*pu-chün t'ung-ling ya-men*), appellants would await cursory examination of their cases and then be returned to their provincial capital for a trial or retrial of the issues by the senior provincial officials. (In instances of grave injustice, the case might be tried by imperial commissioner or moved back to Peking for adjudication by the Board of Punishment.)

Local officials intensely disliked such appeals for they reflected poorly upon them, thereby rendering these officials vulnerable to intimidation by antagonists who threatened appeals on various matters. Furthermore, appeals could be financially debilitating if the magistrate personally bore the expense of transferring the involved people back and forth to the provincial capital.[102] Indeed, while the provincial government allocated funds for custody of appellants at the provincial capital, Ting for some time insisted that the magistrate pay the traveling expenses, for the alternatives were the exaction of fees from the parties to the case and the involvement of irrelevant people to boost income. The longer a case was under adjudication, the greater the fees, as Ting found out upon interrogating an escort officer:

> I asked the escort officer where the 60,000 cash in fees and traveling costs had come from, and he replied "from the relatives of the 'main name' in the case." He called it "assisting public business." When I asked if these payments were voluntary or forced, he told me that it all depended on the "'Five-foot Snake.' When the snake gets to the throat, the money is paid." When I asked about this so-called snake, he laughingly told me that it was a chain.[103]

By shifting the responsibility for escort costs to the magistrate, Ting had hoped to eliminate such extortion; and, to save the magistrate from bankruptcy, he instituted regulations to hasten the handling of appeals. Basic supervisory responsibility for the appeals was entrusted to the Judicial Commissioner, while the Prefect of Soochow had custody of the people and conducted the actual hearing of the case. Control of the cases was supposed to be exercised through the Prefect's regular litigation and prisoner registers; but, with an estimated one hundred appeals a year, backlogs did appear, despite Ting's urgings.[104] Thus, as before, Ting's progressive methods were undermined by lax men. The Judicial Commissioner and the Prefect of Soochow, two of the most important officials in the province, complained Ting, were like "sunflowers that did not turn to the sun. They looked closely without seeing." In a typically self-denigrating and obliquely threatening manner, Ting warned them of the potential consequences of continued inattention:

> It seems to have come to the point where my words must be insufficient to gain your trust for I am unable to move people. I should question myself, take the blame and be ashamed. . . . *If my words are again like water dripping on a stone, then I will be a bad example as a leader and can only ask to be disciplined, to tie my hair up, and go into the mountains.*[105]

The obligatory review of serious cases was also plagued by delays but appears to have been less prone to corruption. Forwarded to the provincial capital by prefects, these cases were first tried by the judicial commissioner, and then reviewed by the governor (but only rarely retried) before being sent on to the Board of Punishments in Peking. The object of this provincial review was to make certain that no innocent people had been falsely involved, that the suspects had been accused of the proper crime, that no suspects had escaped, that the testimony was not contradictory, and that the punishment fit the crime. Like most governors, Ting insisted on a careful trial record, for, as he made clear to his subordinates, he did not like the Board to reject and return cases for retrial.[106] As the *Hsing-an hui-lan* amply illustrates, the Board's particular concern was that the suspect had been properly charged and sentenced; but at the provincial level the review focused on those elements of the case that left Ting free range for his investigative skills.

Reviews and Investigations

Whenever Ting refused to forward a case and returned it to the magistrate, he took the opportunity to instruct the official in how to investigate and hear a case properly:

> Investigation is like reading a book. One must read between the lines, looking for places of doubt, looking for places of articulation. One must seek the reasons therein. When one has plumbed to the bottom, the affair can be seen. When the reasons are correct, then one can know the matter is true. Preconceptions and biases cannot be formed. It is improper![107]

While not offering advice different from that in administrative handbooks, Ting was in a position to reach a broader audience and ostensibly had the power to make them listen; not that he failed to remind his listeners of how inattention affected him:

> For every day a case is unbroken, the grievance of the dead is not repaid. For each day of this, I cannot eat or sleep. And, for each day I go hungry and tired, I'm not peaceful; and the magistrate's reputation is daily endangered.[108]

He complained in particular of the "confused and stupid" Kiangpei Magistrates:

> You dress warmly in the winter and screen yourselves with curtains in the summer. You take good care of yourselves but never think of the people in poor hovels who cannot make an accusation, whose families are broken and unable to respect their ancestors [that is, by leaving their graves behind]. You Magistrates, would a grandfather treat his grandchildren like this?[109]

Ting's instructions and comments to the magistrates are varied: a warning not to discriminate against either Moslems or Kiangpei "guest people" (*k'o-jen*); a query about the competence of a woman forger; a pointed observation on the inconstancy of a suspect's testimony; or simply a rejection of a case on the suspicion that an innocent person was falsely charged. In one such instance, a man charged bandits with murdering his wife, but found himself arrested, tortured into a confession, and forced into confirming it when confronted with an additional charge coerced from his young daughter.[110]

Women suspects in adultery-murder cases were the subjects of Ting's particular moral opprobrium, for their alleged crime was as serious as parricide.[111] Indeed, in Ting's view, as we previously noted, "the relationship between husband and wife is the most basic of human relationships" (*jen-lun*).[112] One woman who murdered her husband and incited her two subsequent lovers to a fatal quarrel had a "poisonous heart." Another who tried to shift the blame to her lover had her argument destroyed by Ting, who stressed that "this kind of licentious, evil woman cannot be allowed to escape the law." Should such crimes go uninvestigated and unpunished, "the laws of the nation could not be made clear nor lewdness punished."[113]

But undoubtedly Ting's teaching was best when he broke open confused cases for magistrates by examining a case socratically. How could a storm at sea selectively wash overboard a boat-owner's family of twelve yet leave the crew unscathed and the goods undamaged? An inability to fathom this case, remarked Ting to the uncomprehending Magistrate, could be explained only by cupidity or absolute idiocy.[114] Of another Magistrate duped by spurious testimony in the case of an 8,000 silver-dollar robbery of a likin post, Ting asked: How could eight men loaded with silver scale a wall before the supposedly hotly pursuing police could catch even one? If the bandits dumped the money in a river when they saw the police coming, why could not the police see them, and why could not the loot be found in the shallow river? And how could two of the alleged suspects who met the reportedly drowned ringleader for the first time in the dead of a moonless night either identify the body or know his name? Angered by this Magistrate's inertia, Ting told him he was "totally without guts"; and he warned other magistrates "not to take on a woman's passive mentality as a virtue."[115]

Examining the Magistrates' performances makes it clear that most of them were hardly the brilliant jurist-detectives of the legal novels, nor were they even familiar with basic procedures. They neither investigated cases on the spot, nor used their logic to break cases with little evidence or muddled testimony; and they were all too prone hastily to conclude cases that they could not understand.[116] To remedy these shortcomings, Ting issued his various circular orders and established the Kiangsu Printing Office for the purpose of publishing simplified versions of the Penal Code and edited versions of magistrates' handbooks. Abuses none the less continued because their underlying cause, socioeconomic inequalities, persisted. Yet Ting achieved a measure of success in his judicial reforms as manifested by a 90 percent decrease in the number of suicides in Kiangpei. As Ting explained it: "Presently even a country bumpkin's simple three-word petition can quickly reach the Governor. When there is no grievance that cannot be assuaged, why must one commit suicide?"[117]

Ting's search for social justice was not, however, simply an end in itself, but equally a means to another end. Litigation, said Ting, was related to the people's livelihood, and through that to taxes and the state's finances (*kuo-chi*):

> Originally, soothing the people and urging taxes (*fu-tzu, ts'ui-k'o*) were carried out together without contradiction. But now prefects and magistrates divide them into two separate things. They do not know that urging taxes "resides in" (*yu-yü*) soothing the people. If one can maintain an attitude of seeking out the people's hardships and showing compassion, then not a single person will lose his home. There will be no one under heaven who cannot be transformed (*hua*). Even among the notorious recalcitrant households (*chu-ming wan-hu*), there will be none who do not turn their heads, change their faces, and enthusiastically provide provisions.[118]

FIVE

Fiscal Affairs

[The state] does not
consider salt or
iron or plan for
waterworks. It
relies only on Kiangnan
where tears are many.
The state taxes three
pints; the people pay
a peck. The oxen are
killed; the fields
cannot be planted.
Kung Tzu-chen[1]

The Taiping Rebellion forced the Ch'ing to broaden its revenue base and introduce fiscal reforms. To finance the suppression of the Rebellion, new taxes were imposed on both domestic and foreign commerce. To assuage the people, waterworks were rebuilt; and tax relief in the form of permanent reductions, temporary remissions, and structural reform was ordered. Yet, the land tax, which actually consisted of two separate levies, a combined land and poll tax (*ti-ting*) and a grain tribute (*ts'ao-liang*), despite a decline in its relative importance, still constituted the bulk of imperial revenues and, accordingly, was seen as the key to the empire's finances.[2]

In 1869, the court instructed the Board of Revenue: "The

way of fiscal management (*li-ts'ai*) consists of nothing more than getting the full benefit of the land and working hard in agriculture. As the amount of land under cultivation increases, so shall our revenues."[3] Correct as the court's basic premise was, it was, nevertheless, an overly simplistic one. Before the state could actually receive a copper in tax monies, settlers first had to be found to bring new land and wasteland under cultivation; once productive, the land then had to be properly surveyed, rated, and enrolled on the tax registers (historically an unsuccessful undertaking);[4] and, finally, equitable rates and corruption-free collection procedures had to be established so that the people would not be exploited and the state not short-changed. First as Financial Commissioner (1867) and then as Governor (1868–1870), it was Ting Jih-ch'ang's duty to accomplish these tasks in order to achieve the coordinate—but sometimes contradictory—ends of protecting the people's livelihood (*min-sheng*) and of ensuring the state's revenue (*kuo-chi*).[5]

RESETTLEMENT AND RECOVERY

The focus of Ting's reclamation activities was in the more severely affected western part of Kiangnan. Resettlement of the east was taken for granted, since the bulk of its original proprietors and cultivators had survived. Indeed, most of the contested territory in the east was resettled and productive less than a year after its recovery and often before tax remissions were granted.[6] Even the famous program of tax reduction, the culmination of ante-bellum efforts, was regarded by some officials and local elite not so much as an inducement to immigration but more as a lever for tax equalization.[7] In the decimated west, despite a lower tax rate than that in the east, and despite tax remissions of three to even six years, the enormous labor of reclamation discouraged settlers; and by 1868 there still remained large tracts of wasteland and numerous hsien unable to resume regular taxation.[8] That year, a dismayed Governor Ting Jih-ch'ang circulated among his colleagues a letter, suggesting improvements in the resettlement program.[9]

Ting focused first on the lack of water-control facilities. In the preceding years of unpredictable weather, the immigrants' crops first had been scorched by drought and then flooded by rains. They had yet to bring in an adequate harvest and had realistically named their fields after their predicament: "depend upon heaven land" (*k'ao-t'ien t'ien*). Ting acknowledged that ordinarily landowners would be expected to subordinate their own needs to the public good and to provide money and labor for the repair and maintenance of waterworks. Indeed, in the east, per-acre assessments of both men and cash were made for work on the Pai-miao and Liu rivers. But, argued Ting, in the west, the new settlers were too dispersed to make such levies practical and, more important, were already too hard-pressed in terms of both capital and time. To repair the waterworks, suggested Ting, unemployed unruly soldiers stationed in Kiangpei should be used.

Yet, even had this scheme been realized and the immigrants thus freed to till their fields intensively, they still would have lacked fertilizer. According to Ting, in combination with their labor, fertilizer could make one acre of land more productive than ten less-hard-worked ones. Obviously, with a sparse population there was a paucity of night soil, and local merchants were financially unable to import an outside supply. To meet the need, Ting suggested that the provincial government use likin revenues to underwrite the purchase of fertilizers. Local officials and gentry directors were to supervise the purchase, shipment, and sale at cost, either of native fertilizer or of the inexpensive Peruvian guano then available in Shanghai. (This marks one of the few instances when Ting's knowledge of *yang-wu* was useful in domestic administration.) Ting hoped that, once the fertilizer reached the immigrants, they would settle down to the backbreaking work of land reclamation.

Ting discovered, however, that no sooner had the immigrants readied their first harvest than they would find themselves dispossessed by the "original owners" of the land. The Restoration's established land policy of recognizing the status quo ante in land ownership not only encouraged the return of refugee proprietors, but also invited chicanery at the expense of the immigrants. Indeed, one of the chief problems in the west was that of local bullies who obtained falsified deeds by bribing the Reclamation Bureau. Such uncertainty discouraged immigrants from settling permanently.[10]

To safeguard the homesteading claims of the immigrants, Ting urged the imposition of a retroactive ten-year statute of limitations. Repossession of newly cultivated land, by either legitimate or illegitimate claimants, would be forbidden if the land had been abandoned and left fallow for the previous ten years.[11] An alternative, but similar, solution was offered by Ma Hsin-i, who was then Ting's superior as Liang-kiang Governor-General. No new land would be opened to immigrants for eighteen months. If during this hiatus the original owner or his survivors did not appear with proper proof, the land and the official deed would be offered to settlers. Since it was difficult to be certain when land had been abandoned, Ma's proposal would have provided the potential immigrants with more secure as well as more immediate benefits. But the basic thrust of both proposals was identical and emphatic: the immigrants would not be used as tools and would not be discarded when the hard work was finished.[12]

Ting perceived still another fundamental impediment to the repopulation of western Kiangnan—a dearth of women. As he cogently observed, "Without them there would be death but no new life."[13] Ting asserted that in Kiangnan the Rebellion had taken a higher toll among women than men. Those women who were not killed were kidnapped either for marriage or sale outside the region. In Kiangpei, however, the foundling homes were glutted with girls rescued from infanticide.[14] Ting logically decided that these girls should be moved south. Steps first had to be taken to protect the girls within the homes, for many of their unscrupulous directors were selling girls into prostitution. Ting immediately prohibited this practice and ordered the provision of adequate funds (without specifying their source or amount) for the proper rearing of all children and for the teaching of weaving to the girls. At eight or nine, the girls were to be sent south to the homesteaders who could either adopt them and arrange a future marriage (which unless it was uxorilocal would have been counterproductive) or raise them as wives for their own sons. In this way, concluded Ting, "the two characters 'to give birth' (*sheng*) and 'to gather' (*chü*) would not be rendered meaningless."[15]

It has been impossible to determine whether any of the above measures were ever implemented; but it is clear that the initial elements in the resettlement program, such as the offers of free seeds and tools, of tax exemptions, and of title to homesteaded wasteland, were drawn from a long tradition of frontier settlement.[16] Ting's efforts to supply fertilizer, to protect claims, and to obtain outside aid for waterworks follow logically from earlier precedents. What does seem unusual is the social engineering involved in the rearing and moving of the young girls. Whatever the ultimate fate of these proposals, immigrants settled in sufficient numbers to affect local customs and to precipitate clashes between themselves and indigenous people.[17] But there was no appreciable decrease in the amount of wasteland, and regular taxation in Kiangning prefecture was not resumed until 1874.[18]

LAND REGISTRATION

In the eastern part of Kiangnan, where the land was quickly repopulated and recultivated, Ting's problems were of a different order. There, regular taxation recommenced in most areas by 1866, but the widespread destruction of tax records permitted the flourishing of the well-refined arts of land concealment and tax evasion. One of the easier dodges was for a newly returned landowner simply not to report that he had reoccupied his land.[19] Perhaps the most prevalent trick was the taxation clerks' old ploy of selling wasteland status and tax remissions to the highest bidders.[20] Although these "wasteland fees" (*huang-fei*) were illegal and were further prohibited by Ting as soon as he became Financial Commissioner, they persisted in Kiangsu throughout his tenure and down to the end of the dynasty.[21] Indeed, anyone who endangered the wasteland-fee racket by attempting to pay taxes instead of fees risked a beating or even illegal imprisonment.[22]

Ting underestimated the severity of the problem. Initially he persuaded himself that the situation was caused by those cultivators who "had a fear of all yamen doors and would hesitate without ever going in." Consequently he accepted the suggestion of the Lou hsien Magistrate to bring the yamen to them. Hence, in each rural district (*hsiang*), a gentry director was to be appointed to check conditions personally, and in conjunction with local officials to file a monthly report on the progress of reclamation.[23] The success of this plan depended on the integrity of these men; yet in some counties it was the gentry director himself who managed the wasteland-fee enterprise.[24] This flaw in Ting's approach was demonstrated by the unreliable registers: the Chen-ts'e Magistrate blithely fabricated a report that 10,000 acres had been reclaimed;[25] the I-hsing register listed long fertile but previously concealed land as newly reclaimed;[26] and Lou hsien itself filed late and incomplete reports.[27] In Fu-ning, where "old disaster precincts" (*lao-tsai t'u*) had endured since the 1840s (apparently without ever coming to the attention of provincial authorities), mobs prevented the Magistrate from conducting a survey. Eventually, in the 1880s, troops and the refusal of the Fu-ning Magistrate to accept litigation over "wasteland" vitiated the practice.[28] Throughout much of eastern Kiangnan, then, there was "land without taxes and taxes without land." In such situations, regulations requried a full-scale clarification of taxes: a cadastral survey and the compilation of new tax maps and registers.[29]

Cadastral surveys were rare in the Ch'ing, "not," as a Chinese historian wrote, "because the state did not want them, but because it was afraid of them."[30] As described by Yeh-chien Wang, a cadastral survey

> aims at proper identification and property valuation. The cadastre, which is the product of the survey and the official record of land property covered by the survey, normally consists of a set of maps on which each plot of land within a specified area appears and corresponding registers which contain the information needed to identify

> each plot . . . The information in the cadastre . . . generally includes the location, size, shape, value, and ownership of each plot of land surveyed.[31]

The hazards of such a survey were many: the survey bow was rarely uniform in size; clerks exacted fees from the people; the wealthy, the very ones whose concealment of land the survey was intended to reveal, bought continued protection from clerks and surveyors; and, finally, an acre-by-acre survey was enormously expensive and disrupted the countryside for three to four years. As several administrative writers concluded, the cadastral survey was more trouble than it was worth; but, because it was a necessity at times, it was never abolished.[32]

In post-Taiping Kiangsu, the survey was used (as Feng Kuei-fen suggested it was best used) only as a last resort.[33] Despite the determined supervisory efforts of Ting, those few surveys that were concluded achieved little more than to provide support for their critics' accusations. The case of K'un-shan is illustrative. In this instance, Ting overcame his suspicion that gentry directors of surveys would misrepresent property rights and ordered the Magistrate to establish a survey bureau staffed by gentry.[34] To supervise the gentry, Ting commissioned an alternate Department Magistrate (*wei-yuan*). After two years of work and an expenditure of 10,000 taels, the Bureau reported completion of its work and asked to be disbanded. Shocked by this news, Ting noted that they had not even finished checking the old registers, much less begun new ones, and asked the *wei-yuan* of what he had been in charge.[35] Ting, in fact, knew full well that, while the *wei-yuan* had sat peacefully unconcerned in his office, bribed register clerks had so falsified the actual survey as to render it meaningless.[36] He therefore instructed the K'un-shan Magistrate to assume supervisory responsibilities and to order the Bureau's gentry directors to finish the survey properly within the year.[37] However, a year, repeated warnings, and another 7,000 taels later, the survey was still unfinished. At this time the Magistrate of K'un-shan, who had already displayed shortcomings in fiscal affairs, in an interview with Ting reported that 30,000 acres—

5 percent of the hsien's taxable land—were still missing from the survey.[38]

As Ting's further investigations confirmed, the chief accomplishment of the survey had been the exaction and embezzlement of considerable funds by the gentry directors and their clerk allies. At the end of the first two years, Ting had asked of the Magistrate and *wei-yuan* a typical rhetorical question: "How can you shamelessly serve as officials?" Sarcastically he urged them to become hermits if the survey was not properly completed within the time limit.[39] But, when they failed, Ting softened. Instead of impeaching the officials or requesting heavy fines, as he could have done, he acted within his gubernatorial discretionary powers and merely deprived the officials and gentry of their buttons.[40] Of all this activity, the K'un-shan Hsin-yang local history, written of course by gentry, simply commented that Ting had sent out an agent to survey by acre those districts that had lost their records.[41]

Other poor surveys were also mildly handled by Ting. After a totally unproductive three-year survey, the Magistrate of Chen-ts'e received just a reprimand.[42] In Li-yang, Ting was patient with a Magistrate who not only had requested survey fees three to five times above the legal rates, but who also had been unable to discover 500,000 acres of concealed fertile land—one half of his hsien's taxable acreage.[43] Neither of these officials had compiled the kind of records that would lead us to expect such leniency from Ting.[44] Indeed, Ting, who considered officials' acceptance of wasteland fees identical to the theft of regular taxes, felt compelled to justify to his Financial Commissioner his deferral of punishment for Magistrates known to be corrupt.

To his apparently puzzled subordinate, Ting explained that to punish without first teaching was to deprive a magistrate of the chance to change himself; only after fruitless admonitions should a magistrate be impeached.[45] Such transformation of official behavior through the arousal of shame was a central element in what Thomas Metzger has called the "probationary ethic."[46] It is difficult to criticize such a principle; but, if a junior official required the capacity to feel shame in order to appreciate why he was being rewarded or punished, the senior official, in order to be effective, had to fulfill his promises to reward or punish. By failing to concretize his verbal ferocity, Ting all too often subverted the impact of his reprimands and warnings. As we shall see in Chapter 6, the reasons behind Ting's ambivalent methods lay not simply within his own personality, but also in structural weaknesses in the Ch'ing administrative system.

Difficulties with the cadastral surveys should not have been unexpected, because a survey had not been conducted in most parts of Kiangsu since the late Ming.[47] Surveys were a regular occurrence, however, in those areas that lay along the Yangtze River. There, the land movements caused by the heavily silted river necessitated quinquennial surveys and adjustments in the tax registers. This schedule was, of course, disrupted by the Rebellion; and, by the time Ting supervised a new survey in 1868, eleven years had passed since the previous one. Still, there remained a reservoir of precedent and experience which should have facilitated the completion of the "alluvial surveys."[48]

Once supervised by imperially appointed officials, alluvial affairs had long since been the prerogative of local officials and gentry directors.[49] In order to start afresh, Ting and Tseng Kuo-fan dismissed these old directors and established an alluvial bureau (*sha-chou tsung-chü*) to handle all surveys and related litigation. To head the main office a Brevet Taotai was appointed, while the branch bureaus (which were essential because of the widely divergent practices in each hsien) were directed by specially selected "official gentry," that is, former officials in retirement or officials home on leave.[50] Originally, the bureau's primary function was to increase revenues for the Nien suppression campaign by collecting from defaulters, adding land to the tax rolls, and setting higher rates.[51] Ying Pao-shih, at the time Soochow Financial Commissioner, unsuccessfully opposed these tax increases as a blatant contradiction of the court's mandate for tax reduction.[52] Soon thereafter, Ting and Tseng did shift the focus of their efforts to reform and relief for the people, but the change reflected the relative abatement of fiscal urgency that followed the pacification of the Nien, rather than Ying's opposition.[53] In any case, as Tseng himself noted, any proclamation that simultaneously announced reform and fund-raising for troops would have been distrusted by the people.[54]

What, in fact, burdened the people was not the basic tax quota, but the manner of its assessment and collection. Fees were demanded simply for reporting land shifts and, as in the cadastral survey, the size of the survey bow was manipulated.[55] The discovery of 1,000-cash-per-acre survey fees in the 1857 survey moved Ting to conclude that Su Tung-po's description of the taxpayer as the clerks' fief was no exaggeration after all.[56] There were also other once legitimate devices for illicit gain, such as setting tax rates on or laying claim to still submerged sandbars (*wang-shui sheng-k'o*), and demanding continued tax payments on eroded land against the eventuality that it might reappear (*shui-ying kuang-t'an*).[57] Not unexpectedly, the result of these malpractices was a distorted picture of alluvial affairs: transfers of land went unrecorded and constant litigation occurred as a consequence of the confusion of ownership claims. The Rebellion, moreover, had exacerbated these problems by destroying records and by forcing the abrogation of land-sale agreements. Once again there was "land without taxes and taxes without land."[58]

The regulations of the new bureau and independent but complementary proclamations were tailored to deal with these specific problems.[59] Claims on still submerged land and advance tax payments were both forbidden. Taxes were to be reassessed without fees on the basis of the survey, and land with established owners was to be exempted from back taxes. A per-acre charge in lieu of full payment of back taxes was to be levied on land on which unreported improvements had been made since 1857. Land unimproved since 1857 was to be rented out by the local government to support charitable institutions.[60] In order to encourage expanded cultivation, newly deposited land was to be offered for sale at 1857 prices, but payment had to be immediate and in full. Finally, all debts on previously contracted for land were rescinded, but this land was still subject to all back taxes.[61] This last measure seems inexplicable and inequitable; yet, for the most part, the regulations were fair and gave promise, if fully implemented, of achieving some important goals: the end of fees, the regularization of procedures, and the removal of entrenched corrupt alluvial bullies (*sha-kun*) and alluvial directors (*sha-tung*).

In his emphatic charge announcing the establishment of the alluvial bureau, Ting had underlined his view that the complete eradication of corruption and maladministration was not an extreme expectation; doubters of such an outcome, he said, were ignorant outsiders.[62] Here again, rhetoric and reality contrast sharply. The dichotomy, though, is not between Ting's words and deeds, but between his public and private voices. Ting himself actually suspected that the eradication of fees was an unrealizable goal. Having found that previously one set of fees had barely been paid when another payment loomed, he resolved at least to limit the opportunities for exacting them.

In an 1868 memorial, Ting requested an extension of the hiatus between surveys from five to fifteen years.[63] His proposal controverted conventional wisdom, such as that of T'ao Chu, the famous Tao-kuang reformist Kiangsu Governor and Liang-kiang Governor-General, who had asserted that Ch'ung-ming's regular three-and five-years surveys had forestalled serious problems.[64] About six months before Ting submitted his memorial, this view had been reaffirmed in the petition of a resident of Ch'ung-ming, who had urged Ting to retain that hsien's triennial surveys. Without them, the petitioner argued, newly arisen land would go unregistered and would be forcibly occupied by local bullies, while eroded land would still be taxed. Ting had already ordered the arrest of Ch'ung-ming's notorious bullies and land-grabbers but still opposed the frequent surveys, which, he claimed, were disruptive and resulted only in duplication of the old registers.[65] He informed the court that, to account for land shifts that occurred between the completion of the present survey and the start of the next, spot checks at the specific request of the landowners would suffice. The court eventually compromised and issued an edict setting a ten-year survey period.[66]

Ting's pessimism about elimination of survey fees was better founded than his optimism, for his reforms were barely effective while he was in office and were inutile after his departure. Purposely sloppy work by the alluvial bureau officials during the 1868 survey led to pervasive large-scale underreporting and undertaxation of land. Remaining ensconced in their yamens, these officials left the preparation of the maps and registers to the local headmen and clerks, whose exactions increased daily.[67] In Chiang-tu, the "evil director" (*lieh-tung*) of an unauthorized bureau accumulated enough fees to build a "mansion" and to purchase an official title. To guard against the repetition of such occurrences, Ting ordered stones inscribed with his prohibition of fees erected in front of all district yamens.[68] At least two hsien properly implemented this instruction;[69] but, as the case of Kao-shun suggests, Ting's order was more honored in its breach than in its observance.

The Kao-shun Magistrate responded to Ting's order with alacrity, and two days before the deadline forwarded a stone rubbing of his proclamation to Ting. Yet, as Ting, obviously stunned, noted, instead of writing, "If land is eroded, it should be reported for an exemption," the Magistrate had inscribed, "If land is eroded, there shall be a [reporting] fee." Ting's bifurcated reaction was typical but curious, if we consider his stern warnings against survey fees. To the official himself, Ting was magnanimous, pardoning his "reprehensible carelessness" in recognition of his promptness. Asperity, however, suffused the covering letter to the Financial Commissioner. Ting asserted that the Magistrate's slip was simply a clear manifestation of his innermost thoughts:

> This Magistrate is like the man who satisfies himself by chewing as he walks by the butcher shop. He should be invigorating himself, combing out the dirt, and scratching the sores. . . . Though the people are barely able to survive, such officials as he and the clerks think it a time of prosperity. They break the bones and suck the marrow [of the common people].[70]

But again, Ting substituted hyperbole for discipline.

A decade later, Ting's own work on the survey came under equally sharp, if more oblique, criticism. At the conclusion of their 1868 survey, in addition to the general report that they submitted, Ting and Tseng were instructed by the court to prepare and send to the Board of Revenue new maps and registers for each hsien surveyed.[71] Yet, they neither produced these papers nor requested the establishment of new and increased tax rates on improved land. Many landowners consequently found themselves in the curious position of requesting tax increases, for without tax receipts as proof, their claim to newly deposited land was easily challenged, and lawsuits were a constant threat.[72]

In 1877 and 1878, the blame for these difficulties was laid upon the official in charge of the new survey, Chu Chih-chen.[73] Chu vehemently denied the charges and shifted the responsibility back in time. In a letter to his immediate superior, Chu cited the specific failures of his predecessors and then asked, "How could one expect that, with Tseng's sageness (*hsien*) and Ting's ability (*neng*), they would not complete their work?"[74] It would seem, then, that, in the matter of the alluvial survey, Ting was guilty of the charge he so often leveled against his subordinates—his words exceeded his deeds.[75]

It would also seem that, by failing (albeit noncollusively) to halt local power-holders from undermining both the cadastral and alluvial surveys, Ting allowed the vital interests of the central government to be compromised. Hilary Beattie has argued that surveys can be seen fairly simply as contests between the central government (which hopes to increase tax revenues and equalize the burden) and local power-holders. Beattie's study reveals that the successful effort of the Anhwei gentry to prevent the rewriting of the tax rolls resulted in the development and long-term survival of large estates, the basis of the gentry's local power.[76] Moreover, although large tracts of land did not accrue to the gentry directors of Fu-ning who engineered the "old disaster precincts," they, too, significantly aggrandized their power. As one Fu-ning Magistrate put it, "The people knew there were directors, but didn't know there were officials" (*min chih yu tung, pu-chih yu kuan*).[77] The challenge confronting Ting was to ensure that another Fu-ning saying that reflected official weakness vis-à-vis local powers—"As soon as taxation begins, it stops"—did not become a province-wide aphorism.

TAX COLLECTION

In the Ch'ing, the process of tax collection entailed three phases: officially reminding the taxpayer of his obligations, or "urging" (*ts'ui-k'o*); receiving the taxes; and forwarding them to higher levels of government. The people were most directly affected by the first two steps, and it was upon them that Ting focused his attention.

Within certain imperial guidelines, Ting and other provincial officials were allowed broad latitude in dealing with problems of urging and collection. In general terms, the court's interest was limited to the collection of full quotas without arousing popular discontent. Successive imperial decisions, however, did establish the desirability of certain specific practices: rural leaders should not be responsible for their entire district's quota; urging should consist only of informing the landowner of his tax bill and reminding him when it was overdue; money should never be handled by urgers or clerks but always placed directly in the collection chest by the taxpayer himself; and there should be no rate discrimination between gentry (*ta-hu*) and commoners (*hsiao-hu*).[78] These standards (which can be grouped under the general themes of individual responsibility and equity), as Ting's official papers show, were rarely applied. Urging was often coercive, and taxpayers with small arrears were hounded into suicide.[79] Gentry were given enormous rate discounts, while commoners made up the shortages.[80] And commoners were bullied into allowing the clerks to pay for them (*ch'ai-tien*), or were so fearful of the clerks that they entrusted their payments to gentry, who appropriated some for themselves before forwarding the rest to the officials for collection (*pao-lan*).[81]

Although some of these problems were particularly severe in post-Taiping Kiangsu, none was peculiar to it; they had been familiar to various provincial administrators in other reigns and were known to contemporary bureaucrats in other parts of the empire. Interestingly, these officials' writings manifest a consensus view on some important aspects of tax collection. The officials generally agreed on the need for the elimination of gentry-commoner differences in payment and for direct personal payment of taxes, though they were divided on the utility of torture and beatings as means for urging taxes.[82] To achieve an end to discrimination, many proposed the use of "easy-to-read tax bills" (*i-chih yu-tan*), in which each taxpayer would receive a simple statement of the total amount he owed.[83] Remarkably enough, none of these proposals ever refers to the established precedents they mirrored.[84]

The officials' views are all distinguished by their emphasis on problems of personnel, though their writings disappointingly offer more in the way of description than corrective prescription. Even when they agreed on a diagnosis, they recommended different cures. Of course, it was essential to choose the right men to sit at the collection chests, but should they be clerks, bonded constables, or "substantial" landowners (that is, holders of more than 100 *mou*)? Substantial families were familiar with tax regulations and were ostensibly honest, but in Soochow they had charged so many fees that they were replaced with clerks.[85] The clerks had their own myriad tricks: "ghost" households,[86] receipts written in purposely confusing cursive scripts,[87] and prepayment of taxes without the taxpayers' knowledge or consent (*ch'ai-tien*).[88] Unquestionably, the clerks had to be made to do the officials' bidding. It was a difficult task, though, when the clerks shared their ill-gotten gains with the officials and had paid handsome fees, subsequently retrieved from the taxpayers, to obtain their posts.[89] Magistrates were urged to exercise control by virtue of their own upright example, but none of the writers surveyed, save Feng Kuei-fen, suggested, as did Ting, that the real solution lay in improving both the status and the income of clerks.[90]

Abuses and corruption had existed throughout the dynasty, but, from their perspective, nineteenth-century provincial officials correctly surmised that the situation had severely worsened by their time.[91] They concluded that, until the inflationary pressure of rapidly increasing population upon limited goods and services had caused prices to soar in the late eighteenth century, tax quotas could be met despite inherent administrative malfeasance. But, with the sharp rise in prices, officials could no longer cover revenue shortfalls out of their own pockets and still maintain their standard of living. This situation gave rise to the practice of collecting customary fees (*lou-kuei*) from subordinates—fees ultimately paid for by the people through extra legal surcharges (*fou-shou*). Magistrates, burdened by their superiors' demands, siphoned tax funds to meet them, and then juggled accounts to meet the tax quotas (*tien-wan*). "Indeed," wrote the scholar-official Hung Liang-chi in a famous 1799 jeremiad:

> it is for this reason that the district officials say plainly to the people: "The reason I am doubling and redoubling your taxes is that the expenses of the yamen at various levels are going up higher and higher from day to day and year to year."[92]

So long as the tax quotas were met, these practices were of little concern to the court; but suddenly in Chia-ch'ing, quotas went unfulfilled. Previously the inflation that buffeted the officials had also meant high rice prices for peasants—an increase which enabled them to remain a step ahead of the surcharges. After 1800, however, rice prices had plummeted (and remained depressed until after the Taiping Rebellion), while silver had rapidly appreciated in price relative to copper. The concatenation of these two events conspired to increase the real tax burden of the people, for, though taxes were assessed in terms of silver, most people paid in cash. Shortages in tax accounts were ubiquitous, and officals were forced to ask for remissions. These were granted, but the court then saddled magistrates with the additional burden of making up the inevitable deficits in provincial administrative expenses as "assigned contributions" (*t'an-chüan*).[93] Thereby the cycle of exactions was perpetuated, for, deprived of this additional income, the magistrate was susceptible to the clerks' corrupt blandishments. By Tao-kuang, failures to meet tax quotas, even through *tien-wan,* were ever more frequent; and in Kiangsu, where tax relief and remissions were allowed after severe floods in 1821, provincial officials falsely reported continued disasters in order to obtain additional financial breathing room.[94]

The official response was not, however, limited only to the superficial and disingenuous. Kiangsu provincial officials such as T'ao Chu and Lin Tse-hsu proposed, in the 1820s and 1830s, fundamental fiscal reforms that adumbrated many of the themes found in Restoration officials' writings. Nonetheless, their experiment in eliminating surcharges by abandoning the enormously expensive shipment of grain tribute by Grand Canal in favor of sea transport was terminated by opposition in Peking, and their plea to rationalize and legitimize customary fees was rejected.[95] The effort to equalize tax rates was vigorously resisted by the influential households (*ta-hu*), which in one Kiangsu county comprised more than nine-tenths of the taxpayers. As one able Magistrate observed, however, it was really the commoners, the ones who had been forced to make up the endemic shortages, who had a reason for creating disturbances and, indeed, in the late 1840s and early 1850s, rent- and tax-resistance riots were a common occurrence in Kiangsu.[96]

The Tao-kuang tax-reform movement was carried into the 1850s by Feng Kuei-fen, renowned Kiangsu literatus and erstwhile secretary of Lin Tse-hsu. Until the late 1850s, Feng had stressed the need for tax equalization, but, unable to obtain support for this idea, he had shifted the focus of his efforts from tax reform to tax reduction—a measure that would directly benefit the gentry households and, it was hoped, persuade them to join the reform cause.[97] Feng's work ostensibly successfully culminated in the famous Kiangnan tax reduction when the court lowered the grain tribute quotas and surcharges and outlawed rate discrimination between gentry (*ta-hu*) and commoner (*hsiao-hu*) households.[98]

This tax reduction, however, as Mary Wright has previously noted, had no significant impact.[99] Preferential rates survived, and the actual level of collection remained high. Moreover, although rents were somewhat reduced in a few scattered areas, this phenomenon was more a function of increased tenant power in a situation of land surplus than it was an intended outcome of the government policy.[100] Actually, notwithstanding an apparent requirement for Kiangsu magistrates to file reports on rents, the issue of rents was a concern neither of the court nor even of reform officials such as Ting Jih-ch'ang; and, in any case, the law calling for rent reductions in times of remissions was toothless. This is not to say that Ting Jih-ch'ang ignored the problem of landlord-tenant relations. Rather, his focus was on protecting the tenant against landlord-induced abuses of official authority. He sought to end magistrates' overzealous punishment of indebted tenants, to control local constables (*ti-pao*) who illegally imprisoned recalcitrant tenants at their landlord's behest, and to make the courts accessible to tenants by eliminating court fees and runners' exactions.[101]

Essentially, the court was so entranced with the idea that reform of the collection process could both increase revenues and decrease the people's burden that it was unconcerned with other matters. It even rejected Li Hung-chang's subsequent request for reductions in the regular land-tax quotas and instructed him to press for further reform.[102] Prodded into action by the court, provincial officials attacked the sources of corruption. Li, Ting, and others pinpointed the magistrate's assigned contributions (*chüan-t'an* or *t'an-chüan*) as one of the chief problems and urged the court to abolish this practice. But their exhortations were to no avail.[103] In 1866, Li enjoyed greater success in obtaining court approval to set median prices for silver and rice, and to establish a standard rice measure, with the aim of ending manipulation of commutation and exchange rates.[104] In succeeding years, acting within his own authority, Ting enacted (but with only temporary success) a series of provincial regulations which prohibited numerous extralegal administrative fees,[105] established payment chests throughout the countryside (*hsiang-kuei*),[106] abolished clerks' posts which had been used to private advantage,[107] and affirmed the principle of gentry-commoner equality.[108] But, of all his measures concerned with tax collection, two in particular, the institution of the *p'an-t'u* urging system and the reinvigoration of the easy-to-read tax bill (*i-chih yu-tan*), are worthy of additional comment because they were conceived by Ting to be long-term institutional solutions to old structural problems.

The success of urging taxes (*ts'ui-k'o*) depended entirely on the proper preparation of tax bills and receipts. These tasks were performed by the office of revenue in the magistrate's yamen.[109] But, since the quotas and rates listed in each hsien's *Fu-i ch'üan-shu* (Complete book of taxes and services) were too general for the proper preparation of the bills, two additional, more detailed registers were required: the household register (*hu-ling-ch'iu*) and the land-maps register (*ch'iu-ling-hu*). Their titles reflected their organization. In the household register, a lineal descendant of the Ming *Huang-ts'e* (Yellow register), each main entry of a household name was followed by information about its landholdings. The land-maps register, also known by its appearance as the *Yü-lin ts'e* (Fish-Scale Register), contained maps of each precinct (*t'u*), on which land was listed by geographic and administrative location, followed by information on that parcel's ownership, fertility, and tax rate.[110] Theoretically, the two registers were the "inner and outer" of tax collection; one was to be used by the clerks to prepare the receipts, and the other was to be retained by the magistrate himself to cross check the clerks' work. In practice, however, officials viewed the two as distinct alternatives and, by the mid-nineteenth century, generally favored the land-maps register because of its supposed accuracy.[111] The household register, nonetheless, was never completely abandoned, for, like the land-maps register, it organized a particular method of urging and collection.

In the spring of 1867, a petition from the energetic Magistrate of Lou hsien stimulated Ting to initiate a circular discussion of the relative merits of the two alternative systems of urging: the land-maps-register-based *p'an-t'u* (by land location) and the household-register-based *shun-chuang* (by family residence). The Lou hsien Magistrate's petition was an advocate's brief for *shun-chuang*. He pointed out that, when one family owned land in many different precincts (*t'u*), *p'an-t'u* required numerous sheets in the registers, while *shun-chuang* made urging and checking payment easier by

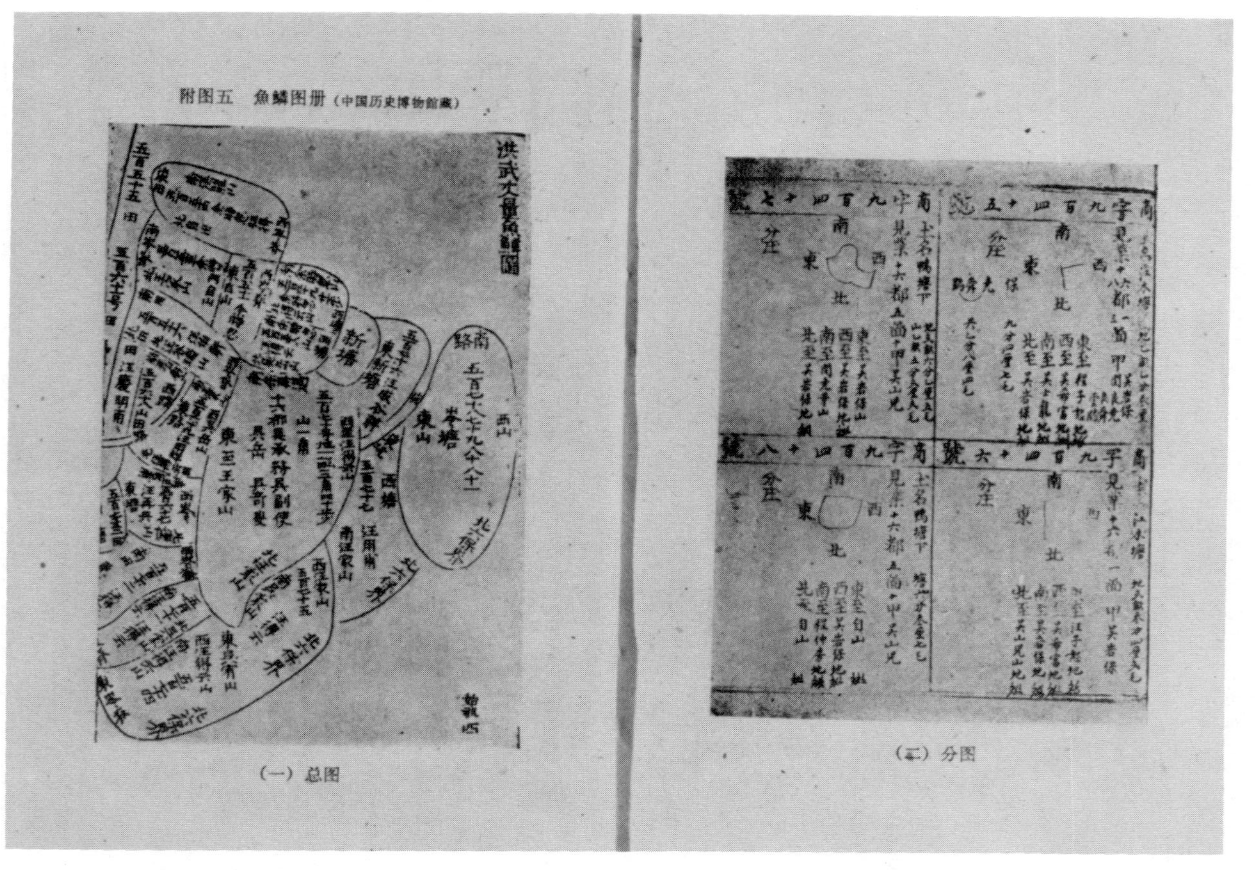

Pages from the Fish-Scale Register, from Wei Ch'ing-yuan, Ming-tai huang-ts'e chih-tu *(Peking, 1961).*

administratively combining their holdings into the single precinct where they lived and by listing them on one sheet. The Magistrate, moreover, implied that *p'an-t'u* owed its popularity among officials and gentry to the deficits which allegedly flourished wherever it was implemented. Nevertheless, like most other officials, he recognized that the two methods should not be mutually exclusive, but mutually supportive; and he reported that he would retain the land-maps register in his office to check on bills and receipts prepared by the clerks using the household register.[112]

After having solicited other officials' opinions, Ting decided in favor of *p'an-t'u*, without indicating whether this choice reflected the majority view of the respondents.[113] At first glance his decision is surprising. Besides the Lou hsien Magistrate's insinuations about the *p'an-t'u* advocates' probity, there were the hard facts that the scattered landholdings in Kiangsu were ideally suited to *shun-chuang,* and that there was a history of gentry sentiment in favor of *shun-chuang*-based tax collection mechanisms.[114]

The appearance in the 1720s of the *shun-chuang* principle of administratively combining dispersed landholdings under the owner's name at his place of residence was linked to the vicissitudes of the *li-chia* registration system and the development in late Ming and early Ch'ing of the equal-field/equal-tax (*chün-t'ien chün-i*) concept. The purpose of the equal-field system was to establish similar-sized taxing units so that the labor service (*i*), which had come to be based on land, would be equitable. In some parts of Kiangsu, adjacent land was first grouped into units of several hundred acres (*mou*), and then households were attached to the land (*p'an-t'u*), but this arrangement meant that one household would have labor obligations in several areas. The alternative approach was to take a natural village (*chuang*) or group of households as a base and attach all its landholdings to the owners' places of residence (*shun-chuang*). Even when the labor-service levy was commuted to cash, thereby eliminating the chief impetus for equalization of labor service, the prompting and collecting of taxes in the natural village retained its attraction. Moreover, prompting by place of residence (*shun-chuang*) facilitated the various rotational methods of urging wherein tax notices were passed from household to household.[115] Thus *shun-chuang* seems to reflect the secular replacement in late imperial China of artificial administrative networks (*li-chia*) by natural ones (the villages).

Ting, however, was not bereft of good administrative arguments to substantiate the case for land-based urging (*p'an-t'u*). In preparing bills and receipts and in urging, *p'an-t'u* showed at a glance all the necessary information about a piece of land: location, dimensions, fertility, tax rate, and ownership. Deception would be less likely under *p'an-t'u,* since land, though alienable, was immobile and, unlike taxpayers, would not slip away.[116] Furthermore, although many of the rotational urging systems had been crippled by serious abuses, Ting did not feel that *p'an-t'u* precluded continued operation of well-functioning ones.[117] But perhaps his best single argument for *p'an-t'u* was that, while many of the household registers had been destroyed, land-map registers were in the process of being prepared by cadastral surveys. For this very reason, even before Ting ordered the implementation of *p'an-t'u,* K'un-shan and Hsin-yang hsien had already adopted the system.[118]

The simple truth was that, regardless of which method was used, regardless of how carefully and honestly the registers and bills were prepared, there remained ample room for chicanery at the actual moment of collection. Although surcharges had been either outlawed or reduced, exchange rates fixed, and gentry-commoner discrimination prohibited, the commoner taxpayer could still be cheated or abused unless he knew the legal rates and the exact amount owed. To protect him from such mistreatment and to guarantee gentry-commoner equality, Ting, as Financial Commissioner, resurrected the moribund "easy-to-read tax bill" (*i-chih yu-tan*).

When first issued to each household in 1650, the *yu-tan* listed all regular and miscellaneous taxes, the rates at which they were levied, and their amounts in cash and kind. In 1667, the court ordered that the arithmetic be done for the landowner and simplified the *yu-tan* to indicate only how much each acre of land was to be taxed. Twenty years later, the *yu-tan* was abandoned, except in Kiangsu, when it was found that officials and clerks were exacting a fee for issuing it.[119] Why Kiangsu alone was allowed to retain the *yu-tan* is unclear. Perhaps it was because the province had more than two hundred tax rates. But the *yu-tan* continued to be plagued with abuses; and, with the brief exception of a period in the 1830s, its issuance was strictly *pro forma.*[120]

Ting himself did not initiate the revival of the *yu-tan;* this honor must go to the able Magistrate Shen Hsi-hua, a former clerk whose six-year tenure in Wu-chiang was the longest of any T'ung-chih Kiangsu magistrate.[121] Shen, moreover, made an important modification in the notices. He not only issued to each household a *yu-tan* listing the amount per acre to be paid on variously rated land, but he also posted several thousand colloquially phrased notices of tax rates, commutation and exchange rates, shipment fees, and carrying charges, which could be understood by peasants from their knowledge of a few simple characters.[122] Adjudging that, for once, Shen's deeds matched his words, Ting immediately seized upon Shen's idea. He ordered other magistrates to follow suit and to send in samples of their own *yu-tan,* rate notices, and tax receipts. Urging their rapid compliance, Ting exhorted them not "to let Shen alone be the *chün-tzu.*"[123]

Yet, before the officials could even respond, Ting revised Shen's original format. Having discovered that few people knew how their land was rated, Ting concluded that posting rates would be of little help to most taxpayers. At the most, some remembered the rate at which their land had been assessed previously; at the least, some recalled how much they used to pay. With more than two hundred different rates in the province (nearly sixty in one hsien), this already complex situation was further complicated by the tax reduction.[124] After that, only the revenue clerks knew precisely which rate was applicable and the total amount owed.

Therefore Ting ordered that each household be issued a revised *yu-tan* which showed simply the amount per acre owed (including all fees and carrying charges) in all the alternative forms of payment: copper, cash, silver, or rice; and the exchange rate based on market conditions, at which cash or foreign money could be converted into silver, and rice commuted into silver.[125] This was essential information, for the price ratio of copper to silver and the commutation rate of rice into silver both varied according to market conditions; and uncertainty over official standards could erupt into capital appeals and riots.[126] In Kiangsu in the late 1860s, rice was decreasing in price, while silver was becoming more expensive relative to copper, thereby increasing the real tax burden of the peasants, who used copper cash to pay their taxes. In addition to notifying taxpayers of the rates, Ting tried to hold down the price of silver and set a mean price for rice, so that the smaller taxpayer could get the same return on his crop regardless of whether he sold it when demand was high or low.[127]

To discourage the clerks from withholding the individual "easy-to-read" notices, Ting instructed Magistrates to post throughout each rural district (*hsiang*) a general notice which contained the information in all of that district's individual notices. He did not, however, specifically incorporate Lin Tse-hsu's principle of allowing taxpayers to submit a complaint if the individual notice was not received, though he clearly had demonstrated his willingness in other instances to hear personally the people's grievances.[128] Nonetheless, satisfied that his measure was effective, Ting included the new procedures in the tax-collection regulations he issued in 1867 and later extended the entire set of regulations to Kiangpei when he became Governor.[129]

The revised *yu-tan* met its first test well but unequivocally failed its second. Despite a mediocre fall harvest in 1867, taxes, according to Ting, were both enthusiastically and completely paid because of generally uniform compliance with his newly instituted methods.[130] However, the following spring, well after tax collection had begun, only two Magistrates had sent in sample *yu-tan;* the *yu-tan* were both not only unclear but also as yet unposted. Ting charged that the officials' lackadaisical attitude toward issuance of the *yu-tan* demonstrated their acceptance of the clerks' obstructions and exactions as routine occurrences. He complained to the Financial Commissioners, with characteristic self-mocking irony, that the Magistrates considered his orders utterly useless but those of the clerks divinely intelligent; and he demanded to know just who these Magistrates thought they were (*tzu-ming ho-teng*) to divorce themselves from the people's suffering and immerse themselves in poetry the minute they became officials. Concluding that verbal lashings were insufficient for such men, Ting ordered that magistrates remiss in printing and posting the *yu-tan* be given a major demerit (*chi ta-kuo*). He also strongly hinted that the Financial Commissioners ought to impeach one or two officials to demonstrate that he was not "all talk and no action (*mi-yun pu-yü*)."[131] At least on this occasion Ting carried out his threat, but he still sought, apparently successfully, to give added weight to his new measure by gaining court approval.[132]

As enunciated by Ting, the basic purpose of the *yu-tan* was "to take the minute, enlarge it and make it known; to take the secret, expose it and make it known" (*wei-che chang-shih shih-cho; mi-che chieh-chih shih hsuan*).[133] By requiring the magistrates to submit copies of the actual individual *yu-tan,* posters, receipts, and price lists, Ting also applied this theme as a standard to official performance.

Over the following three years (1868–1870), as he uncovered officials' numerous shortcomings, he used them as a guide for further improvements in the *yu-tan* procedures. One of the officials' most common failings was not indicating on the *yu-tan* and on the posters themselves that money could be exchanged at the market price rather than at the fixed official rates. Magistrates also often posted out-of-date exchange rates and listed the in-kind, but not the commuted, rate per acre.[134] To correct these problems, Ting, at the suggestion of one of the Magistrates, required that a separate sheet of exchange rates and prices marked in red be attached to both the individual and the composite *yu-tan.*[135] He developed a similarly simple solution to the problem of composite notices being posted by magistrates only at the yamen door and city gates. Magistrates were ordered to print and post at least 1,000 of the composite *yu-tan* in large hsiens and at least 600 in small ones.[136] But the practice of posting only a few notices continued. In a letter to one Magistrate guilty of this offense, Ting asked him if he were more interested in splitting illicit income with his clerks than in properly using the authority of his office.[137]

For the most part, however, Ting faulted the Magistrates not for their cupidity but for their stupidity. In a letter to the Financial Commissioner, he reasoned that, since the Magistrates were men of self-respect and did not want the money, they would not coerce payments. Yet, he noted, they stupidly allowed the clerks to enrich themselves while they bore the final responsibility for any abuses. To save the Magistrates from the consequences of their own neglect, Ting begged the Financial Commissioner personally to urge upon Magistrates the importance of searching out and eliminating corruption themselves before the people's complaints brought it to the attention of higher authorities.[138] While the Financial Commissioner persuaded the Magistrates, Ting warned them that,

> if the secret agents I have sent out to investigate find one *hsiang* or one *t'u* that does not post the notices or that goes so far as to collect surcharges, the [responsible] Magistrate will be impeached for dismissal without leniency. Take Care! [139]

Ting had previously informed one difficult Magistrate that in matters of general concern he would not "let numerous families cry so that one would not";[140] and he manifested his anger at the continuance of extralegal surcharges by rephrasing the *Shih-ching* ode:

> *Do what is good for the people, good for the people*
> *Receive emoluments from heaven.*

to:

> *Do what is right for the officials and clerks;*
> *Spread poison to the people.*[142]

Here once again we have an example of Ting's bluster. When his agents reported to him that there were few notices in the countryside of Ch'ing-chiang hsien, and that the Magistrate's laxness allowed the corrupt clerks free rein, he ordered the Financial Commissioner to punish the Magistrate with merely a reprimand and a major demerit.[142] Impeachment was mentioned only as a warning against repetition of such behavior. When news of similar incidences in T'ai-chou came to him, Ting replied that he would first give the T'ai-chou Magistrate a chance to arouse shame within himself and correct the problem on his own. But, at the slightest hint of backsliding, Ting admonished, "I will have to lower my eyebrows and take on an angry appearance."[143]

Ting must have been of perpetually choleric mien, for few Magistrates were able to submit consistently satisfactory reports on *yu-tan* to him. (See Appendix C-2.) Of the forty-four hsien for which we have two or more comments from Ting, only five were judged up to standard each time; and this number included just one of the three head hsien in Soochow. Although there is no clear correlation between the quality of response to the *yu-tan* order and a hsien's location or tax burden, as Ting noted, if the head county of the provincial capital had malpractices, it was hardly strange that magistrates who might be anywhere from 100 to 1,000 *li* away looked upon the law with disrespect.[144] Apparently, it was precisely because noncompliance was so widespread that Ting was reluctant to enforce the new regulation harshly. He admitted that it was unreasonable to expect within one day to eliminate one-hundred-year-old abuses; and he acknowledged that, if one tried to fulfill this expectation with newly minted regulations, not a single magistrate's record would go unblemished. Yet this seems a weak rationalization for not forcefully disciplining poor magistrates. As Thomas Metzger has noted, officials considered it impossible to avoid some blemishes on their career records. Indeed, discipline for public offenses (*kung-tsui*) was so routine, states Metzger, that it had lost its punitive effect.[145]

Nonetheless, despite Ting's leniency, opposition to his measures appeared, particularly in Kiangpei which had the greatest disparities in gentry-commoner rates.[146] This resistance took the guise of personal defamation (of which we unfortunately do not have an example), but with a tinge of self-pity Ting announced to the reporting Prefect that he had anticipated the obloquy:

> If one wants genuinely to aid the people, one cannot concern oneself with the poisonous vilification that will arise. Considering the situation, one can only bear up under slander, swallow one's anger, press on with the business at hand, and then save the lives of several poor commoners. I have written this out quickly [and hope that you] do not consider it too maudlin.[147]

Ting had hoped that the *yu-tan* in combination with his other measures—elimination of fees, strictures on clerks, setting fair exchange rates, and reduction of the price of silver—would eliminate corruption and inequities; but their net impact was inconsequential. Illicit surcharges, gentry tax evasion, commoner rates eighteen times gentry ones, corrupt clerks, and incompetent officials—all continued to plague Kiangsu throughout Ting's tenure in office and on into the next reign.[148]

Official inability to reverse or even impede these tendencies stimulated among the people efforts at self-protection. The voluntarily organized rotational urging groups known as "equitable precincts" (*i-t'u*) established a set of rules, including fines for delinquency, that were designed to ensure prompt full tax payments and to avoid dunning harassment by yamen underlings. Similarly, the gentry-managed bursaries could guarantee to the noninfluential landowner both the collection of his rents and the payment of only his legitimate taxes. Official reaction to these institutions was ambivalent: tolerance because both seemed to promise ease of tax collection; suspicion because both violated the longstanding principle of direct tax payment. Perhaps because neither the bursaries nor the "equitable precincts" were widespread, they never became a major cause of official concern.[149]

Still, the question remains—could any reformist official have corrected the fiscal abuses? In 1876, an editorial writer for Shanghai's Chinese newspaper *Shen Pao* answered negatively. Such able officials, he asserted, became the enemy of the gentry and clerks who together manufactured defamatory rumors and pretexts for accusations. The harassed and discomfited officials then became a warning to future magistrates that this would be the fate of all reformist officials.[150]

Ting and subsequent administrative reformers were rarely deterred by slander, so we must seek another reason for the persistence of fiscal corruption. I would suggest that reform failed mainly because most elements of the population shared, or imagined they shared, the profits of corruption. Scorned for their evil, petty, profit-seeking ways, clerks and runners were generally the first to be charged with guilt. But, as we have noted, Ting and others recognized that corruption was their only source of income, and that officials, were they so inclined, could control their yamen underlings. For some officials, inaction could be attributed to implication in the clerks' schemes, as they, too, depended upon corruption for supplementary income; for others, stupidity appears the only explanation, since for just a small percentage of the illicit gains they had to assume complete responsibility.[151] Both gentry and commoners were stricken with greed—they "did not know when enough was enough" (*pu-chih tsu*).[152] The gentry were not satisfied with their social and political advantages and fought to maintain economic ones as well. The commoners, as Feng Kuei-fen wryly noted, "just cannot accept that land is taxed, and that there is no heavenly place to which they can flee."[153] Ting's experience confirmed this assessment, for, even though he halved the price of tribute grain through the elimination of surcharges (albeit temporarily in some instances), when he instituted an emergency grain reserve contribution equal to one fiftieth the former surcharges, the people still complained vigorously.[154]

On paper, the state had the coercive powers to force these various groups to adhere to the standards of honesty and equity in tax matters. From the inception of the dynasty, stiff administrative and penal measures, applicable both to general problems of corruption and malfeasance, and to almost every aspect of fiscal chicanery, were at officials' disposal: a four-grade demotion for officials, and permanent disbarment from official service and confiscation of their land for gentry guilty of purposeful concealment of taxable arable land; confiscation of anyone's land who illegally dispersed it (*fei-sai*) with officials and degree-holders being punished more severely than commoners for such tax evasion;[155]

beatings and the cangue for those who paid others' taxes (*lan-na*), and possibly tatooing and banishment for those who embezzled tax monies in the process (*pao-lan*);[156] penal or military servitude for officials who shifted funds or whose accounts were short, even if no dishonesty was involved;[157] and dismissal and beatings for gentry and officials who defaulted on tax payments.[158]

In practice, these measures were rarely, if ever, fully implemented, especially after the late 1840s. We have already seen that Ting was reluctant to impeach and dismiss officials who seriously mishandled fiscal affairs (even at the risk of potentially endangering his own career).[159] It would seem that he did not lack replacements for them; there was a plethora of alternate officials in Soochow eagerly awaiting an opportunity for office.[160] The quality of this "talent" pool was highly uneven, however, and, as we have argued in the Introduction and Chapter 6, a governor's ability to make appointments was increasingly restricted. Thus, apparently, unless a magistrate was totally derelict in his duties, Ting employed the "probationary ethic." Indeed, despite the central importance to his career of his ability to deliver full tax quotas, a magistrate dismissed because of shortages could generally be restored to his rank and office once he had made up the deficits.[161]

In the case of gentry, fiscal malfeasants were given a similar chance to nourish their shame. Although a Tao-kuang Kiangsu Literary Chancellor complained that lower gentry were bearing more of the guilt for tax problems than were the clerks, there is strong contrary evidence which indicates that gentry were not consistently held to the letter of the law.[162] In mid-Chia-ch'ing, over three hundred *chien-sheng* involved in a *pao-lan* scheme that deprived the state of nearly 40,000 taels were spared punishment "in order to open to them the road of self-renewal" (*yu-i tzu-hsin chih-lu*).[163] Such leniency was apparently not uncommon, for, by the end of the dynasty, gentry tax delinquents were so infrequently punished that, according to the eminent legal official and scholar Hsueh Yun-sheng, the relevant section of the Penal Code had become a dead letter.[164]

For its treatment of officials, the state had a developed rationale, but there was none for the gentry. That the prevalence of this permissive attitude coincided with a period of increasing tax abuse suggests that the extent of participation in tax evasion and fraud constrained the enforcement of punitive measures. While the state's attempts at vigorous enforcement of the moral parts of the Penal Code—those concerning robbery, rape, burial, and marriage—served to consolidate its support among the Confucian gentry backers, the state's fiscal pressure was thoroughly offensive to them on both practical and Confucian grounds, and in inflationary times sharply tested their loyalty. In the wake of the Taiping Rebellion, it was a question for the state of how rigorous the test could be without engendering open hostility.[165] For the gentry it was a question of what upright behavior entailed; knowing that their evasions shifted their burden to the commoner, could they still characterize themselves as Confucian gentlemen, as leaders of society? Significantly, reform officials appealed to gentry not as Confucians, but as men who could see that reform was also in their own self-interests.

The fiscal conduct of Restoration Kiangsu's gentry has been a source of controversy, some of which mirrors—albeit not explicitly—the debate between exponents of moral and political peasant economies.[166] The central issue has been whether Feng Kuei-fen and his influential gentry confreres (in James Polachek's words, "the Soochow patriciate") granted their tenants rent reductions commensurate with the tax cuts.[167] Whatever the case, rent reductions are not the standard by which to judge a Restoration fiscal policy that never encompassed the question of rents. However shortsighted we may adjudge this approach, however pernicious we may find its long-term consequences, the omission was not inadvertent. Restoration reforms were designed to increase revenues by eliminating corruption and inequalities at the point of collection, not to transform landlord-tenant relations.

Influential gentry supported this program (which did not threaten their vital interests) in order to obtain in return decreased taxes, and, like their late Ming and early Ch'ing predecessors, in order both to insulate themselves from and attack the abuses of their more rapacious colleagues. As Polachek and Dennerline have argued, such financial manipulation was seen by politically influential men as likely to provoke a central government attack on the privileges of all gentry.[168] However genuinely felt such fears may have been, in the post-Taiping world they were unfounded, for the state was reluctant, if not unable, to challenge its ostensibly most loyal supporters. Moreover, the central—even the provincial—government was often ignorant of gentry depredations. Capital appeals (*ching-k'ung*) by the aggrieved could be buried by unsympathetic provincial governors, and violent public protest could be suppressed while being dismissed as the work of "tricksters." Even after peasants in Szechuan in the late 1870s raised flags and attacked government forces, it took repeated investigation before the source of discontent was revealed and the gentry-managed tax collection bureaus were permanently prohibited by the court.[169]

Although the influential gentry of the Soochow hinterland had established similar bureaus to collect rents and later to levy surcharges for reconstruction purposes, the Kiangsu provincial government, at least under Tseng Kuo-fan and Ting Jih-ch'ang, worked to restrain the fiscal and political power of such institutions.[170] Coincidentally, the gentry began to batten on the likin as a more lucrative source of revenue for their projects, thereby alleviating some of the direct pressure on peasants.[171] Not only was likin an increasingly productive levy; but also the gentry's perennial competitors, the yamen underlings, were not so well entrenched, and accounting procedures were not so strict as they were in the land tax. While land-tax-related gentry chicanery waxed healthy in Kiangpei, in the South, gentry-managed land tax surcharges and their attendant tensions seem to have waned until their reimposition at the turn of the century in the guise of indemnity and modernization fees.

A delimiting of the role of the gentry, a restructuring of local government and society, and an improvement in the status of the clerks, were the *sine qua non* of a fundamental solution to fiscal problems. Provincial officials—even ones as determined as Ting

Jih-ch'ang—could not achieve such transformations on their own. They could intitiate the ideas for institutional change, but the impetus for success could come only from the court. Without such structural reform, the impediment to long-term change was the very same one the Chinese Communist Party would have to face later in each newly liberated district: it was difficult to offer guarantees against the recrudescence of vengeful old enemies to those who had supported the new. Magistrates moved on in T'ung-chih Kiangsu, averaging only one and one-half years in office; and Ting was Governor of Kiangsu for barely two years.[172] Officials, gentry, clerks, and commoners all knew that the odds militated against his successor's being as vigorous an administrator.

Could not virtuous officials have smoothed the way for their successors by making negative exemplars of recalcitrants, just as the recalcitrants sought to humiliate and constrain their successors? In theory, the answer is yes. But we have seen that, in practice, this rarely happened. For reforms to succeed, then, their advocates had to ensure a continuity of vigorous administrators who would not only protect and consolidate their predecessor's reforms but also advance their own.

Yet, the vital imperial support for sustaining a reform regime that we noted above was not forthcoming. In the late Ch'ing, the court's good Confucian official, imperial edicts notwithstanding, gave primacy to the people's livelihood (*min-sheng*) only insofar as it advanced the state's revenue (*kuo-chi*). Liu K'un-i, Governor of Kiangsi, 1865–1874, epitomized this type. Liu remained Governor by deleting the people from his political thinking and sedulously focusing on meeting all imperial demands for funds.[173] Ting Jih-ch'ang could easily have addressed to his gubernatorial colleague Liu the same angry query he directed toward a subordinate:

> Why is it that officials pride themselves on being Neo-Confucians (*i li-hsueh wei tzu-ming,* viz. scholars) until they have power in their hands, and then suddenly consider raising revenue important and loving the people trivial?[174]

SIX

Personnel

Now in this time of difficulty,
men of talent are few.

Ting Jih-ch'ang, 1865[1]

One of the most basic themes in Confucian political writings is that good government comes from men, not from laws.[2] Prevalent throughout the Ch'ing, this view is epitomized by Wang Chih-i, a late-eighteenth-century Governor-General:

> Since ancient times, there has been rule by men but not by methods (*yu chih-jen, wu chih-fa*). Because of a problem, a rule was established; but the rule could not be perfect and, consequently, another problem arose for each new rule; and in the end none of the problems could be eliminated. Moreover, the tighter the rules are, the more they will be perverted and evaded, and the greater will be their uselessness. From this, one can see that, rather than make detailed proposals of rules, it is better to select and use men carefully. If the men are upright, then the problems will get rid of themselves.[3]

The need for regulations was accepted by most officials, however, because they were aware of their own shortcomings—in particular, their susceptibility to socioeconomic pressures.[4] Yet, Ting was perhaps too quick to decide that a problem could be resolved once proper guidelines and forms had been developed. Hence his career was highlighted by the tightening of old regulations and the establishment of new strict ones, and also often darkened by officials' immediate evasion of them.

Ting obviously did not ignore the problem of personnel. He was fully aware of man's ability to subvert and circumvent any procedure; indeed, he attempted to fulfill T'ao Chu's advice that "the best administrative results are obtained if one finds a good man and then subjects him to rewards and punishments."[5] The key was to recruit men good enough to be influenced by either the carrot or the stick. Yet, of the three basic personnel elements in local administrations–yamen underlings, local elite, and officials, Ting was involved only in the selection of a small number of the officials. He had negligible control over the other two groups, and his supervision of them was indirect and dependent upon the officials' execution of his policies. Finally, Ting had to confront the issue of spheres of responsibility, since, despite the large area and the population of many hsien, there was little formal government below the magistrate; and the yamen underlings and local elite competed to fill that void.[6]

YAMEN UNDERLINGS: CLERKS AND RUNNERS

The vast sub-bureaucracy of clerks and runners kept the Ch'ing bureaucratic machine functioning. Although these underlings were limited in number and length of service by statute, as a result of official need and their own manipulation, in almost every yamen they exceeded not only their quota but also their legal tenures.[7] As we have seen, the clerks controlled the preparation, flow, and storage of documents within the yamen, while the runners served as policemen, jailers, tax-urgers, despatch-carriers, and warrant-servers. Though most of the runners were legally classified "mean people" and barred from the examinations, they received a wage (albeit barely a subsistence one). The clerks, however, were not given a salary or even their stationery supplies and were thus forced, as were the runners, to collect various fees (*lou-kuei*) in order to maintain themselves.[8]

The imaginative and lucrative chicanery of the clerks and runners has been amply illustrated in the preceding chapters and in the works of Ch'u T'ung-tsu and Hsiao Kung-chuan, so there is no need to recatalogue it here. However, it is worthwhile reiterating that officials perceived the clerks' power as great enough to block official decisions at all levels, to manipulate the official appointment and disciplinary process, and even to subvert imperial desires substantially.[9]

Why, Ting asked rhetorically in an 1868 memorial, had such power reverted to the clerks and accumulated in their hands? First, he replied, officials normally served only two to three years in office and frequently less, while clerks "raised their families in office." Since "the energy of a man was limited, while the changes in regulations were endless," the official could never master the complex regulatory material in which the clerk, always willing for a price to fit the precedent to suit the case, became a specialist. Second, despite this de facto authority, the clerks had no status. It was, quipped Ting, "like handing them a knife but forbidding them to kill a man." Third, wealth could compensate for status (*kung-ming*) denied, so the clerk's paltry wages compelled them to build their fortunes illicitly.[10]

Ting's analysis of the problem, although more colorfully phrased than that of others, is not unique. Nor was his immediate response, the provision of necessary stationery monies and the prohibition of all extralegal fees, uncommon.[11] Nonetheless, Shen Pao-chen felt that these measures had had an extraordinary effect: "Within two years after Ting became Governor, the rapacious underlings stayed their hands."[12] Tseng Kuo-fan, however, considered that Ting's approach was mistaken:

> He wants to eliminate his subordinates' rice bowls completely. I do not agree. Certainly there is no one in the empire who can do without a rice bowl. You take their one bowl away and they'll simply find another. This is of no benefit to public affairs. It will simply cause the common people to suffer (*ch'ih-k'uei*), that's all.[13]

We have seen that Tseng's assessment was more accurate than Shen's; the impact of Ting's effort to eliminate fees was short-lived. But it was, after all, only a short-term approach. Like generations of previous officials, Ting also sought more enduring solutions to the problem.

Officials first had to accept the complicitous role their own incompetence played in enhancing the clerks' influence and to stop scapegoating the clerks as some evil force incarnate. As epitomized by the insightful Tao-kuang official, Liang Chang-chü:

> Clerks are not all goblins and monsters. . . . They are simply people. Who, after all, seals and issues documents after clerks alter them? If I accede to their actions, who is responsible, if not me? . . . Officials are ignorant of administrative practice yet want to eliminate abuses. There is nothing to be gained from "killing clerks." If I want power in my own hands, I must take up the burden.[14]

The key then, argued administrative writers, to ending the clerks' chicanery was the improvement of the quality of officials and the status of clerks. Officials trained intensively before their appointments in the codes and regulations of the empire and in the routines of their appointive offices would not be dependent upon the expertise of clerks. (Many officials did not even know the procedure for taking up a new post and indebted themselves to the clerk in the process of "buying" the proper forms.) If officials were kept at their posts longer, they could become close to the people and prevent the clerks from interjecting themselves as intermediaries. The fewer levels between people and officials, then the less paper work and the fewer clerks, noted one writer who proposed the elimination of senior provincial officials and a sharp increase in the number of magistrates.[15] Still a better method of ensuring closeness between the people and the officials, suggested some, was to abolish the rule of avoidance (which prohibited officials from serving in or near their home districts) and thus end the outside official's dependence on native clerks.[16] Finally, many writers, all referring to Han high officials who rose from clerkships, urged that either the clerks be allowed to improve their status through examination and appointment to subgrade posts, or that their duties be redefined and men of higher status be appointed to clerkships.[17] Ting's long-term approach does not differ greatly in its broad outlines from the above ideas, but the details of his proposals push this generally accepted thinking to its logical and sometimes startling end.

Ting had been attentive to the problems of clerks since his days as a Kiangsi Magistrate, and his concern was heightened by the magistrates' need to hire additional clerks for compiling the various monthly registers he required.[18] But, significantly, Ting's first extensive discussion of clerks was in an 1867 statement on treaty revision, thereby demonstrating his view that domestic political reform was the keystone of self-strengthening. In this document, Ting specified how officials could be better trained and selected, and called for longer tenures in office and higher salaries. In regard to the clerks, he urged the refinement of selection, the strengthening of rewards and punishments, and an increase in salary. By eliminating the corrupt and superfluous, argued Ting, additional revenue would be produced, which in turn could be awarded to the remaining honest clerks in order to ensure their continued good performance.[19]

But the heart of Ting's proposal (reiterated a year later in a famous memorial attacking perfunctoriness) was that the clerks *and runners* be allowed to improve their status (*ch'u-shen*) through examination; thus "the able could rise and the bad be eliminated." Ting's inclusion of the runners was a radical and unique step, for it would have required a basic readjustment of their legal status. Ting also asked that petty officials (*tso-tsa* and *tso-erh*) be allowed to serve as clerks; and he expressed the striking, if forlorn, hope (the example of the Han ministers notwithstanding) that even scholars who did not dread starting their official careers by studying the precedents would serve as clerks. In 1867, Ting had specified that successful candidates in the examination for clerks and runners could be appointed to magistracies, but had appeared reserved about their appointment to senior posts.[20] In 1869, however, he flatly stated that recommended candidates should not be distinguished from those who had taken the regular examinations.[21]

This final element in Ting's proposals is distinctive. Yuan

Shou-ting, a skillful Magistrate and respected administrative writer, despaired of ever controlling the clerks;[22] and Feng Kuei-fen, who felt that all present clerks had to be eliminated, still would have restricted his new-style clerks from ever serving in the Grand Secretariat or the Hanlin Academy.[23] That clerks could serve ably, at least as low-level officials, was an idea actually long enshrined in the *Hui-tien,* which provided for a gubernatorial examination and recommendation of clerks with five years' good service.[24] Indeed, two of the most competent Magistrates serving in Kiangsu during Ting's tenure were former clerks.[25] But so rare were clerks who rose to magistracies that the people did not bother to distinguish them from other "yamen grubs" (*ya-i*), and Ting and other officials seemed unaware that such procedures were established precedents.[26] Still, Ting alone was willing to extend to clerks and runners the concept of self-renewal (*tzu-hsin*), and to express confidence in their ability not only to turn from private interests toward public ones, but also to serve at any level. That it was an unfulfilled and unrewarded trust does not diminish its distinctiveness.

By including the runners in the examination Ting demonstrated his reluctance to prejudge them on the sole basis of their status, although he did deal severely with the notorious bullies and incorrigible incompetents among them. To his Judicial Commissioner Ting wrote:

> *The runners are low people under the officials, but unless they have violated the law, they are still our children* (ch'ih-tzu). *How can we not distinguish black from white, but simply see the two characters* ch'ai-i *and treat them all as bullies and bandits.*[27]

The *ch'ai-i* ranked the lowest in status among the runners (a group already considered mean) and had as their chief duties making arrests and escorting prisoners between trials. For the latter, often expensive task, the runners were expected to pay all expenses.[28] Understandably, they were lackadaisical about being on time and often harsh in their treatment of their charges. To prevent the runners from extracting the cost of the journey from their prisoners,

Ting had ordered Magistrates to pay all escort fees. But many of the Magistrates had no funds for this, and both they and their runners were subject to unceasing exactions from superior yamens at which the successive retrials were held.[29] Ting ordered the superior yamens to halt this practice and also adopted from Soochow a technically illegal system by which *ch'ai-i* subcontracted their escort duty to beggars. Impressed by the reliable service provided by the beggars in return for adequate housing, clothing, and food, Ting substituted them for the runners.[30]

Ting's willingness to employ and thereby legitimize unauthorized—even unlawful—but effective practices was characteristic of him. It was, moreover, an approach that he extended to people, too. For instance, when a Magistrate complained that he had been unable to break a case, Ting instructed him to use two recently dismissed runners, for, though "there was no evil they would not do," they were able.[31] Interestingly, Tseng Kuo-fan regarded Ting in a similar light: a suave and evasive fame-seeker whose considerable ability, nonetheless, had to be utilized.[32]

LOCAL ELITE

By the mid-nineteenth century the term "gentry" (*shen*) by itself and in such phrases as "gentry director" (*shen-tung*) and "evil gentry" (*lieh-shen*) was being applied rather loosely by contemporary officials and writers. Of late, historians seeking to avoid the intellectual baggage associated with the word "gentry" and to underline their own broad definitions of the term have taken to using in its place the phrase "local elite." But in so doing we must not forget the banal but essential parameter of perspective. The bully or trickster who appeared to peasants in the far corner of a backward country to be a man of influence might seem nothing more than a troublesome country bumpkin to the local elite in the environs of the provincial capital. The shape of power in the subprovincial political landscape was complex, similar in appearance to a pointilliste painting. We must not, like a casual museum-goer, take only the general impression and ignore the detail. Rather, although it is beyond the purpose of this section to dissect completely the structure of the local elite, we must retain an awareness of the individual matrixes of varying intensity and tone.

Hence, the local elite should be seen as encompassing not only degree-holders (both by examination and purchase) without office and active and retired officials, but also powerful merchants, rich commoner landlords, and local bullies. Possessing one or some combination of the attributes that generally characterize elites—wealth, prestige (exacting respect from officials and the people in the area), power (in the sense of the ability to coerce either by mobilizing the forces of law or one's own followers)—the local elite was as essential to local administration as were the yamen underlings.[33] Viewing itself as the proper agent to fill the vacuum between the magistrate and the people (there being only one magistrate for every 250,000 people), it sought to maintain order and to represent the people to the magistrate as well as the magistrate to the people. We have seen that, to the detriment of the common people, the local elite and yamen underlings often cooperated; but they were also competitors for political power; and, though the local elite was far less subject than commoners to the underlings' depredations, it was not wholly free from harassment.[34] So long as this struggle did not become disruptive, it was advantageous to the magistrate, for an increase in the influence of either group would come at his expense.

Since the local elite was not a homogeneous group, however, there was not a community of interest among its constituent elements. Nor, consequently, was there a uniformity in their modes of operation or in the official response to them. Most noticeable, perhaps, were the clashes of interest within the group of degree-holders between those who had served as officials and those who had not and between urban- and rural-based local elites.

Scattered across Kiangsu's countryside was a profusion of quasi-formal sub-district officers, serving as sorts of general factotums, but whose status and function are not now, and were not even to contemporary officials, always clear.[35] In addition to the general rubric "gentry director" (*shen-tung*), which was normally applied without concern for territorial jurisdiction to managers of charitable institutions, land surveys, and irrigation projects, we find rural township directors (*hsiang-tung*), precinct directors (*t'u-tung*) (identified in some sources with the constable [*ti-pao*] that headed the *pao-chia*), village directors (*ts'un-tung, chuang-shou*), polder directors and heads (*yü-tung, yü-chia*), and stockade directors and chiefs (*sai-tung, sai-chu*). While, owing to the diversity and particularity of conditions, it is impossible to generalize with certainty about their duties, on the whole their bailiwick seems largely to have been fiscal affairs (including relief administration) and, where tolerated, preservation of order; or, as Ting said of one village director, "to handle the management of all officially ordered things."[36]

Table 2 illustrates how the various levels mentioned in the sources might be organized, but it must be emphasized that, by the 1860s, the rural townships (*hsiang*) (except where they were small) and the ward (*tu*) divisions were simply geographical expressions without official function.[37] It was the *t'u* (the old *li* transformed into a territorial unit roughly equivalent to the *pao* and comprising some 120,000 families) that was preeminently the realm of the rural gentry director.

While local officials appointed gentry directors of "officially ordered" charitable schools and granaries, irrigation projects, and land surveys, these men had probably already achieved that status in some other capacity over which the officials had no direct control. Many precinct and village directors were the consensus choices of communities whose respect they had earned. Others, especially where local defense was important, drew upon their resources of wealth, personal physical strength, or loyal followers to assert themselves.[38] The officials' role was one of acquiescence, one in which they both acknowledged and employed as local leaders those presented to them as such.

It is clear that in less developed rural areas a degree was not a prerequisite for gentry directors, though it was a perquisite of office that could be obtained with the proceeds (legitimate or otherwise) from incumbency.[39] Given the enormous surplus of

TABLE 2 Types of Sub-District Government in Kiangsu

---

hsien => *hsiang*[a] =>

- *tu*[b] => *t'u*[c] =>
  - *chen*[d]
  - *ts'un*[e]
  - *sai*[f]
  - *yü*[g]
- *tu* => *yü*
- *t'u* =>
  - *chen*
  - *yü*
  - *ts'un*
  - *chuang*[h]

Sources: Hsiao, *Rural China*, pp. 10–12, 521–548.
Wu-hsien chih (1936), 21 (*shang*) 1, 45:2b-3.
Su-chou fu-chih (1883), 29:1.
Kun-hsin. . . ho-chih, 8:11–15.
Han Wen-ch'i, *Kung-shou t'ang tsou-i,* 6:67.
Wang Jen-k'an, *Wang Su-chou i'shu,* p. 463.
Juan Pen-yen, *Ch'iu mu ch'u-yen,* p. 76.

Notes: => indicates administrative control
[a]*hsiang* (rural district)
[b]*tu* (ward)
[c]*t'u* (precinct)
[d]*chen* (market town)
[e]*ts'un* (village)
[f]*sai* (stockaded village, usually in Kiangpei)
[g]*yü* (polder, i.e., area within an embankment)
[h]*chuang* (village, usually part of linked village system in Kiangpei)

unemployed degree-holders, however, it is equally certain that they indeed filled many directorships. Unfortunately, Ch'ing sources are contradictory on both how many and at what levels. On the one hand, we might suspect that a magistrate's report to Ting that all the precinct directors were *chu-jen* and *kung-sheng* was exaggerated in order to justify their apparent considerable accretion of power, and might also consider the doubts of later Kiangsu provincial officials that precinct directors held degrees.[40] On the other hand, we know that, as early as the mid-eighteenth century, village heads in Chekiang (a province comparable in social composition to Kiangsu) were *sheng-chien,* and that, in the late nineteenth century, Chekiang *kung-sheng* administered charitable institutions in market towns.[41] Furthermore, in the 1870s in Funing, a commercially important Kiangpei hsien not renowned for a large population of degree-holders, precinct directors included a military *chu-jen, pin-sheng,* a *sheng-yuan,* a *fu kung-sheng,* and a *chien sheng.*[42]

Whatever the numbers of degree-holders in the rural precincts, at this level of society a degree was not as important as other attributes, namely the power to organize the local population. Significantly, one did not have to put this ability at the service of the state in order to acquire prestige, especially when one was leading tax resistance. In one Kiangpei hsien, tax directors at the precinct level, encouraged by the spinelessness of local officials, connived with village heads to falsify disaster reports and prevent taxation for decades. Even when the elite-led *t'uan-lien* was mobilized against them, timorous magistrates avoided confrontation. The consequent loss of respect meant loss of control. As one writer observed, such an official might claim that the *t'uan-lien* were his, but in fact they had become synonymous with "gathering to resist."[43]

Effective as they were against reluctant magistrates (or dissident neighbors), the forces at the *t'u* level were vulnerable to attack by a determined local official and certainly to provincial forces. Local elites, however, possessed other weapons that enabled them to achieve their ends without provoking such escalation. The most important of these was the capital appeal. Since any but the most trivial charge was accepted for adjudication, it was not necessary for the local elite to have high degrees or be well connected at the provincial capital or Peking in order to intimidate a susceptible magistrate. If the aim was to see the appeal through to a favorable conclusion, influential friends were certainly a necessity, but this was often not the intent. Rather, it was to use the threat of appeal with its potential for temporary removal of magistrates and discovery of magisterial misdeeds to bend the official to the elite's will.[44] Hence, while a degree added a patina of cultivation and prestige, the respect (albeit at times begrudging) of the magistrate, power, and influence could be attained without one.

A degree, moreover, was not an unalloyed advantage, for in theory it gave the officials another handle by which to control the local elite. On paper, a magistrate could readily have the educational commissioner discipline the directors if they were *sheng-yuan* or *chien-sheng,* but the supervisory responsibility was delegated to the prestigeless local teaching officials, and such sanctions seem to have been neither common nor effective.[45] Regardless of their status, gentry managers were an irritant to Ting, who considered it "most difficult to obtain good men from among them."[46] Furthermore, he despaired that the power of bad directors could be destroyed. To the Hsu-hai Taotai he wrote:

> *The evil of gentry managers (*shen-tung*) with no self-respect is far worse than that of the clerks.* The clerks at least are somewhat fearful of the control that officials can impose, but the gentry have ties within the yamen and outside of it connections with local bullies (*t'u-hao*) and can do what they want. Even if there were an earnest capable magistrate who wanted to control them with the law, they probably still would not budge when ordered.[47]

His advice to the planners of a waterworks project to take care that "the people will not suffer from the directors before they do from the floods" was clearly nothing more than a forlorn hope.[48]

At the opposite end of the political spectrum from the rural gentry directors were the holders of higher examination degrees and former officials, who by virtue of their elevated status were the most influential members of the local elite, and who regarded the more predatory activities of the directors as inimical to their own interests. The scholar-official local elite's *modus operandi* paralleled that of the clerks. As natives of a district or province, the scholar-official elite could offer an official expert advice but (unlike the clerks) could unabashedly claim to be speaking in the people's interest. From compiling gazetteers they often knew as much about taxes as did the clerks, and they were equally familiar with administrative precedents on subjects ranging from dike and *pao-chia* management to the erection of honorific arches. Scholar-official elite, moreover, were in a position to bestow administrative advice, no doubt accompanied where appropriate by references to their superior rank.[49] The value of drawing broadly from the ideas of local elite to supplement his own judgment before acting on important matters was acknowledged by one Magistrate. But this same man emphasized that, while popular opinion could be allied with, it should never become the controlling factor. Disorder, he concluded, was inevitable if the official was the manipulated rather than the manipulator in any relationship with the elite.[50]

At both the local and provincial levels, scholar-official local elite could also effectively oppose officials' policies by appealing to influential friends in higher offices. (This produced the same result as a capital appeal, but circumvented the distasteful involvement with the law that a formal capital appeal entailed.)[51] From the official viewpoint, this was the most pernicious type of elite activity. Indeed, one Governor made a particular effort to maintain his distance from scholar-official elite, for he feared that, if he saw them, his local officials would conclude that his policy decisions were directed by his visitors.[52] As one official writer phrased it, "The gentry cannot be allowed to look upon the officials with disdain. Once they are given their rein, their oppression will daily increase."[53] The problem, of course, was that official local elite were themselves officials. Yet, once they left office, even temporarily, many of them seemed to protect their own or local interests more than those of the state they but recently had served.

For officials, the most immediately threatening role played by all sorts of local elite was that of agents in the preservation of local order. The state acknowledged that the elite were respected by common people, and it accepted their intermediary functions of forwarding the people's grievances to the officials and transmitting official orders and imperial teachings to the people. But the state considered it imperative to prevent the elite's involvement in taxation, litigation, or policing; and it allowed, as Philip Kuhn has shown, elite organization of militia only in the direst emergencies.[54] The state's suspicions, moreover, were directed not simply against the bad gentry (*lieh-shen*) who led tax resistance struggles, smuggled salt, and even hid criminals, but against all gentry.[55] For, as the state discovered during the Taiping Rebellion, authorizations for gentry to raise funds and militia, and the issuance of seals, even to the most upright gentry, led inevitably to infringements on and usurpations of official authority.[56]

The local elite's most readily accessible point of pressure on officials and the weakest link in the chain of official responsibility was the petty official (*tso-tsa*)—in particular, the sub-district assistant magistrate (*hsun-chien*) who was stationed in market towns. Isolated and vulnerable to the local elite's political and economic pressure, the *hsun-chien* (together with all petty officials) nonetheless were given the important responsibility of selecting the local constables (*ti-pao, yü-chia*) who headed the *pao-chia.* The constables' supposed duty was to control itinerant vagrants (*liu-min*), but, at the behest of landlords, they often also collected back rents and illicitly detained recalcitrant tenants.[57] Moreover, despite strict regulations against the practice, they sometimes even heard litigation.[58] Significantly, it was at the level of the *ti-pao* that Feng Kuei-fen wanted to create a new group of popularly selected officials to handle minor disputes and suits.[59]

In the Ch'ing, however, only magistrates were authorized to accept petitions, and one of Ting's first steps as Financial Commissioner was to issue a stern circular order reiterating the prohibition against the involvement of *tso-tsa* in litigation. But the problem was deep-rooted and resisted Ting's repeated attempts to eliminate it.[60] Although Ting frequently warned against gentry interference in litigation, in this instance he did not explicitly connect them to the *tso-tsa;* rather, he blamed the resistance on the petty officials' desire to defray the cost of purchasing their offices. Yet, there are implicit indications that Ting perceived a tie between the gentry and the *tso-tsa*'s unauthorized courts. He urged strict officials not to be deterred by hostile placards or defamation, which were almost always concocted by gentry; and he removed the authority to appoint the *ti-pao* (who forwarded litigation to the petty official) from the *tso-tsa* to the magistrate himself. Comparing the situation to the one that prevailed in the imperial stables, where the horses became proportionally thinner for each new administrative level, Ting wrote that he had taken this step because layers of supervisory control too readily became layers of exploitation.[61] But, deliberate or not, this action served to undermine the power of the local elite, who recommended to the *tso-tsa* candidates for *ti-pao* and then used the *ti-pao* to further their own interests. Indeed, the court considered the *tso-tsa* so susceptible to this type of local influence that, like the clerk, they were specifically forbidden to retain their posts beyond their stipulated tenure. And, significantly, this is one measure that Ting enforced.[62]

As both Financial Commissioner and Governor, Ting vigorously opposed the involvement of gentry directors, not only in litigation but also in the leadership of *pao-chia* or other policing organizations. He did, however, specifically order the participation of Soochow gentry and official households in the onerous task of providing someone to serve a rotating turn as ward watchmen.[63] Unlike some other mid and late Ch'ing officials, Ting was clearly determined to deny local elite both leadership and supervisory responsibility in the maintenance of local order.[64] He squelched any suggestions that the *pao-chia* be supplemented with Chou-style village officials appointed by the magistrate with the argument that, during the Rebellion, serious abuses had arisen whenever elites had been awarded official seals to assist their militia activities. And he sharply opposed the proposal to allow gentry directors to police the enforcement of the ban against armed boats and to make secret accusations.[65]

The issue here was the same one recently contested with the Taiping—the control of the countryside. Indeed, one can argue that what we see are two divergent currents of reform: the "unofficial" and the "official." The scholar-official local elite in the 1860s, and again in the 1890s, envisaged reform as the devolution of formal power from the hands of the magistrate and his surrogates, the yamen underlings, into their own hands. It was decentralized, local reform that was to be manned by influential village leaders and by the thousands of unemployed holders of examination degrees. It was reform that would, moreover, eviscerate the influence of the purely power-oriented bad gentry and local bully gentry director types at the rural precinct level.[66] The official reform movement, what we know as the T'ung-chih Restoration, was characterized by centralization, regulation, and an effort to establish direct communication between the people and the magistrate, thereby eliminating all middlemen, were they yamen underlings or local elite. For the state to achieve these goals, exceptional local officials were required.

OFFICIALS

As Mary Wright has stated, during the Restoration there was a great assemblage of talent in "high places."[67] But what of the local officials? Their malfeasance, charged Ting, had created rebels by forcing the common people into banditry, yet their wisdom and virtue (*hsien-liang*), said the court, were essential for the reconstruction of the devastated areas.[68] It was as critical for the empire to have men, said Ting, as "a fish to have water, a tree to have roots, a fire to have oil." The provision of good government in a single hsien by an able magistrate was the foundation of good government for the empire. But, continued Ting, "if without judging a man's ability we suddenly commit to him the power of magistrate, it is like assigning a porter capable of carrying only ten catties the responsibility of carrying one hundred. How can we expect him not to fall?"[69]

To some extent, Ting's criteria for a good magistrate are not that different from the requirements for a good cadre in the P.R.C. Ting believed that a magistrate was appointed not to serve his superiors or himself but to serve the people. He advised magistrates that they need adhere only to one fixed rule: "Based on what is good for the people, do what is the good."[70] By following this precept, a magistrate could establish between himself and the people a mutual trust, without which his efforts to have the people do things would be like "trying to put a square handle into a round hole."[71] The magistrate could not hold himself apart from the people, but had to put himself in their place so that official and people "could breathe together as if one" and eliminate divisions into which clerks could insert themselves.[72] As Ting counseled one Magistrate:

> *If a magistrate can treat himself as a local constable (*ti-pao*) and not as an important official, then the superior and subordinate (*shang-hsia*) will be mutually close and the people of the hsien will have some hope.*[73]

And, though the magistrate as the "father and mother official" (*fu-mu kuan*) caring for his "children" (*ch'ih-tzu*) was inevitably somewhat removed from the people, he was also like a visiting merchant who had to satisfy his customers:

> *If he opens a shop and his goods are new and fresh and his prices low, his trade will be great.* But if his goods are of low quality and the prices high, the market people look and run away. How can the merchant expect business to expand?[74]

To continue Ting's metaphor, the magistrate had to know his market well and work it intensively. Ting expected magistrates to endure hard work (*nai fan-lao*) and fulfill the lessons in magistrates' handbooks. Immediately upon taking office they were to inspect all the tax registers and prepare records and receipts for the next collection. In addition, they were to clear up backlogged official papers and judicial cases. Regardless of the size of their districts, they were to travel to all corners of their jurisdictions to check on the condition of the people, not by relying only on the old and influential, but also by seeking out comments on administration from farmers or anyone of intelligence or virtue.[75] Doorkeepers, clerks, and runners should be tightly controlled; gentry behavior should be assessed; and alleged abuses should be investigated.[76] In sum, as Ting repeatedly said, an official should treat the people's affairs as attentively as his own.[77]

As we have indicated, Ting felt that, before the Rebellion, such officials were all too few. (Feng Kuei-fen considered unlikely even their existence.)[78] The problem was not necessarily evil intentions but merely a lack of trade skills. Any skill, said Ting in his 1868 memorial, had to be studied and practiced. "To repair a house, one asks a carpenter; to cure an illness, one invites a doctor. Any country bumpkin knows this." But, he lamented, what had been recognized as dangerous for the military had not been considered so for civil officials: "What they studied was of no practical use, and what was of practical use was never studied." It was like "forcing a carpenter to cure an illness or a doctor to repair a house." Although the sickness might worsen or the house fall, such mishaps were of minor consequence compared with the fate of the state:

> The house and the illness are the concerns only of an individual or single family, yet they would not be so reckless. But, though being a magistrate is an important business, we allow them recklessly to pick up a knife and try to cut.[79]

If administratively skillful men were to be obtained, however, changes had to be made in the examination system; and, in his 1867 statement on treaty revision, Ting suggested what they should be. As one who had suffered from the eight-legged essay (*pa-ku wen*), Ting urged its elimination, but suggested the retention of some traditional sections: loyalty and respect to evaluate the candidates' conduct; the Classics and hundred schools to evaluate their learning; and poetry writing to demonstrate their talent. A section on current events, in earlier dynasties the crux of the examination, should be reincluded to elicit their views (*shih*). But there also should be entirely new sections on: punishments and finance to evaluate administrative strengths; geography and military tactics to test ability with troops; calculation and geology to assess thoroughness (*t'ung*); machinery and construction to measure ability (*neng*); and finally, foreign languages, affairs, and policy to ascertain whether or not the candidate could avoid causing incidents. Moreover, both in 1867 and 1868, Ting proposed the establishment of a special bureau to invite recommendations of men with unusual talents and of officials with outstanding substantive performances. Ting, of course, was not alone in expressing such views; but his proposals underline his feeling that the times required officials of unusual administrative competence and keen sensitivity to new ideas.[80]

Whatever his estimation of his personnel needs, a governor could not unrestrainedly remold the provincial bureaucracy to suit his own tastes, for the appointment process was a delicate balance of the interests of the metropolitan bureaucracy (representing the throne) and the governors. Magistracies within each province were graded according to difficulty (simple, medium, important, and most important) and assigned from a set group of characters (*nan*—insecure, *fan*—busy, *ch'ung*—trade center, *p'i*—unremunerative) a one-, two-, three- or four-character designation that accurately reflected their attributes.[81]

The simple and medium posts were filled by the Board of Civil Office from its lists of newly minted inexperienced officials. There was, however, no guarantee that the appointee would immediately take up the seals of office, since the governor could retain Board appointees in the provincial capital for evaluation through a series of temporary assignments (while filling the post with an acting magistrate of his own choosing). The governor could furthermore, within six months of a new incumbent's assumption of his assigned office, remove him for cause.[82]

Those Board appointees who, in the course of five years' service in the province, had demonstrated their capacity to govern, together with experienced officials transferred from elsewhere by the Board, constituted the candidates for the more difficult "important" and "most important" positions known as transfer and preferment posts.[83] In recognition of his need for tough, experienced men in critical positions, the governor was essentially accorded control of these posts, with the Board's approval of his selections after the fact. Generally, ratification was *pro forma,* for governors were careful about whom they nominated in order to avoid the embarrassment of rejection; but, when the Board felt its authority being trifled with, it was not averse to exercising its own obstructionist devices. Since most magistrates served their entire careers in a single province, we might think of the process in terms of the Board's stocking the pool of talent and the governors' culling it.[84]

Given the large number of three-and four-character posts in Kiangsu and its ravaging by the Rebellion, one would expect that metropolitan and provincial officials would have cooperated to ensure that a particularly distinguished group of officials would serve in Kiangsu during the 1860s. But such was not the case, despite the Restoration's emphasis on the quality of local officials. (Few T'ung-chih officials' biographies appear in *fu* and hsien gazetteers.) Disconsonant views on what made a good official may account for this dearth. Not everyone shared Tseng Kuo-fan's premise that, since the highest priority of the period was the reassertion of Confucian obligations, *chin-shih* made the best local officials.[85] Indeed, in terms of degree status, Kiangsu's Restoration magistrates' only marked difference from other samples is that there is a lower percentage of *chin-shih* and a higher percentage of *chien-sheng* among them, thereby reflecting the sharp increase in purchase of rank during the Hsien-feng reign and the preference of holders of purchased rank for service in Kiangsu[86] (see Appendix B). Yet, interestingly, while the degree status of officials who held more than one post largely correlates with the percentages among officials as a whole, there is a slightly higher number of *chin-shih* in the Kiangsu sample (see Appendix D). Most striking, however, about the status/career relationship among Kiangsu magistrates is that during this period two clerks held magistracies in the province, serving repeatedly and capably.[87]

In light of the court's interest in appointing "wise and virtuous" (*hsien-liang*) magistrates to devastated districts, it is also worthwhile to examine the record of magistrates appointed to Kiangsu hsien which received three-year tax exemptions after the Rebellion (Appendix F).[88] The most ravaged were several normally easily governed districts in Kiangning (Nanking) prefecture. Extraordinary measures, such as temporarily upgrading the difficulty rating of the post or allowing the governor to make acting appointments of particularly capable officials, were abjured.[89]

Instead, the court proceeded as if conditions were usual and, following the regular appointment process, selected (with but one exception) officials with no prior experience in the province. The challenge these novices confronted was formidable; some apprehensive officials simply refused to take up office in recovered areas, thereby discouraging resettlement.[90] Furthermore, of the fourteen who received appointments in Kiangning prefecture, only four distinguished themselves sufficiently to be reappointed to other posts within the province. This same pattern also holds true for other badly damaged hsien.

Equally of interest is the type of man appointed to serve as magistrate in the three head hsien—Wu, Ch'ang-chou, and Yuan-ho—which formed the city of Soochow. G. William Skinner has suggested that we ought to find serving in high-revenue areas such as Soochow the ablest and most trustworthy men in the imperial bureaucracy. In the post-bellum period, however, only one of these head Magistrates, a former clerk, had had prior experience within the province; and, in ironic contrast with Soochow's reputation as a literati center, only one was a *chin-shih.*[91] Moreover, these officials, the supposed exemplars for the rest of the province, were a constant disappointment to Ting.

Not peculiar to Kiangsu, this apparent abasement of the head magistracy was created, complained a Censor, by governors who were conned by the smooth ways of those who had purchased degrees and offices. They, rather than the socially inept scholars, were obtaining the governor's recommendation to these preferment posts. Although the Board of Civil Office rejected the Censor's proposal that head magistracies be reserved for holders of high examination degrees, it acknowledged that bad character was a more common attribute among those who had earned their candidacy for office through military merit or purchase, and it instructed provincial officials to give priority to those who had risen through the examinations (*cheng-t'u*). If, and only if, these men seemed genuinely unsuitable (viz., too inexperienced) for a head magistracy, could the governor recommend someone of other status. But the Board demanded a detailed defense of any substitution and ominously reminded governors that they would be held fully responsible for any adverse consequences arising from a poor selection.[92]

This exchange on the head magistracies was a small symbolic piece in large mosaic-like struggle over the appointment process. In Kiangsu, in the 1820s and 1830s, and then in the 1850s and 1860s in the Rebellion-scarred provinces of Hupei, Hunan, and Kiangsu, gubernatorial discretionary control over appointments was tolerated in order to enhance provincial officials' ability to respond quickly and effectively to crises.[93] Ordinary standards were an impediment. "A good choice [of an official]," observed Governor Hu Lin-i of Hupei, "is only possible when there is a departure from the rules."[94] Yet, while Hu's colleague Tseng Kuo-fan admired his practice of employing alternate officials as acting magistrates instead of those chosen in Peking, by the early 1860s the metropolitan bureaucracy was tiring of this usurpation of its prerogatives.

Specifically, the Board of Civil Office had three concerns: one, that governors were improperly blocking Board-appointed magistrates from assuming their duties; two, that governors were manipulating procedures to appoint unqualified people to important posts; and three, that, as a consequence of the first two, people with examination degrees were being denied their proper opportunity to hold office.[95] The Board did not deny that provincial officials had the right to retain in the provincial capital all appointees for office and weigh their qualifications by employing them first as alternates. Indeed, it reaffirmed this gubernatorial function. The Board firmly asserted however, that alternate officials' probationary appointments were not in force until it approved them, and that, once the approval was received, the official had to be sent out immediately.

The Board also made clear through a series of circular orders that it would not tolerate dilution of the pool of officials eligible for three- and four-character posts. Especially distressing was the sudden influx of men from the ranks of petty officials (*tso-tsa*). A routine had apparently developed in which men purchased a petty official rank, joined the military, gained rapid promotions on the basis of military merit, obtained exemptions (legally until 1870) from service as alternate officials, and received appointments to important magistracies. Decrying this syndrome, the Board emphasized to governors that inexperienced alternate officials with military merit and military merit types with poor records in their initial posts were wholly unsuitable for preferment posts and laid down the order of eligibility: first, those presently serving in substantive posts; next, alternates with significant previous administrative experience; then, *chin-shih.* The constant reiteration of basic rules underscores not only the growing plasticity of the appointments process but also the determination of the Board to reintroduce into it structure and regularity.

The sale of rank and office to raise revenue was an old custom in China, but the Ch'ing had refined and expanded the system so that, by the early nineteenth century, purchasers held many substantive posts.[96] Despite the presence of outstanding officials (such as Ting himself) among the holders of purchased ranks, the rapacious ones were sufficiently numerous for the group as a whole to be blamed for bureaucratic corruption and subversion of the judicial process. An end to, or at least control of, the sale of rank was a clarion call of the Restoration.[97] Opposition to the practice was not based simply on the grounds that it led to corruption, cheapened officials in the eyes of the people, and even degraded China in the eyes of the foreigners; it was founded also on the claim that the provision of posts for all buyers occasioned a rapid turnover of officials and severely impeded the appointment prospects of long-waiting *chu-jen* and *kung-shen,* who, out of frustration, took lesser posts beneath their qualifications.[98]

By the time Ting memorialized in 1868 on the sale of rank, the debate had been joined for several years. It focused not on the majority who bought merely brevet ranks, but on the one-third whose purchased titles and degrees gave them access to office. In the early 1860s, the court had initiated and then abandoned an attempt to end the sale of substantive office. But, in 1866, it took a tentative step toward its original goal by disallowing requests for substantive offices from gentry and official contributors to *t'uan-lien* and by restricting their rewards to brevet ranks, merits, posthumous honors for parents, and increases in subranks.[99] In his memorial, Ting raised the critical but little discussed issue of what the actual income from sale of office was. In his view, the real amount of income was negligible when the revenues gained from the reduced prices for offices were measured against those lost through poor government.[100] "It was," said Ting, "like a rich family short of cash letting its lands at low rents to tenants and then permitting them to destroy the houses and ruin the land [rather than lose the tenants]. Can the state afford such practices?" Until the court could make this calculation and plan to substitute likin or customs revenues, Ting asked that the court temporarily stop further payments from those who had not yet been awarded ranks.[101]

Meanwhile, Ting was, nonetheless, still left with more than a thousand holders of purchased ranks awaiting appointment to the magistracies, and with sixty to seventy others hopeful for appointment to only two available taotai posts.[102] There were so many of these men in Soochow, commented Ting, that "they were standing back to back looking at each other."[103] While they waited without salaries, their savings evaporated. Some borrowed from and indebted themselves to rich local elite, yamen underlings, merchants, or *mu-yu*.[104] Others used their credentials of rank to encroach on regular revenues, bully the people, make false accusations to foment litigation, and even hear suits. After a wait of sometimes up to ten years, one Censor observed, they might have merely one year in office before being transferred or removed to make way for their fellow purchasers of rank. In that single year, commented Ting, the official would try to recoup what he had spent in the previous ten and accrue enough to cushion himself for the next decade. "If you place a dog or a goat in front of a hungry tiger," concluded Ting, "but want him not to bite, even if you try to stop him with a strong bow and poisoned arrows, you certainly cannot do it."[105]

Indeed, Ting was far more successful at preventing the bad purchasers of rank from receiving substantive appointment than he was at controlling them once they were in office. Finding himself, as Financial Commissioner, inundated with the credentials of these men and unable to distinguish the good from the bad, Ting decided to examine them. Fortunately for us, the *North China Herald* obtained copies of Ting's examinations and translated them. His questions were not traditional ones, but dealt with the duties of office; and, with a sense of irony, Ting required the candidates to resolve some of the problems that they were charged with creating:

1. By what plan would you propose to prevent the irregularities that exist among the under-officials of the yamen?
2. What would you propose to do with the veterans to insure their settling down as peaceful subjects now that their services are no longer required?
3. At the present time, the candidates for official appointments are very numerous, while there are but few appointments to give them. By what plan would you propose to overcome this difficulty?
4. The petty officials take it upon themselves to judge cases that ought to be referred to the district magistrates. How would you propose to remedy this evil?

The examination was given to three separate groups of candidates. In the first group, none passed. In the second, which answered the first two questions, and in the third, which answered the last two questions, some but still negligible numbers of candidates passed.[106] One wonders if the subsequent groups had the sense to answer the third question by suggesting that office be awarded to the authors of the best examinations.

Purchasers of rank were not the only ones scrutinized. Governors regularly tested all alternate officials (*hou-pu*), those awaiting an appointment, with temporary assignments and could delay a Board-appointed magistrate's assumption of duties if they considered him unequal to the task. Moreover, many appointments were for just one probationary year (*shih-yung*).[107] In the view of one Censor, alternate officials provided a pool of upright men who could at once gain experience and constrict the influence of yamen underlings through assignments to escort prisoners and to expedite paper work.[108] But alternate officials—both degree-holders and purchasers of rank—had no income unless selected for a commission and were consequently subject to extreme economic pressures. Ting assessed alternate officials as a group equally divided between good and bad with a tendency for the latter portion to enlarge once out of the capital on commission. This element claimed the rank of the official to whom they were assigned, bullied the people, and struggled with their retinues over even a "fly head" of a fee. Disdainful of their superior, the commissioned officials (*wei-yuan*) milked him while out in his district and slandered him upon their return to the capital. Consequently, Ting urged that *wei-yuan* should be used only if it were absolutely unavoidable and advised local officials to impeach strictly any *wei-yuan* guilty of extortion.[109]

Ting instructed the alternate officials to devote themselves to training in public affairs instead of to personal enrichment so that they would be useful when they became probationary officials (*shih-yung*). Ho Shih-chun, a skilled statecraft official, was more specific in advising the *hou-pu* to read provincial gazettes, the *Lü-li,* and the *Hui-tien shih-li;* to discuss affairs with senior officials and experienced *mu-yu;* and to be generally upright and cautious in their personal and public conduct.[110] But again, as Thomas Metzger has shown, most officials assumed that their own and their colleagues' probity and conscientiousness were infirm without external constraint.[111]

Characteristically, Ting's solution was to institutionalize and refine the existing but relatively relaxed established system of mass "interviews" at which all the *hou-pu* milled about hoping to be noticed by the governor.[112] Designed to distinguish the able from the incompetent, Ting's new regulations required the *hou-pu* to prepare diligently:

1. Excluding those presently in office or out on commissions who would form one group, one group of ten *hou-pu* are to be inteviewed each [unspecified] period of time. Those

wei-yuan working in bureaus or assisting in trials are to present background reports on their work before their interview.

2. Each official will present a brief statement of local conditions, taxes, litigation, and foreign affairs at the time of the interview. You are to be straightforward about anything of advantage to the nation.
3. Each report shall list no more than four items, and each item should contain just the essentials and absolutely no glossy verbiage. I shall discuss the essence of each report, *trying to get to the core of it with my questions, while giving the candidate the opportunity to amplify his ideas.*
4. I shall retain for personal reading anything critical or secret and shall discuss it with the official at a personal interview the following day to prevent leaks.
5. If the candidate's talents are exceptional and his writing excellent, I shall set a time for another personal interview. If there is something inappropriate in the proposals, I shall instruct you.[113]

For some, this examination was an insurmountable hurdle. One alternate Assistant Magistrate proved to be fundamentally illiterate. Concluding that he would be of little assistance to the hard-pressed Magistrate of Shanghai and that he would become an object of derision to foreigners, Ting delayed his assignment and detained him in Soochow. Retention in the provincial capital was not, however, always a stigma. In the case of a *chien-sheng* with a purchased magistracy and good administrative experience in Kweichow, Ting sent him to the Judicial Commissioner's auxiliary court for orientation and training in order to eradicate an unfamiliarity with Kiangsu that Ting feared would hinder him in coping with the powerful gentry directors who had held sway over Wu-hsi's previous Magistrates.[114]

On the other side of the coin were those *hou-pu* rewarded after successful commissions with merits and recommendations to posts for which their paper qualifications were technically inadequate. In Tao-kuang, the court had regularly approved such extraordinary appointments, and, in T'ung-chih, Ting and his colleagues accelerated the practice when the court agreed to compromise regulations for filling vacancies.[115] Nevertheless, the court was determined to hold the line against complete abandonment of regular procedures and periodically rebuffed provincial officials' recommendations.[116] Indeed, in 1871, a Censor complained that governors' lackadaisical recommendations for appointments, which rarely considered either an official's qualifications or the difficulty of the post, were making an empty letter of established regulations.[117]

Regardless of a man's credentials, once appointed, he had to be supervised and controlled by exhortation, rewards, and punishments. A central theme in many T'ung-chih memorials was the necessity of clarifying rewards and punishments, for the writers felt that the exigencies of the Rebellion had caused such a dilution in standards that "rewards no longer encouraged and punishments no longer frightened" their recipients.[118] Significantly, Ting's comments elucidating the effectiveness of the carrot-and-stick approach for officials are almost identical to those discussing clerks.[119] They moreover suggest that Legalism and Confucianism had become so intertwined by this time that it was pointless to try to separate the two.

In Ting's view, the most effective reward was an increase in official remuneration. A magistrate's formal income had not increased between the early eighteenth and mid-nineteenth centuries. Out of a salary of 45 to 80 taels and a supplementary salary (*yang-lien*) of 1,000 to 1,800 taels, a Kiangsu magistrate had to do the following: pay a good *mu-yu* upwards of 1,000 taels, provide office supplies, make exemplary contributions for flood relief and charitable institutions, buy presents for senior officials, pay his assigned contribution (*t'an-chüan*) to make up deficits in provincial accounts, pay fees to runners and clerks in superior yamens; and, of course, support his family and its servants.[120] Clearly, in order to meet these expenses a magistrate had to generate substantial outside income, and for T'ung-chih Kiangsu officials the strain was still greater because, in many areas of the province, they had not received their *yang-lien* payments. As an expedient measure, Ting fruitlessly proposed that officials be allowed to convert their back pay, totaling a staggering 260,000 taels, into contributions for substantive posts.[121] He made the equally unsuccessful—yet in hard times striking—suggestion that, for the long run, metropolitan officials be awarded tenfold salary increases, and that taotais, prefects, and magistrates be given substantial increases in administrative fees.[122]

To his opponents, who feared that there were no revenues to meet the larger outlays, Ting explained that they did not see the two benefits that would produce the needed income:

> The obvious benefit is that higher pay will lead to improved administration, which in turn will mean fewer shortages and less defalcation of regular revenues. The hidden advantage is that, with good government and no oppression, the common people will not be forced into banditry; and the government's military expenses can be reduced.

The first step toward increased salaries, said Ting, was the legitimation of customary fees (*lou-kuei*).[123] Previously, Tao-kuang's efforts to achieve this had been opposed by officials on the ground that it was improper; but Ting, as had Tao-kuang before him, considered central regulation of *lou-kuei* preferable to local discretion.[124] Moreover, legitimation would eliminate "the obligation of the recipient and the strings attached by the giver," the very elements of *lou-kuei* that corroded the governmental process.[125]

That *lou-kuei* within the bureaucracy and surcharges imposed by the bureaucracy on the people were an inevitable consequence of inflationary pressures on fixed salaries had been recognized as early as Tao-kuang's reign.[126] Similarly, we can see that assigned contributions (*t'an-chüan*) were a manifestation of the state's inability to live on a fixed income in times of mounting costs. From Ting's perspective, first as a Magistrate in Kiangsi and still later as Governor of Kiangsu, the people could have no rest until superior yamens relaxed their demands on subordinate ones, and senior officials ceased their harrassment of junior ones. Throughout his career, Ting set a personal example for his subordinates. As Financial Commissioner and again as Governor, he issued and enforced a circular order forbidding subordinates to send their superiors congratulatory birthday and holiday notes, which he dismissed as tendentious flattery (*t'ao-yu*) paid for by the people.[127] He also instructed superior offices to eliminate their staffs' exactions from subordinate officials and their staffs. In judicial appeals, said Ting, the fees were so numerous that officials were more worried about the "fellow in front or behind" than concerned with expediting the case. After all, he reasoned,

> If we prohibit *chou* and hsien runners from demanding money from the common people, it is especially necessary to forbid the runners of superior yamens to demand it from the district magistrates.[128]

To ferret out and document such cases was difficult, however, since magistrates were leery of embarrassing or offending senior officials with accusations against their staffs. Even when Ting himself documented that clerks in his yamen exacted fees from magistrates, he was unable to pinpoint the responsibility. Ordering the clerks to his office for interrogation, Ting concluded:

> *If we cannot prevent our clerks from wanting the magistrates' money, how can we keep the magistrates from taking the people's money?* We talk about eliminating abuses, but they are right in front of our eyes though we are ignorant of them.[129]

Ting's *mu-yu,* Lin Ta-ch'üan, had a far more positive assessment of Ting's measures. Not only were they conceptually acute, he wrote, but also effectively executed. Unlike other officials who issued similar orders but never carried them through, Ting, said Lin, "stirred up such a fuss everywhere that the fault of superiors and subordinates fighting over small profits was avoided."[130]

On his own, however, Ting could do nothing about the struggle between the state and its officials over *t'an-chüan.* Actually, since officials' *yang-lien* were garnished to pay for *t'an-chüan* before they even received them, they had little means of protest. Indeed, deprived of this income, officials were forced to juggle funds (*no-tien*) to meet mandated and customary administrative expenses. Since officials would eventually run out of accounts to juggle, additional deficits would have to be made up by subordinate offices or, in the magistrate's case, by the people.[131] In light of this problem, Ting repeatedly sought relief for his subordinate officials. As Shanghai Taotai, he sought unsuccessfully to exempt officials of the Kiangnan Arsenal from their *t'an-chüan,* and later, as Governor, he made a similar request for Kiangpei magistrates.[132]

Ting's concern for Kiangpei was motivated by the aforementioned inability of the magistrates to pay runners' escort fees without shifting funds from regular tax accounts. "Is it right," he asked, "to expect a magistrate in debt to be a good one. . . . How, when they can barely support themselves, can we expect them to nurture and teach the people?" To alleviate the pressure on the magistrates, Ting sought an exemption for them not only from the *t'an-chüan* but also from penalties for *no-tien. T'an-chüan* remissions had just been approved, but he recognized that such requests were granted only as a rare imperial favor.[133] To ensure success, he solicited Tseng Kuo-fan's support. When Tseng hesitated, Ting felt impelled to address an interesting letter to the concerned Magistrates:

> If Tseng does not memorialize, the Board [of Revenue] will surely reject our request. Tseng's youthful experience was as a Hanlin, so he has never tasted the bitterness of a magistrate. Therefore I look to you to turn yourselves inside out and come out in support of it.[134]

Tseng never seconded Ting's proposal, and we may surmise that the anticipated failure ensued.

There was, of course, no guarantee that, had Ting been able to increase officials' salaries, an improvement in government would have followed. Indeed, quoting an old saying, "Peace is destructive" (*yen-an jen tu*), Ting complained that officials in the three head hsien had revived the custom of extravagant banquets. Tseng-tzu's (a disciple of Confucius) epithet for meat-eaters, "parasites" (*jou-shih-che pi*), epitomized the cruelty of these times, said Ting, when soldiers had to fight on empty bellies and emaciated commoners could barely obtain congee. "Think of them," Ting instructed the officials, "and you will be unable to swallow even the greatest delicacy placed before you." In any case, it was unlikely that the banqueters would see a delicacy, because, according to Ting, the messengers pocketed the tips for the cooks, who angrily used dirty, stale ingredients to prepare dishes of poor color and awful odor. Not only were they unpalatable, Ting remarked, but they were also probably unhealthy. Ting forbade excessive banqueting and ordered the officials to set a frugal example for the people by limiting their dinner parties to five large dishes and eight small ones.[135] Obviously, Ting's supervision and discipline of officials focused on weightier matters than this; yet, this affair is not so inconsequential as we might think. For, despite the emphasis in the *ch'u-fen* on rewards and punishments, the Confucian belief in the power of moral example remained as strong as ever.

To assess officials' performances, Ting always required complete information. He had a wide variety of sources: monthly registers, official correspondence, appeals, "chair petitions," personal tours, interviews, rumors, and confidential agents. Ting employed his agents when discrepancies in documents suggested abuses, when serious accusations were made in an appeal, and when he desired detailed general intelligence.[136] As agents he used alternate officials (*hou-pu wei-yuan*) commissioned either in Soochow or in other districts; but, fully aware of their slanderous tendencies, he acted on their reports only when there was sufficient corroborating evidence.[137]

Neither the agents' reports nor the officials' reports and registers were meaningful, however, when their despatch to Ting had been delayed by postal breakdowns. Thus, to those who questioned the relevance of his postal reforms to administration he replied:

> *Delays in documents are like blood not circulating freely in a person. Does not the person dry out when his pulse does not flow freely?* Can we delay even for a minute requests for flood relief, a release order for a falsely accused prisoner, or calls for troops to pacify bandits?[138]

The delays that confronted Ting were certainly serious, and proximity to Soochow was no guarantee of rapidity. Documents from

Shanghai arrived in sixteen hours instead of the required seven; from Hsu-chou in six days instead of two; from Hai-chou in nine days instead of three; and in some cases from the far north in forty to fifty days instead of three.[139] This ineffective postal system consisted of stations (*p'u*) managed by petty officials (*p'u-ssu*) and staffed by runners (*p'u-ping* or *p'ao-fu*).[140] Throughout the province it had been disrupted by the Rebellion, but most serious was the four-year interruption of communication between Soochow and Kiangpei. In handling this problem, Ting devised the mechanisms to cope with the symptoms and even reveal the cause, but he seems to have neglected effecting a complete cure.

Huang Liu-hung, in the seventeenth century, had charged that runners vindictively delayed and destroyed documents in order to protest their maltreatment. He had urged that they be fed and housed properly, and that time sheets be applied to all envelopes so that the runner responsible for any delay could be pinpointed.[141] Huang's analysis still held true in the nineteenth century; and Ting adopted from Chekiang province the time sheets, which he ordered printed on every envelope and filled out by every station at the time of arrival and despatch. But Ting, uncharacteristically, made no reference to the difficult conditions under which the runners actually served. Instead of alleviating their difficulties, he attended to the establishment of halfway stations (*yao-chan*), to be staffed in rotation by runners from the main stations, as the key to improved service. Though Ting claimed success in accelerating the delivery of documents, problem areas remained; and documents frequently arrived in his office not only late but also with a blank time sheet.[142]

Even before he attacked the postal system's defects, Ting, as Financial Commissioner, had moved to improve the handling of documents within officials' offices. He sent out a circular order establishing his own procedures as a model. First, he categorized all official papers as "most important," "secondarily important," and "routine," and then personally considered them. Next, they were stamped in red ink with a time limit and sent for copying to clerks who were dismissed for delays. He also instructed the magistrates to notify him immediately upon receipt of any important document and to observe carefully the time limit he had set for them. Routine matters were exempt from the deadlines, but Ting warned that procrastination on urgent ones would be swiftly punished.[143]

Within a week of this initial order, Ting issued new instructions revised to fit the example of the Ch'ang-chou Prefect. Repeating his complaint that his official letters repeatedly went unanswered, Ting ordered the local officials to indicate their receipt of important documents by immediately returning to him the attached red slip. At the end of the month, they were to compile a list of both routine and urgent matters, indicating the day of their receipt and categorizing their status as "managed and replied," "managed but unreported," "presently being managed but not yet reported," "replied but not yet begun to be managed," or "not yet replied." Within a month, all but one Magistrate had filed their reports; and, though many of them were excellent, Ting was disturbed by omissions and inconsistencies of format. Accepting the blame for these problems, he issued a style sheet. At the same time, however, he sharply admonished the Magistrates that he sought facts, not shallow promises of a response forthcoming, nor vague references to respectful management of orders received.[144]

Ironically, with the form available to them, the Magistrates' performance worsened the next month. Four instead of one failed to reply at all, and most of the submitted registers had shortcomings: the form was incorrect; circular orders were not listed; there was no indication of how a matter had been handled; days of receipt of important documents and references to them were omitted; and, in one instance, the Soochow Prefect reported the elimination in Yuan-ho of an abuse that Ting knew to be still rampant.[145] Yet, these deficiencies did not discourage him, as Governor, from ordering the Financial and Judicial Commissioners to implement similar procedures or from extending his order to Kiangpei.[146] However, like the tax-rate notices, these regulations were not implemented without opposition. As Ting wrote to the Nanking Financial Commissioner:

> *Resentment is certainly great when one wants to change rapidly the accumulated bad practices of several hundred years. When I changed the way official papers were handled, it generated hatred and malignancy. Truly I was the center of resentment* (yuan-fu). *But I notice neither the increase nor the decrease of vilification.*[147]

Ting returned Kiangpei's antipathy in full measure. He considered it a pit of incompetence, capable of entrapping even the most diligent magistrate; and northern officials' haphazard compliance with the directives on documents did nothing to mitigate this view.[148] The Hai-chou Magistrate requested an exemption from the registers, whereupon Ting asked him if he was "turning into an old, confused, arbitrary man."[149] The T'an-yuan Magistrate, repeatedly impeached yet leniently unpunished, let his clerks fill out the registers as they pleased, for which misdemeanor the already dismissed chief clerk was given another month in the cangue.[150] The Tang-shan Magistrate, commented Ting, "was really taking a holiday," for he had failed to compile or send a single one of the registers that Ting had ordered.[151] And in Hsu-chou prefecture and Feng hsien, where the officials were "a bunch of puppets moving and stopping when the clerks desired," every routine administrative housekeeping matter was red-tagged, while the more than two hundred pieces of back litigation were treated routinely.[152]

According to Lin Ta-ch'uan, Ting's supervision of officials was so close that, during his governorship, "Magistrates imagined they saw Ting in front of them every time they opened their eyes."[153] As impressive as this sounds, it is certainly an exaggeration; and, as the preceding paragraph evidences, many Magistrates never bothered to awaken. One then still must ask if the severe discipline, vital to the ultimate achievement of an enduring improvement in the quality of governance, accompanied the strict supervision.

The answer is no. Despite his fierce reputation, Ting's actual record does not suggest that he was indeed a "hatchet man." With his gubernatorial powers he could inflict major and minor demerits—both of which led to dismissal, remove an official from his post, fill any office up to first-class prefect without first memorializing, and remove an official's seal of office and button of rank. To fine, demote, transfer, dismiss, or permanently bar an official from office, Ting had to memorialize the throne.[154] Of all the punishments at his disposal, Ting most commonly inflicted demerits. Yet, only twice did officials accumulate enough to be dismissed, and one official who did reach the limit apparently was retained in office. Next in frequency was the removal of a magistrate's button, but not uncommonly on public occasions officials flouted the penalty in order to avoid the intended shame, and Ting seems nearly always to have restored buttons in recognition of good work.[155] Rarely did he have officials removed from office; at most, 9 percent of local officials were dismissed. (Of all the local officials who served through the course of the dynasty, some 10 percent were removed from office.)[156] Of the twelve who were dismissed, there were three *chin-shih,* four *chu-jen,* two *fu-kung,* and one *chien-sheng.* Two of the *chin-shih* and one of the *chu-jen* whom Ting impeached while he was Financial Commissioner were recommended by Tseng Kuo-fan and Li Hung-chang to serve as educational officials, but, in two cases, the court preferred a "cleansing of officialdom" to such leniency.[157]

Even parents' pleadings with their sons, commented Lin Ta-ch'üan, could not compare with Ting's repeated entreaties to, encouragement of, and admonitions to his subordinates.[158] Ting hoped to arouse lethargic officials to "renew themselves" (*tzu-hsin*) in order to retain their hard-won status. To the Judicial Commissioner and to the Nanking Financial Commissioner, he explained his technique of carefully escalated threats:

> First I use gentle words, then I warn them [the recalcitrant Magistrates]. If a minor demerit is insufficient, then I remove their button. But some Magistrates are undisturbed and show no sign of anger or happiness. When I have exhausted my cunning, what can I do? ... Able men are hard to get so I don't shrink from talking till my tongue is dried and my lips bleed, subtly encouraging, subtly warning. But, if they are [impervious] to my words like rocks on which water drips, I will have to dismiss one or two as a warning to the rest.[159]

While the oratorical and literary style Ting employed in these exercises is not unique (Hu Lin-i's directives are similarly sharp-edged in tone), few officials' comments to their subordinates contain more bite and sarcasm.[160] Because of Ting's belief that the regular examinations produced men who knew nothing about governance, one would expect to find that he reserved his harshest words for *chin-shih* and *chu-jen.* There are scattered examples of such an attitude: an observation that a certain Magistrate immediately could announce his judicial decision only because he had been a *mu-yu*;[161] and a comment (apropos of efforts to get additional funding for dike work) that "those who call themselves Neo-Confucians (*li-hsueh chih-jen*) are not willing to give a bit of thought to the suffering of the common people; they merely sigh, 'What can be done, what can be done?'"[162] But there is no consistent correlation between an official's degree status and Ting's tone. Nor is there any indication that senior officials were spared his sharp tongue.[163]

But was Ting's hyperbole an effective substitute for discipline? Could not his accusation against the Magistrates of "talking without communicating" be lodged against him? When Ting, speaking of the notorious T'an-yuan Magistrate, asked the Judicial and Financial Commissioners, "How can I bear to disturb him when I know that he likes peace and quiet and dislikes being bothered?" these senior officials probably could appreciate the irony.[164] But what impact did such comments have when they were addressed directly to Magistrates? For instance, Ting wrote the unresponsive Hai-chou Magistrate, "If you in your heart think I am being a busybody, then naturally I will apologize for stepping out of line."[165] If the Magistrate was as confused an old man as Ting believed him to be, he most likely thought that this threatening specious self-deprecation actually was an apology. Surely, much of Ting's carefully conceived sarcasm (which we have previously encountered) was equally lost on other Magistrates. If his sarcasm had any influence upon those officials who he felt were willfully disrespectful, it certainly would have been a negative one. They probably first would have been angered by his sharpness, and then pleased at his discomfiture. In sum, Ting's overly subtle use of the probationary ethic often backfired.

Had Ting strictly adhered to his own teachings, had he moved more often from warnings to action, he would have been indeed a stern and effective administrator. But he was like a bad parent whose increasing frustration at repeatedly ignored warnings finally culminates in dire fulminations—fulminations either never fulfilled, or realized only after futher provocation. We have already seen many examples of such behavior, but the case of the T'an-yuan Magistrate gives us a significant insight into Ting's character. Ting repeatedly awarded demerits to him and threatened him with impeachment, yet, for a year of continuing difficulties, he eschewed all intermediate steps at his disposal before finally requesting the court to remove the Magistrate from office.[166] Since, in this case, the probationary ethic was clearly inoperative, and since the Magistrate had no political influence and was easily the worst official in the province, it is important to find an adequate explanation for Ting's hesitancy.

One can account for Ting's disciplinary behavior in terms both of his personal background and of institutional and political factors that impinged upon all late Ch'ing officials. Ting's rapid rise, despite his lack of a high degree, was undoubtedly enormously satisfying to him; but it also seems to have made him uncertain in the use of his great authority. As he himself acknowledged, he knew better than most how difficult it was to obtain an official position.[167] His constant references to himself as a "man up from the fields," while giving him claim to a special understanding of the people's problems, take on a poignantly defensive note in a province renowned for its literati elite. Thus, Ting sensed, perhaps, that his office alone was insufficient to command respect; social standing and style were more important credentials. In any case, because of his insecurity in high office, Ting was, indeed, easily provoked by officials' disregard (real or imagined) of his orders, and was particularly sensitive about the performance of officials whom he had personally recommended for their posts.[168]

If, however, we allow Ting's personality to dominate, we diminish the significance of the problem and obscure the political and institutional milieu in which he functioned. Of pivotal importance in this era was the previously noted contraction of the provincial officials' role in the appointment of their subordinates. In the late 1860s the metropolitan bureaucracy still grudgingly accommodated the needs of governors to make expedient irregular appointments, but it accompanied its approval with stern reminders that its tractility was specific to the case and was not to be taken as a precedent. This hardening vividly delineated for provincial officials the shape of things to come and induced in them a defensiveness which suffused their recommendations.[169] Tseng Kuo-fan, hardly an enthusiast of the ambitious uncultivated careerist, ruefully concluded that

> The high authorities are no longer willing to make frequent exceptions to the personnel regulations so as to allow for [those who may be regarded as] opportunists. Everything has to go by qualifications and regular procedures and everyone continues to play the old tune.[170]

Even within the permissible parameters of personnel management, governors lacked flexibility, for there was simply a limited number of competent people. The transfer of an able magistrate to resolve a crisis, retrieve another official's failed administration, or assume a difficult post merely created a new vacancy. The plethora of alternate officials was no panacea; amidst that throng was a paucity of skilled men. Hence a replacement might be worse than an incumbent. There was, in a word, famine in the midst of plenty. The beneficiaries of this anomaly were often the "wily and cruel" or corrupt officials who, possessed of special expertise, deployed their indispensability to forestall dismissal.[171]

Removal, then, of a baneful official from office afforded no certainty of an enduring or even an immediate improvement in governance. The frequently lengthy hiatus between an official's receipt of the order to vacate his office and the arrival of his replacement allowed the incumbent to avenge his dismissal at the expense of both the people and his successor.[172] Moreover, the officials whom Ting dismissed had an excellent chance to be reinstated through recommendation because of scholarship, monetary contributions, or military merit. In 1870, a Censor charged that such officials probably had learned nothing in the interim (implicitly prophesying the deleterious consequences), but the practice seems to have remained acceptable.[173] *Chin-shih* and *chu-jen* who had been unable to comprehend the lessons of office were designated educational officials, in which role they were expected to assume, in addition to their lecturing responsibilities, the difficult task of supervising the obstreperous *sheng-chien.* And one Magistrate removed from office by Ting in 1868 for judicial incompetence was reappointed in 1873 to an even more important post within the province.[174] Committed by its ideology to recognizing the right to an office of those who ostensibly had demonstrated their moral leadership through the attainment of a high degree, and myopically obsessed by its short-term revenue needs, the Ch'ing ignored the question of whether it could afford such practices.

Yet, just as Ting's discipline of officials was vitiated by elements beyond his control, so, too, could another type of outside force ensure that predatory officials ultimately would be punished. For, beyond any temporal sanctions, there was heavenly retribution (*kuo-pao*). As the couplet Ting placed on the door of his governor's yamen said, ". . . If everywhere there is perfunctoriness and evasion of responsibility, though punishment by law may be evaded, in the end there will be retribution in another life."[175] (And there was a similar warning at the entrance in every magistrate's inner quarters.)[176] Although Ting had complained occasionally that the people wasted their time by listening to stories about moral retribution, clearly a belief in it must have been common to the elite as well for him to have had recourse to it. Indeed, the renowned eighteenth-century Magistrate Wang Hui-tsu had openly discussed his conviction that his commitment to good government would redound to his benefit in the afterlife.[177] Admittedly, said Ting, *kuo-pao* was not discussed by Confucian scholars; and an official was actually lowering himself to speak of it. But, continued Ting, Confucian scholars would certainly accept the essential truth of the phrase, "The result [in your next life or for your descendants] of accumulated good actions is prosperity; the result of accumulated bad actions is calamity" (*chi-shan yü ch'ing, chi pu-shan yü ts'an*).[178]

SEVEN

Conclusion

The interlude between the Ch'ing's triumph over the Taiping and its collapse in 1911 was not the conscious creation of T'ung-chih statesmen. The "temporary stabilization" before the "final catastrophe" constituted survival, not the revival Mary Wright called it.[1] The dynasty suppressed the Rebellions and forestalled foreign calamity; the centrifugal forces at the provincial level were checked and the center held.[2] However, as the Empress Dowager's use of naval construction funds for a marble boat and the metropolitan bureaucracy's exclusion of talented "irregulars" who would have provided leavening for a "flat" bureaucracy suggest, the consequences of reassertion of central control over personnel and finances were not always beneficial. More important, because the dynasty never took into account the post-Rebellion absence of imperial leadership and the solidified position of local elites, it never met the agenda of civil measures that composed the heart of the Restoration program. With neither enthusiastic direction nor support from above, nor a responsive, competent bureaucracy below, provincial governors, upon whom fell the burden of restoring good governance, could accomplish little.

The dynasty's inability to restore a system of rule by superior civil officials and its consequent patent failure to reform local government impeded and attenuated every element of the Restoration agenda. There was no fundamental equalization or reduction of the tax burden, thereby leaving largely disembodied the "Restoration's" policy axiom (as stated by Mary Wright) that "political control could not be effectively reasserted until the burden of the land tax was lightened and more equitably distributed."[3] Heterodox customs were not exterminated, and Confucian values were not uniformly reaffirmed; nor was the dynasty's presence in the countryside and in networks of local control effectively reestablished. The judicial system, although it retained the capacity occasionally to right outrageous wrongs, remained inefficient, while banditry was sufficiently pervasive to justify the retention of draconian summary executions.[4] In sum, viewed in terms of its own goals, there was no T'ung-chih Restoration.

K. C. Liu, however, argues that to judge the Restoration by its own aspirations is to apply too strict a standard. "Given the best of intentions," he asks in his essay, "The Ch'ing Restoration," in the *Cambridge History of China* "was it possible for a few statesmen to change the customs and institutions of the *pre-Taiping* [emphasis added] local government?" Liu responds negatively to his own rhetorical question, but concludes that a restoration nevertheless was achieved in the sense of a return to the status quo ante—perfunctory bureaucracy, corrupt yamen underlings, widespread tax evasion and inequalitites, tax and litigation mongering by unemployed lower-degree-holders.[5] Clearly, although Ting and his contemporaries never themselves spoke of a Restoration, had they used the term it would not have denoted a return to the ante-bellum quality of governance. For Ting the Tao-kuang reign (1821–1850) was not a model period of a truly vital Confucian order; it was instead a time of an exemplary struggle against institutional decay, a struggle he and others sought to continue in the 1860s. In this light, the Taiping Rebellion may be seen not as the cause of a Restoration effort but as the occasion for the renewal of an earlier campaign. It seems to this historian, and would probably appear to Ting, that Liu's dreary characterization of the 1860s and 1870s (which is congruent with my own) affirms not the success of T'ung-chih officials but rather their failure.

What, then, accounts for the modicum of tranquillity enjoyed by the Ch'ing in the last quarter of the nineteenth century? The relief from social tensions provided by the extraordinary population losses is obvious and cannot be overemphasized. Less obtrusive is the dampening of social tensions by the expansion of social welfare institutions under the direction of the scholar-official elite and by the consolidation of the rural power-holders' control in the countryside. Essentially, though, the Ch'ing's immediate survival is attributable to military victory. It was, moreover, as K. C. Liu has noted, a remarkable triumph, for the leaders of the Ch'ing armies, unlike the T'ang Restoration's commanders, were scholar-officials far removed from military aristocratic culture.[6]

Yet, paradoxically, because it vitiated the urgent impetus to reform, it was the very success of the Ch'ing armies that contributed to the dynasty's failure to realize and consolidate a Restoration. Although the Nien and Moslem Rebellions continued after the Taiping, and banditry persisted, none of these replicated the Taiping challenge to Ch'ing sovereignty. Nonetheless, both the Nien and Moslem suppression campaigns drew attention and funds away from problems of civil administration.[7] Hence, while self-strengthening advanced haltingly forward in response to periodic foreign intrusions, domestic reform no longer had such a stimulus; and it would be nearly two decades before the strong indigenous impulse to reform fully surfaced again.

In the absence of threats to the established order and with a reduced population to govern, most officials lapsed into complacency. By as early as 1868, widespread perfunctoriness within the bureaucracy so disturbed the court that it solicited opinions on how to *reinvigorate* the empire's administration! [8] In his response, Ting Jih-ch'ang asserted that the presence or absence of perfunctoriness determined the condition of the state. In peaceful times people avoided discussing—much less acting upon—the elimination of the bad for fear of stepping on someone's toes. Yet, unless such timid behavior was vigorously discouraged, there could be no hope for peaceful and enduring rule. When officials finally realized that they were trapped by perfunctoriness, it would be, averred Ting, too late for them to arouse themselves:

> It is like sailing in a small boat on a river. When it is shallow, you start to think about abandoning the boat, but because you are afraid of getting your feet wet you do not. Soon the boat is out in the middle of the river. Your strength is insufficient, your hands and feet can do nothing. You can only sit and let things happen.[9]

Ultimately, Ting's metaphorical analysis proved to be correct, and for the remainder of its existence the dynasty was borne by currents on a course not of its own making. Nonetheless there were those (*inter alia* Ting, the Ch'ing-i ideologues in the metropolitan bureaucracy, and the local elite reformers) who refused to let matters drift. Strikingly, despite their different perspectives, they unknowingly shared an agenda for change that adumbrated many of the 1898 reformers' concerns: an end to corruption, improvement in communication between above and below, and the search for and promotion of new men. The possibility of a coalition for reform was foreclosed, however, not only by institutional constraints against faction-building but also by divergences on how and by whom change should be wrought. For instance, while Ting shared the Ch'ing-i's moral fervor and aversion to perfunctoriness, as a provincial Governor gripped by the problems of daily governance, he was primarily concerned with managerial and organizational matters. His approach to reform was utilitarian and rule-oriented. The Ch'ing-i, on the other hand, emphasized the transformative power of moral leaders at the center. Separating Ting and the Ch'ing-i was a dichotomy between "administrative and political renovation."[10] Although, in the twentieth century, it was a political renovation that transformed China, between 1870 and 1895 the center of the stage in the small theater of reform activity was dominated by provincial officials and local elites striving for "administrative renovation." It is toward these two groups that we direct our attention.

For their part, the scholar-official local elite advanced the thesis that the administrative paralysis in local government, and penultimately in the entire bureaucracy as well, was created by the divorce of local officials from the countryside. Not only were these men "outsiders," often possessed of merely purchased credentials; they also employed as their eyes and ears, or sometimes more accurately their "teeth and claws," the lowest of the local residents, the yamen underlings. Isolated in his yamen, kept ignorant by his underlings, the local official could hardly serve the needs of his district, much less represent them to his superiors. Drawing from the early Ch'ing scholar and Ming loyalist Ku Yen-wu, Feng Kuei-fen suggested the corrective of a restructured sub-district government in which the appointed agents of the magistrate would be replaced by consensually selected local notables.[11] In combination with the elite's dominant role in schools and welfare institutions, Feng's proposal would have enabled them to fulfill their goal of gathering important local functions into their own hands. With the activities of yamen underlings thereby circumscribed and the magistrate more responsive to "public opinion," a significant measure of power would have ineluctably devolved from the magistrate to the scholar-official local elite.

Philip Kuhn has played down the invidiousness of this apparent power grab. The objective of Feng, he argues, was to create "a more highly bureaucratized and codified system of local rule. . . . to gather up dispersed power [personified by the gentry directors] and to regularize and control it." They in no way, concluded Kuhn, desired to weaken "the power of the imperial state which guaranteed their status.[12] Indeed, asserts David Faure in a recent Princeton dissertation, the expansion of the local elite's role in sub-district government and social welfare institutions halted dynastic decline.[13] Still, there is a suggestive continuity between the localism of non-bureaucratic reformers (who were intellectually influenced by Ku Yen-wu) and the burgeoning anti-Manchuism of later local-elite parliamentarians. Although we should not infer anti-Manchuism carelessly, students of the Ch'ing, as Jonathan Spence admonished his graduate students, should never forget that it was a conquest dynasty and always "think Manchu."

At the time, however, Ting and later reform Governors certainly did not question the loyalty of local elites (whether scholar-official or gentry director), but neither did they regard the growth of the local elite's independence and power as a sign of dynastic health, for the elite's interests and objectives often diverged from the dynasty's.[14] Hence, while Kiangsu local elites were a pale shadow of Han notables, and the Han example was never cited by T'ung-chih officials, the debilitating impact of powerful local families upon the Han Restoration may have been a subliminal goad to those committed to strengthening the center. As representatives of the center, Ting and other reform Governors had no quarrel with the local elite's view that a gap existed between local government and society. Nor did they disagree with the premise that incompetent magistrates and unrestrained yamen underlings were causative factors. But, as representatives of the center, provincial officials could not concur that the remedy was a reversal of the "political flow" from center downward to local elite upward, for they had found that elite intercession in the critical areas of finance, justice, and personnel was antithetical to the implementation of the center's policies.

Inevitably, then, the question of whose agents would control the countryside divided the official reformers from the like-minded local elites. Ting Jih-ch'ang's attacks on lackadaisical magistrates, conniving gentry directors, and rapacious yamen underlings earned him Feng Kuei-fen's paean as Kiangsu's best Governor since Lin Tse-hsu.[15] Yet, Ting's attitude on the potential uses of clerks and runners was anathema to Feng, who wanted to eliminate them and instead staff the bureaucracy from top to bottom with men of educational attainments. Ting's writings suggest that he understood that yamen underlings constituted not only a potential source of talent but natural allies for the center as well. Unlike the local elites, whose legitimacy by the late nineteenth century was arguably somewhat independent of the center, but like the poor peasants elevated to cadre positions in the 1940s by the Communist Party, former underlings, "turned" by the inducements of legitimacy and appointed to office, could reasonably be expected to serve the interests of the state from which they had obtained their new status. (Ting's suggestion to transform the underlings' status is one of the few proposals of that time that bordered on genuine social change.) Feng Kuei-fen understood the ramifications of such a possibility. Indeed, one can read his call to "kill" the clerks as less an altruistic desire to eliminate predators upon society than a bid to eliminate bona fide potential rivals for political power.[16]

Unifying above and below (*shang-hsia i-t'i*) was a focal political issue in the second half of the nineteenth century. Perhaps stimulated by the Rebellions to recall the teachings of Mencius, there was across a wide spectrum of officials, from Ch'ing-i to Ting, a correct recognition that China's resurgence depended ultimately on her real strength, her people. Nothing could be accomplished without their assistance. As Ting once advised the Nanking Financial Commissioner, in words that would have been counsel well taken by the 1898 reformers and the Kuomintang:

> It is essential first to get the people's trust before one can get them to labor [for one]. A magistrate, of course, should think about whether or not he has a definite plan [for change] in his mind; but, if he hasn't the people's confidence, no matter how good the plan or fine his intentions, there can be no sudden change in the old established regulations; and the magistrate will lose control of the situation.[17]

By never effectively countering the power of the local elites, the dynasty foreclosed the possibility of a restoration of previous levels of governance, since it ensured that its attempts to get the people's trust and implement its policies would be filtered through as well as impeded by the political (and in the last decades–racial) interests of the local elites. Until the first decade of the twentieth century, these elites continued to support the dynasty because it served their interests, but, when it became clear that even a "reformed" one was no longer advantageous to them, many of the elite reversed their attitude of the 1860s, abandoned the dynasty, and joined the opposition.

In the end, the Ch'ing lost control because it waited too long to undertake aggressive survival measures. Like an apathetic forest ranger resting after the immediate threat has passed, the Ch'ing assumed that, because the "tree of state" was still standing after the flames of rebellion had subsided, it needed no strengthening. The military victories afforded the dynasty a hiatus, but the vigorously enunciated plans of reform were timorously enacted. Independently of official initiatives, traditional Chinese culture and values (broadly defined and distinct from Confucian scholarship) flourished and, to varying degrees, perdure today, but, while the overlying political superstructure may have lasted another fifty years, it was not revived. As Ting Jih-ch'ang gloomily concluded in 1873:

> *The "tree of state"* (she-mu) *is so big that ten men surround its girth, so big that it can shade an ox*
> *From without it appears tall and beautiful;*
> *Within it rots.*[18]

Appendixes

Abbreviations

Notes

Bibliography

Glossary

Index

Appendix A
Degree Status of Local Officials: Kiangsu, 1864–1870

The data presented here confirm the findings of Li Kuo-chi and others that an increasing percentage of magistrates had obtained office by purchasing degrees. Indeed Li's findings suggest the phenomenon peaked in T'ung-chih. The *Chin-shen ch'üan-shu* data cover every county and the gazetteer data are nearly complete. Although I have been unable to cross-check every official, my initial and tentative conclusion from a comparison of the two sources is that a large number of officials listed in the *Chin-shen ch'üan-shu* either never actually served in their appointed posts or served in another post within the same province. This situation may have resulted from provincial officials' reviews and reassignments of Board-appointed magistrates, a process that appears to have taken a disproportionately heavy toll of Manchu candidates.

See pp. 146–147; Li Kuo-chi, *Chung-kuo ti-fang chih*, pp. 28, 212–213; T'ung-tsu Ch'ü, *Local Government*, p. 20; Ping-ti Ho, *Ladder of Success*, pp. 48–49.

	Chin-shen ch'üan-shu		Gazetteers	
Background	Number of Persons	%	Number of Persons	%
By examination:				
chin-shih	48	21.62	19	14.50
chu-jen	65	29.30	42	32.08
pa-kung	11	4.95	3	2.30
fu-pang			2	1.52
sui-kung	1	0.45	2	1.52

Background	*Chin-shen ch'üan-shu* Number of Persons	%	Gazetters Number of Persons	%
ling-sheng	1	0.45	1	0.76
fu-sheng	10	4.50	2	1.52
sheng-yuan	4	1.80		
Total	140	63.07	71	54.20
By purchase:				
ling-kung	8	3.60	9	6.90
tseng-kung	1	0.45	1	0.76
fu-kung	7	3.15	10	7.63
kung-sheng	6	2.70	1	0.76
chien-sheng	50	22.53	35	26.71
Total	72	32.43	56	42.76
By other channels:				
li-yuan	2	0.90	2	1.52
kung-shih	5	2.25	1	0.76
pi-t'ieh shih			1	0.76
i-hsu (meritorious record)	3	1.35		
Total	10	4.50	4	3.04
Grand Total	222	100.00	131	100.00
Social background				
Manchu	10	4.50	3	2.29
Mongol	1	0.45	1	0.76
Chinese bannermen	3	1.35	3	2.29

Sources: The following gazetteers were used in the preparation of Appendix A and in the preparation of Appendixes C, E, F.

Chen-yang hsien T'ai-ts'ang chou ho-chih, 1918.
Chia-ting hsien-chih, 1880.
Chiang-yin hsien-chih, 1878.
Chin-t'an hsien-chih, 1885.
Ch'ing-p'u hsien-chih, 1879.
Ch'uan-sha hsien-chih, 1935.
Ch'uan-sha ting-chih, 1879.
Chung-hsiu Ching-chiang hsien-chih, 1879.
Ch'ung-ming hsien-chih, 1881.
Feng hsien-chih, 1877.

Hsu-hsiu Chiang-ning fu-chih, 1880.
Huai-an fu-chih, 1884.
I-hsing Ching-ch'i hsien-chih, 1882.
Kan-ch'üan hsien-chih, 1885.
Kan-yü hsien-chih, 1888.
K'un-hsin liang-hsien hsu-hsiu ho-chih, 1880.
Li-yang hsien hsu-chih, 1897.
Nan-hui hsien-chih, 1878.
P'ei hsien-chih, 1918.
Su-chou fu-chih, 1883.
Tan-t'u hsien-chih, 1879.
Tan-yang hsien-chih, 1885.
Tsai-hsu Kao-yu chou-chih, 1883.
T'ung-chih Hsu-chou fu-chih, 1874.
T'ung-chih Shang-hai hsien-chih, 1871.
T'ung-chou chih-li chou-chih, 1876.
T'ung-shan hsien-chih, 1923.
Wu hsien-chih, 1933.
Wu-chiang hsien-chih, 1879.
Wu-hsi Chin-kuei hsien-chih, 1881.

Appendix B
The Correlation Between the Length of Tenure and a Post's Degree of Difficulty

The only conclusion that can be drawn on the basis of the data presented below is that, at least for the T'ung-chih period, no clear correlation can be established between the difficulty of a post and an official's length of service. Hence, these data do not lend themselves to testing Skinner's argument ("Cities and the Hierarchy of Local Systems," pp. 338-339) that the existence in revenue-producing counties of local elite parapolitical structures alleviated the administrative burden of local officials.

Moreover, without two additional pieces of information—the reasons for an official's departure and the actual administrative burden in a post—it is dangerous to put too much weight on these statistics. A capable magistrate might be repeatedly transferred to deal with troublesome areas, and a hsien's rating did not always accurately reflect its condition.

Post	Degree of Difficulty[1]	Post Designation[2]	Average Length of Service (in years)[3]	Special Characteristics
An-tung	3	FPN	1.16	
Ch'ang-chou	4	CFPN	1.50	
Chen-yang	2	F**	3.25	shares city with T'ai-ts'ang
Chia-ting	2	PN	1.60	
Chiang-ning	3	CFN	1.40	
Chiang-p'u	1	C	1.20	
Chiang-tu	4	CFPN	1.00	
Chiang-yin	3	FN**	2.00	area of missionary problems
Chin-kuei	2	PN	1.50	
Chin-t'an	2	PN	1.30	
Ching-ch'i	2	PN	1.60	
Ching-chiang	1	N	4.00	
Ch'ing-ho	4	CPFN	1.60	
Chü-jung	2	CN	1.60	
Ch'uan-sha	3	FPN	1.40	
Ch'ung-ming	3	FN**	1.60	in mouth of Yangtze
Feng h.	1	no characters	1.00	
Feng-hsien	2	PN	1.60	low in administrative and economic hierarchies

Post	Degree of Difficulty[1]	Post Designation[2]	Average Length of Service (in years)[3]	Special Characteristics
Fu-ning	3	FPN	1.40	
Hua-t'ing	3	FPN	3.00	
Hsiao h.	1	N	1.60	
Hsin-yang	2	PN	1.20	low in administrative and economic hierarchies
Kan-yü	1	N	1.40	
Kao-shun	1	no characters	3.30	
K'un-shan	2	PN	1.60	low in administrative and economic hierarchies
Li-shui	1	no characters	1.00	
Li-yang	2	FN	1.50	politically senstivie
Liu-ho	1	no characters	1.60	
Lou h.	2	PN	0.90	low in administrative and economic hierarchies
Nan-hui	3	FPN	2.60	
Pao-shan	3	FPN	2.30	
P'ei-chou	3	CN**	1.00	on the Grand Canal
P'ei h.	1	C	1.60	
Shan-yang	4	CPFN	2.00	
Shang-yuan	3	CFN	2.00	
Su-ch'ien	3	CFN	2.00	

Post	Degree of Difficulty[1]	Post Designation[2]	Average Length of Service (in years)[3]	Special Characteristics
Sui-ning	1	no characters	0.90	
T'ai-ts'ang	3	FPN	1.75	
Tan-t'u	4	CPFN	1.30	
Tan-yang	4	CPFN	1.60	
T'an-yuan	3	CFN	3.00	
Tang-shan	3	FPN	1.00	
T'ung-chou	3	FN**	1.50	on sea near mouth of Yangtze; politically sensitive
T'ung-shan	3	CFN	2.50	
Wu h.	4	CPFN	1.40	
Wu-chiang	4	CPFN	3.30	
Wu-chin	4	CFPN	1.25	
Wu-hsi	3	CFN	1.50	
Yang-hu	2	FN	3.60	politically sensitive
Yen-ch'eng	2	FN	4.00	politically sensitive
Yuan-ho	4	CPFN	1.40	

Sources: See pp. 182–183.

Notes: 1. The importance rating, or degree of difficulty, is based on the categorizations listed in the *Ta Ch'ing chin-shen ch'uan-shu*, 1864–1870. The equivalents are:

1 = easy
2 = medium

3=difficult and important
4=extremely difficult and most important

2. Each letter represents a particular characteristic:
N (*nan*)=difficult or insecure
F (*fan*)=troublesome or busy
C (*ch'ung*)=frequented or trade center
P (*p'i*)=fatiguing or unremunerative

G. William Skinner, observing that the degree of difficulty sometimes exceeded the number of characters in a post designation, has suggested that the absent character be considered a "secret" signifier of a post's strategic importance. I have flagged these with a double asterisk (**) and noted their geographical location. Skinner furthermore advises that we distinguish between the two character designations. Thus CF (*ch'ung*, trade center; *fan*, busy yamen) is a post with an economic level higher than its administrative rank. FN (*fan*, busy yamen; *nan*, insecure) is a post whose administrative rank is higher than its economic level. There are a number of FN posts in the above table,and three of them—Chiang-yin, Ch'ung-ming, and T'ung-chou—possessed the "secret signifier" of security importance. See Skinner, "Cities and the Hierarchy of Local Systems," pp. 316-317.

3. These figures exclude "temporary" officials (*tai-li*) who served as short-term fill-ins, but include "acting" (*shu*) officials. These findings are similar to those of Li Kuo-chi, *Chung-kuo ti-fang chih*, pp. 386, 777-778. For a more detailed study of magistrates' tenures in Su-sung-t'ai, see Lojewski, "Confucian Reformers," pp. 362-422.

Appendix C.1

Compliance to Orders on Registers for Documents and for Litigation and Prisons

Place (Rating)		Documents Register	Litigation and Prison Register
Ch'ang-chou	(4)	5/67, date of receipt of important document not shown 6/67, lists order but does not report implementation of order	ligitation register unclear
Ch'ang-shu	(3)		should not omit minor cases from the register
Chao-wen	(2)		both registers totally unclear and not in accord with form
Chen-chiang fu	(4)	response fine	
Chen-ts'e	(2)	6/67 report merely duplicates previous one without indicating how matters handled; both not in accord with form	both registers unclear and not in accord with form
Chen-yang	(2)		5/67, clear and good 6/67, not in accord with form
Chia-ting	(2)		5/67, conscientious 6/67, good, large number of cases concluded
Chiang-yin	(3)		demerit, prison registers not in accord with form
Chin-kuei	(2)	4/67, makes no mention of circular orders 5/67, important documents not listed 6/67, documents still missing; register not in accord with form	deliberately and disobediently delayed sending the litigation register

Place (Rating)		Documents Register	Litigation and Prison Register
Chin-shan	(2)		5/67, too general and vague 6/67, not in accord with form
Chin-t'an	(2)		6/67, prison register should be submitted even if there are no prisoners
Ching-ch'i	(2)		registers clear
Ching-chiang	(1)	5/67, omits the circular order forbidding *tso-tsa* from accepting litigation 6/67, this document still not listed	litigation register not in accord with form prison register not even prepared
Ch'ing-p'u	(3)	does not list circular orders	5/67, prison register not in accord with form; too many unsettled cases 6/67, both registers totally disorganized and incomprehensible
Ch'uan-sha	(3)		registers not in accord with form; too many unsettled cases
Ch'ung-ming	(3)		5/67, prison register not in accord with form; too many open cases 6/67, numerous mistakes in litigation register; demerit for failure to make prison register
Feng-hsien	(2)	5/67, two important documents omitted	not in accord with form and unclear
Hsin-yang	(2)	lists all documents but does not say how they were handled	not send in prison register

Place (Rating)		Documents Register	Litigation and Prison Register
Hua-t'ing	(3)	4/67, register very late	5/67, not in accord with form; too many old unconcluded cases 6/67, good detailed report
I-hsing	(2)	5/67, omits the circular order forbidding *tso-tsa* to accept litigation 6/67, not in accord with form; too much unfinished business	
K'un-shan	(2)	6/67, fine	both registers deliberately delayed; litigation but not the prison register is in accord with form
Li-yang	(2)	not in accord with form	5/67, 6/67 registers identical; no progress in any cases
Lou h.	(2)	5/67, important documents omitted	too many unsettled cases; prison register not in accord with form, unclear
Pao-shan	(3)	3,4/67 fine 5/67, omits order to speed up handling of public business	prison register not sent
Shang-hai	(3)	not in accord with form, unclear	not in accord with form, though magistrate able
Su-chou fu (Soochow)	(4)	5/67, not include order on distribution and reading of *Sacred Edict* 6/67, erroneously reports Yuan-ho tax surcharge eliminated	
T'ai-hu ting	(2)	fine except lacks dates	omitted summary of cases; next month form is still too general
Tan-t'u	(4)	5/67, omits orders dealing with taxes	5/67, prison register not in accord with form 6/67, unclear which cases are closed

Place (Rating)		Documents Register	Litigation and Prison Register
Tan-yang	(4)		5/67, sends only the ligitation register 6/67, again omits prison register; litigation register filled with errors
Wu h.	(4)	6/67, lists an order but does not report on its implementation	5/67, too many open cases 6/67, extremely unclear and not in accord with form
Wu-chiang	(3)	4/67, 5/67 both excellent	fine; should take and record chair petitions
Wu-chin	(4)	lists all documents, but fails to give details on response to circular orders; doing poor job 6/67, filled with errors; not in accord with form	no one listed in prison register; too many unsettled cases
Wu-hsi	(3)	important documents not listed	
Yuan-ho	(4)	6/67, lists order but does not report on its implementation	registers extremely unclear and not in accord with form

Sources: For documents registers, *TCCCS:FanWKT*, Chapter 5.
For litigation and prisons registers, ibid., chapters 8–9.

Appendix C.2
Compliance to Orders on Tax Rate Notices

Place	1867		1868		1869	
	Land	Tribute	Land	Tribute	Land	Tribute
An-tung					demerit; no copies of rates or receipts	
Ch'ang-chou	clear			per-*mou* rates in rice only no commutation rates		
Ch'ang-shu	no warning against surcharges		did not list foreign dollar price			
Chao-wen	no foreign dollar rate or encouragement to pay at market rate		did not list foreign dollar price or say it can be done this way			
Chen-ts'e	clear, detailed		clear and simple			
Chen-yang	clear, detailed			lists payment deadlines		
Chia-ting	nothing against abuses			late, but fine and detailed		
Chiang-tu				separate list with rates, should be on proclamation	no receipt forms	proclamation only, no receipt forms

Place	1867		1868		1869	
	Land	Tribute	Land	Tribute	Land	Tribute
Chiang-yin	clear; foreign dollar price the highest					
Chin-kuei	nothing against abuses			per-*mou* rates in rice only; no commuted rates		
Chin-shan	clear; foreign dollar rate too high	did not post enough notices	proclamation did not give exact price			
Chin-t'an				submitted only the form instead of printed copy		
Ching-ch'i			proclamation did not give exact price	per-*mou* rates in rice only; no commuted ones		
Ching-chiang	clear but foreign dollar price too high				did not post enough notices	
Ch'ing-ho		demerit: did not post enough notices		notices omitted foreign dollar and silver prices	demerit: did not send copies of rate notices or receipts	

Place	1867		1868		1869	
	Land	Tribute	Land	Tribute	Land	Tribute
Ch'ing-p'u	no statement on the reduction of fees		proclamation did not give the exact price	required contributions to charitable granaries listed in detail		
Ch'uan-sha	did not distinguish amounts to be paid in fall and spring					
Ch'ung-ming	detailed but last one in					
Feng h.				did not give exact rates	did not indicate can pay in foreign dollars and according to market price	
Feng-hsien	clear, detailed			detailed foreign dollar price within the notice		
Fu-ning		demerit: did not post enough notices			proclamation only; did not send copies of receipts	
Hua-t'ing	sloppy; unclear on rules for paying in foreign dollars			detailed foreign dollar price within the notice		

Place	1867		1868		1869	
	Land	Tribute	Land	Tribute	Land	Tribute
Hsiao						fee shown must be a mistake
Hai-chou				first to be ready, clear, detailed	no receipt forms	proclamation only no receipt forms
Hsin-yang	lacks detail and refinement		all fees listed, good and detailed	survey fees listed in detail within notice		
Hsing-hua				detailed statement against corruption	demerit: did not send copies of rates or receipts	sent only proclamation; no copies of receipts
Ju-kao					as above	as above
Kan-ch'üan		separate list with the rates, not correct form			demerit: did not send rate notices or copies of receipts	
Kan-yü				rates not detailed; deficient in warnings against corruption	did not indicate can pay in foreign dollars according to the market price	per-*mou* rates not given in cash, but in rice only

Place	1867		1868		1869	
	Land	Tribute	Land	Tribute	Land	Tribute
Kao-yu					demerit: did not send copies of rates or receipts	
K'un-shan	lacks detail and refinement		all fees listed; good and detailed	survey fees listed in detail within the notice		
Lou h.	clear, but foreign dollar rate is too high		proclamation did not give the exact prices	foreign dollar price detailed within the notice		
Nan-hui	clearest most detailed			sent form only, not printed copy		
Pao-shan	sloppy careless		proclamation did not give the exact price	late, but simple and clear		
Pao-ying				no foreign dollar price or commutation rates		
P'ei h.				simple and clear		
Shan-yang		unequal rates *ta-hu, hsiao-hu*		clear and simple		
Shang-hai	too brief		proclamation did not give the exact price			

Place	1867		1868		1869	
	Land	Tribute	Land	Tribute	Land	Tribute
Shu-yang					no receipt forms	proclamation only, no receipt forms
Su-ch'ien				did not make blocks and print up notices		rates only in rice per *mou*, no cash equivalents
Sui-ning					demerit: did not send copies of rates and notices	
T'ai-chou				proclamation did not list foreign dollar price		proclamation only, no receipt forms
T'ai-hu	simple and clear					
T'ai-hsing					demerit: did not send copies of rates and notices	
Tan-t'u	clear but foreign dollar rate too high					
T'an-yuan		demerit: not enough notices posted			demerit: no copies of rates or receipts	demerit: no copies of rates or receipts

Place	1867		1868		1869	
	Land	Tribute	Land	Tribute	Land	Tribute
T'ung-shan						demerit: no copies of rates or receipts
Wu h.	clear			detailed clear		
Wu-chiang	clear and detailed		clear and simple			
Wu-chin	foreign dollar rate based on market price; rates not too clear		proclamation did not give the exact price	per-*mou* rates not commuted but shown in rice only		
Wu-hsi	clear on commutation rates		did not list foreign dollar price or state that taxes can be paid in them			
Yang-hu	foreign dollar rate based on market price; rates not too clear		proclamation did not give the exact price			
Yen-ch'eng		delayed in posting		unclear	demerit: did not send copies of rates or receipts	
Yuan-ho	detailed			total amount given instead of commuted per-*mou* rate		

Place	1867		1868		1869	
	Land	Tribute	Land	Tribute	Land	Tribute
T'ung-chou				fine report	demerit: did not send copies of rates or receipts	
T'ai-ts'ang	did not eliminate fees, no foreign dollar price					

Source: FWKT, 12:6–6b; 33:7–10; 44:8b–10b.

Appendix D
Officials with Repeated Service in Kiangsu

Name *Status*	Post (degree of difficulty)	Dates of Service	Comments
Chang Chen-huang *chu-jen*	An-tung (3) (acting)	1868–1870	new but able
	T'ung-shan (3)	1870	
Chang Ch'iao-lin *ling kung-sheng*	Wu h. (4)	10/1863–2/1864	
	Ching-ch'i (2)	1867–1868	impeached and dismissed for excess collections
Chang Chin *chu-jen*	Chia-ting (2)	9/1862–1/1863	
	I-hsing (2)	2/1864–6/1864	
	K'un-shan (2)	1866–1868	unable to complete survey
Chang Hung-sheng *chu-jen*	Kan-yu (1) (acting)	1868	impeached and dismissed for backlogged litigation
	Yen-ch'eng (2)	1873	
Chang I-meng *chien-sheng*	Liu-ho (1)	185?	
	Chiang-ning (3)	1865–1867	
	T'ai-hsing (2)		button returned for capture of suspect
Chang Pao-heng *chin-shih*	Wu h. (4)	8/1865–9/1866	
	Tan-yang (4)		major demerit for surcharges
Chang Ts'e-jen *chien-sheng*	Lou h. (2)	11/1865–8/1867	
	Hua-t'ing (3)	8/1867–9/1873	biography in gazetteer
Ch'en Ch'i-yuan *lin kung-sheng*	Nan-hui (3)	1867–1869	major merit, charitable works major demerit, no tax notices promoted for good judicial work

Name *Status*	Post (degree of difficulty)	Dates of Service	Comments
	Hsin-yang (2) (acting)	10/1870–4/1871	
Ch'en Mao-ai *chin-shih*	Wu h. (4) P'ei chou (2) Hai-chou (2)	1857–1858 1862–1865	 delays documents; controls runners; promoted for good judicial work
Ch'eng Tsu-yin *chu-jen*	Li-shui (1)	1864–1865 1867–1869	
Ch'i Te-ch'ang *chin-shih*	Pao-shan (3) Tan-t'u (4)	8/1865–8/1866 1868–1870	
Ch'ien Pao-chuan *fu kung-sheng*	Ch'ing-p'u (3) Ch'ang-chou (4) Ch'ing-p'u (3)	1866–1868 5/1868–2/1869 1870–1871	
Ch'ien Te-ch'eng *chien-sheng*	Kao-shun (1) Ch'ung-ming (2) Yuan-ho (4) (acting) Soochow fu (4) (acting) Chiang-ning fu (3)	1848 1862–1863 4/1862–1868 1868 1869–1870	personally captures locusts good response to land tax regulations
Chou Chi-lin *fu-kung*	Ju-kao (2)	1864 1866–1870	trouble with litigation banned from office forever
Chou Ting	An-tung (3) Ch'ing-ho (4)	1870 1870–1875	
Chu Chia-hsiang	P'ei chou (3) Sui-ning (1)	1867 1869	

Name *Status*	Post (degree of difficulty)	Dates of Service	Comments
Chuan Lin-sen	Wu-hsi (3)	1867	held in Soochow for additional training
chien-sheng	Ching-ch'i (2)	1869–9/1873	easier post suited to his talents
Feng Hung-hsiang	Wu-hsi (3)	1868–1869	
chu-jen	Chiang-yin (3)	1869–1871	
Feng Wei	Tan-yang (4)		
chien-sheng	Hsin-yang (2)	7/1867–10/1868	
Han P'ei-chin	Feng-hsien (2)	1862–1865	
		1868–1870	two major demerits for too many unsolved robberies
Hsu Pi-t'ing	Feng h. (1)	1861–1862	
chien-sheng	T'ung-shan (3)	1862–1864	
	Feng h. (1)	1864–1865	
	P'ei h. (1)	1865–1866	
	P'ei chou (3)	1866–1867	
Kao T'i	Ch'ang-chou fu (4) (temporary)	1865	
chu-jen	director Ch'ang-chen ch'üan-neng chü	1866	
	Hsu-hai tao (?)	1867–1870	Board of Civil Appointments opposes since he had had no audience; Chao Lieh-wen calls him an "operator"; Ting says an excellent judge
Kao Yun-ku	P'ei chou (3)	1865	
chin-shih	Hsu-chou fu (3)	1865–1868	dismissed for remissness in judicial affairs
Ku Ssu-hsien	Lou h. (2)	2/1865–1872	
chu-jen	Ch'ang-chou h. (4) (acting)	7/1868	

Name *Status*	Post (degree of difficulty)	Dates of Service	Comments
K'uai Te-mo *fu kung-sheng*	Ch'ang-chou h. (4)	8/1864–4/1868	one major merit for concluding litigation; Chao Lieh-wen accuses of bribing Ting
K'uang Mao-lun *chu-jen*	Li-shui (1) (temporary)	1867	
		1869–1870	
Kuei Ya-heng *chin-shih*	Wu-chin (4)	3/1865–2/1866	
	T'ai-chou (3)	1867–1870	promotion for good judicial administration
Li K'o-chin *li-yuan*	Yuan-ho (4)	12/1861–4/1862	
	Chia-ting (2) (acting)	4/1862–9/1862	
	Ch'ing-p'u (3)	1863–1864	
	T'an-yuan (3)	1868–1870	replaces the worst magistrate in the province
Li Shuai-lien *chin-shih*	Shang-yuan (3) (acting)	1865–1867	
	Lou h. (2)	8/1867–1/1868	in arrears in transfer of Shang-yuan tax funds
Liang Tui-sheng *chu-jen*	Ch'ung-ming (3)	1863–1865	
	T'ung-chou chih-li chou (3)	1865–1868	recommended for post by Li Hung-chang and Tseng Kuo-fan
Lu Hsiang-yun *chu-jen*	T'ang-shan (3)	1863–1864 1865–1866	
Lu Hung-k'uei *chu-jen*	I-hsing (2)	7/1867–1870	long on virtue, short on ability; deprived of button for failure to hang prisoner in custody board; button returned for burying all coffins
	Chia-ting (2)	7/1870–8/1871	
Ma Pu-ying	Sui-ning (1)	1863–1864	
	T'ang-shan (3)	1864–1865 1866–1868	fails to report on robberies and inquests

Name *Status*	Post (degree of difficulty)	Dates of Service	Comments
Mo Hsiang-chih	Liu-ho (1)	1865–1867	
fu-sheng	Chiang-ning (3)	1867–1869	
		1869–1871	
	Shang-yuan (3)	1873–1874	
	T'ung-chou chih-li chou (3)	1874–1876	
Ni Pao-k'un	Kan-ch'üan (4)	1863	
	Ch'ing-ho (4)	1867–1870	energetic superior official two major merits
	An-tung (3)	1870–1871	
Pai Han	Hua-t'ing (3)	4/1863–9/1865	
chien-sheng	Lou h. (2)	1–2/1865	
Pao Chia-ch'eng	Kao-shun (1)	1861–1865	
pa-kung	Su-ch'ien (3)	1865–1868	
	T'ai-ts'ang chou (3)	1868–1870	promotion for good judicial administration
	Soochow fu (4) (acting)	1868–1869	
	Chiang-ning fu (3)	1870–1871	
Shen Hsi-hua	Wu h. (4) (acting)	1861	
	Yuan-ho (4)	3/1863–7/1863	
	Wu-chiang (3)	9/1862–8/1868	idea for tax rate notices; degraded and transferred because of a case
		8/1869–6/1870	

Name *Status*	Post (degree of difficulty)	Dates of Service	Comments
Shen Wei-t'ien	Wu h. (4)	1861	
chu-jen	Ch'ing-p'u (3)	1865–1866	
	Ch'ang-shu (3)		one major merit for arresting pirates
Sung T'ing	Chiang-tu (4)	6/1865–3/1866	
fu kung-sheng (Chinese bannerman)		4/1867–2/1870	broken old bad habits; promotion for good judicial administration
	Yuan-ho (4)	3/1870–8/1870	
T'ang Han-t'i	T'ung-chou chih-li chou (3) (temporary)	1864–1865	
ling-kung	Ch'ing-p'u (3)	1865–1866	
	Wu h. (4)	9/1866–9/1867	
	T'ai-hu ting (2)	1867	
T'ang Ling	Shang-yuan (3)	1859–1865	
chien-sheng	Kao-yu (3)	1865–1868	
	P'ei chou (3)	1869–1871	
T'ao Shou-lien	Yuan-ho (4)	2/1864–8/1867	
chu-jen	Pao-shan (3)	8/1867–9/1868	not especially good reputation but no big errors
T'ien-tso	Chiang-tu (4) (acting)	3–10/1866	
chu-jen	Wu h. (4) (acting)	9/1867–7/1868	good reputation, capable; one major merit for concluding litigation
	Chia-ting (2) (acting)	7/1868–7/1870	
Ts'ao Wen-huan	Ching-ch'i (2)	1865–1867	
fu-kung	Ch'ung-ming (3)	1866–1869	did not forward all contributions for Nanking reconstruction

Name *Status*	Post (degree of difficulty)	Dates of Service	Comments
Ts'en Ch'ang-wu *chin-shih*	Tan-yang (4)	1866–1867	97% short in amounts forwarded in lieu of taxes; when transferred takes the records; biography in gazetteer
	Lou (2)	8/1868–10/1868	of four previous magistrates greatest in arrears in transfer of funds
Tseng Hui *chien-sheng*	Chiang-p'u (1)	1862–1863	
	T'an-yuan (3)	1864–1868	worst in province; tried for gross malfeasance
Wan Hsueh-ch'ao *fu kung-sheng*	Ching-ch'i (2)	10/1864–1865	
	Hua-t'ing (3)	9/1865–8/1867	
	Yuan-ho (4)	8/1867–3/1870	
	Ch'ang-chou (4)	4–5/1868	
Wan Yeh-feng *chu-jen*	Sui-ning (1)	1864–1865	
	Kan-yü (1)	1869–1870	
Wang Ch'i-chin *ling-kung*	Wu-chin (4) (acting)	2/1866–7/1867	good reputation and ability liked by scholars and people
	Nan-hui (3)	1868	can handle an important post
Wang Fu-an *chien-sheng*	Chia-ting (2) (acting)	9/1863–7/1868	
	Wu h. (4) (acting)	7/1868–5/1870	
Wang Hou-chuang	Feng h. (1)	1862–1864	
	Kan-ch'üan (4)	1868	
Wang K'un-hou *fu chien-sheng*	Chiang-yin (3) (acting)	1867–1869	promotion for good judicial administration
	Tan-t'u (4)	1870	
	Lou (2)		

Name *Status*	Post (degree of difficulty)	Dates of Service	Comments
Wang Tsung-lien *chien-sheng*	Yuan-ho (4)	11/1860–12/1861	
	Tan-t'u (4) (acting)	1867	
	Shang-hai (3)	1867–1870	NCH calls him an "incubus" and reports his removal
	Wu-chin (4)	11/1870–11/1871	
Wang Pao-ch'ang *chien-sheng*	Feng h. (1)	1866–1868	stops warder's extortion; omits litigation registers
	Su-ch'ien (3)	1868–1869	
	Ch'ung-ming (3)	1869–1870	
Wang Yun-hou	Ch'ung-ming (3)	1858–1859	
		1865–1866	did not forward large sum collected for Nanking reconstruction
Wu Ch'eng-lu *chin-shih*	Ch'ang-chou (4) (acting)	7/1869–7/1870	
	T'ai-ts'ang chou (4)	7/1870–1878	biography in gazetteer describes an extraordinary official
Wu Shih-chien	Hsiao h. (1)	1863–1866	
	Feng h. (1)	1870–1872	
Wu Yuan-han	Su-ch'ien (3)	1862–1865	
	Sui-ning (1)	1866	
	Kan-yü	1871	
Wu Chih (Cheng?)-hsiang *chu-jen*	Wu-hsi (3)	1865–1867	diligent and knowledgeable
	Chin-kuei (2) (acting)	1867–1870	deprived of button for not hanging prisoner board; button returned for establishing charitable schools

Name *Status*	Post (degree of difficulty)	Dates of Service	Comments
Yang Te-chang	Shan-yang (4)	1865–1868	
	Kao-yu (4)	1868–1872	Board of Civil Appointment initially denied appointment because he had not had an audience
		1873–1879	
Yen Jung-chi *chin-shih*	Ching-ch'i (2)	1863–10/1864	
	Chiang-yin (3)		appointed but did not serve
	Ch'uan-sha ting (3) (acting)		donates his *yang-lien* for coffins; recommended by Ma Hsin-i
	Pao-shan (3)	9/1869–5/1872	
Yu Ming-hou *chien-sheng*	Chen-yang (2) (acting)	10/1867–8/1869	recommended by Tseng Kuo-fan
	Chin-kuei (2)	1867–1870	
Yü Liang *chien-sheng* (Manchu bannerman)	Ch'ing-ho (4)	1863–1865	
	Kan Yü (1)	1866–1868	

Appendix E
Magistrates Appointed to Devastated Hsiens and to the Head Hsiens

Post (degree of difficulty)	Name, *Status* Date of Service	Prior Posts	Subsequent Posts
Chiang-ning fu (3)	Tu Tsung-ying, *chu-jen* 1864–1869	military merit	Su-Sung-T'ai Taotai
Chiang-ning h. (3)	Wang Hung-hsün, *chu-jen* 1865, acting		Shan-yang (4) 1868–1869
	K'ang Pa-yü, *sui-kung* 1865, temporary		
	Chang I-meng, *chien-sheng* 1865–1867	Liu-ho (1) (1850s)	T'ai-hsing (2)
	Mo Hsiang-chih, *fu-sheng* 1867–1871	Liu-ho (1) 1865–1867	Kao-yu chou (3) 1872–1873 Shang-yuan (3) 1873–1874 T'ung-chou chih-li chou (3) 1874–1876
Shang-yuan (3)	Li Shuai-lien, *chin-shih* 1865–1867, acting		Lou h. (2) 8/1867–1/1868
	Chang Kai-ch'i, *fu-pang* 1867–1871		
Kao-ch'ang (1)	Chang Chin-ch'üan, *chien-sheng* 1865–1868		
	Yang Fu-ting, *chu-jen* 1868–1871, acting		

Post (degree of difficulty)	Name, *Status* Date of Service	Prior Posts	Subsequent Posts
Li-shui (1)	Tseng Shao-chuan, *kung-shih* 1863–1864		
	Ch'eng Tsu-yin, *chu-jen* 1864–1865, 1867–1869		
	Ch'a Hsiang-kao, *chien-sheng* 1865–1867, acting		
Liu-ho (1)	Tai Yuan-fu, *chien-sheng* 1864, acting		
	Yu Kuan-chih, *fu chien-sheng* 1864, acting		
	Mo Hsiang-chih, *fu-sheng* 1865–1867, acting		see Chiang-ning h.
Tan-yang (4)	Feng Wei, *fu-kung*		Hsin-yang (2) 7/1867–10/1868, acting
	Shen Hua-ch'eng		
	Chang Pao-heng, *chin-shih*	Wu h. (4) 8/1865–9/1866	
	Chin Hung-pao, *fu-kung*		deprived of rank and office (*ko-chih*) for over-collection of taxes
	Ts'en Ch'ang-wu, *chin-shih* 1867		Lou h. (2) 8/1868–10/1868
	Wang Wan, *chu-jen*		

Post (degree of difficulty)	Name, *Status* Date of Service	Prior Posts	Subsequent Posts
I-hsing (2)	Chang Chin, *chu-jen* 2/1864–6/1864		K'un-shan (2) 8/1866–7/1868
	Chang En-p'ei, *fu-kung* 6/1864–12/1864		
	Ch'eng Chi-lu, *chin-shih* 12/1864–7/1867		impeached and dismissed for over-collection of fees
	Lu Hung-k'uei, *chu-jen* 7/1867–1870		Chia-ting (2) 7/1870–8/1871
Ching-ch'i (2)	Yen Jung-chi, *chin-shih* 1863–10/1864		Ch'uan-sha ting (3) 1869, acting Pao-shan (3) 9/1869–5/1872
	Wan Hsueh-ch'ao, *fu-kung* 10/1864–1865		Hua-t'ing (3) 9/1865–8/1867 Yuan-ho (4) 8/1867–3/1870
	Ts'ao Wen-huan, *fu-kung* 1865–1867		Ch'ung-ming (3) 1867–1869
	Chang Ch'iao-lin, *ling-kung* 1867–1868	Wu h. (4) 10/1863–2/1864	impeached and dismissed
	Chang Shang-te, *chien-sheng* 1868–1869		
Ch'ing-p'u (3)	Li K'o-chin, *li-yuan* 1863–1864	Yuan-ho (4) 12/1861–4/1862 Chia-ting 4/1862–9/1862, acting	T'an-yuan (3) 1868–1870

Post (degree of difficulty)	Name, *Status* Date of Service	Prior Posts	Subsequent Posts
Ch'ing-p'u (3)	Shen Wei-t'ien, *chu-jen* 1865–1866	Wu h. (4) 1859–1861	Ch'ang-shu (3)
	T'ang Han-t'i, *kung-sheng* 1866		Wu h. (4) 9/1866–9/1867
	Ch'ien Pao-chuan, *fu-kung* 1866–1868, 1870–1871		Ch'ang-chou (4) 5/1868–2/1869, acting
	Ch'en Ch'i-yuan, *ling-kung* 1868–1870	Nan-hui (3) 1867–1868	Hsin-yang (2) 10/1870–4/1871
Yuan-ho (4)	T'ao Shou-lien, *chu-jen* 2/1864–8/1867		Pao-shan (3) 8/1867–9/1869
	Wan Hsueh-ch'ao, *fu-kung* 8/1867–3/1870	see Ching-ch'i (2)	
	Sung T'ing, *fu-kung* (Chinese bannerman) 3/1870–8/1870	Chiang-tu (4) 1865–1866, 1867–1870	
Wu h. (4)	Chang Ch'iao-lin, *ling-kung* 10/1863–2/1864		Ching-ch'i 1867–1868, impeached and dismissed
	Ts'ao I-chih 3/1864–8/1865, acting		
	Chang Pao-heng, *chin-shih* 8/1865–9/1866		Tan-yang (4)
	T'ang Han-t'i, *ling-kung* 9/1866–9/1867	T'ung-chou chih-li chou (3) 1864–1865, temporary Ch'ing-p'u (3) 1866	T'ai-hu ting (2) 1867–?

Post (degree of difficulty)	Name, *Status* Date of Service	Prior Posts	Subsequent Posts
Wu h. (4)	T'ien-tso, *chu-jen* 9/1867–7/1868	Chiang-tu (4) 3/1866–10/1866	Chia-ting (2) 7/1868–7/1870
	Wang Fu-an, *chien-sheng* 7/1868–5/1871	Chia-ting (2) 9/1863–7/1868, acting	
Ch'ang-chou (4)	K'uai Te-mo, *fu-kung* 8/1864–4/1868		T'ai-ts'ang chou (3) 1867–1870 Chiang-ning fu (3) 1870–1871
	Ch'ien Pao-chuan, *fu-kung* 5/1868–2/1869	Ch'ing-p'u (3) 1866–1868	Ch'ing-p'u 1870–1871

Abbreviations

CFTL	*Ch'in-ting liu-pu ch'u-fen tse-li.*
CMCY	Juan Pen-yen, *Ch'iu-mu ch'u-yen.*
CP (Chü-heng)	*Ching-pao,* Chü-heng edition
CP (Shantung)	*Ching-pao,* Shantung edition.
CPLKI	Feng Kuei-fen, *Chiao-pin-lu k'ang-i*
CT:KCW	*Tsung-li ko-kuo shih-wu ya-men ch'ing-t'ang: Chiao-wu pu, Kiangsu chiao-wu.*
FO	Great Britain Foreign Office
17	*General Correspondence, China*
228	*Embassy and Consular Archives, China*
FHCS	Huang Liu-hung, *Fu-hui ch'üan-shu*
FWKT	Ting Jih-ch'ang, *Fu-wu kung-tu*
HAHL	*Hsing-an hui-lan*
HCCSWP	*Huang-ch'ao ching-shih wen-pien*
HCCSWHP	*Huang-ch'ao ching-shih wen hsu-pien*
HCTK	Feng Kuei-fen, *Hsien-chih-t'ang kao*
HT	*Ch'in-ting Ta-Ch'ing hui-tien*
HTSL	*Ch'in-ting Ta-Ch'ing hui-tien shih-li*
IWSM:TC	*Ch'ou-pan i-wu shih-mo,* T'ung-chih reign
KH	Kuang-hsu reign
MLSCY	Ting Jih-ch'ang, comp., *Mu-ling shu chi-yao*
NCDN	*North China Daily News*
NCH	*North China Herald*
PLSK	Ting Jih-ch'ang, *Pai-lan-shan-kuan ku-chin t'i-shih fu-tz'u ying-lien*
SL:TC	*Ta-Ch'ing Mu-tsung-i (T'ung-chih) huang-ti shih-lu*
TC	T'ung-chih reign

TCCCS	Ting Jih-ch'ang, *Ting Chung-ch'eng cheng-shu*
FanWKT	*Fan-wu kung-tu*
FWTK	*Fu-wu tsou-kao*
HHKT	*Hsun-hu kung-tu*
TCLL	*Ta-Ch'ing Lü-li hui-t'ung hsin-pien*
TCSMS	*Kiangsu Ts'ai-cheng shuo-ming shu*
THTKTI	*Tao-hsien-t'ung-kuang ssu-ch'ao tsou-i*
TLTI	Hsueh Yun-sheng, *Tu-li ts'un-i*

Notes

1. INTRODUCTION

1. See, for example, Kung Tzu-chen in Ping-ti Ho, *The Ladder of Success in Imperial China* (Chicago, 1964), p. 266; Chang Hsueh-ch'eng in David Nivison, *The Life and Thought of Chang Hsueh-ch'eng* (Stanford University Press, 1966), p. 268; and Wang Hui-tsu in James H. Cole, "Shaohsing: Studies in Ch'ing Social History" (PhD dissertation, Stanford University, 1975), p. 62.
2. Yuan Shou-ting, *T'u-min lu,* 1836. Yuan was a magistrate in the 1740s and 1750s.
3. On the political ambiance of the early nineteenth century, see James Polachek, "Literati Groups and Literati Politics in Nineteenth Century China" (PhD dissertation, University of California, Berkeley, 1976), pp. 29–32; and Hao Chang, *Liang Ch'i-ch'ao and Intellectual Transition in China, 1890–1907* (Cambridge, Mass., 1971), pp. 7–34.
4. The phrase was used by Mary Wright to describe T'ung-chih officials, but it is equally appropriate for the earlier period; Mary Wright, *The Last Stand of Chinese Conservatism: The T'ung-chih Restoration, 1862–1874* (New York, 1966), p. 66.
5. Thomas A. Metzger, *The Internal Organization of Ch'ing Bureaucracy* (Cambridge, Mass., 1973), pp. 76–79; and Metzger, *Escape from Predicament* (New York, 1977), pp. 154–158.
6. The phrase "exemplary center" is drawn from Hao Chang's description of Tseng Kuo-fan in "The Intellectual Context of Reform," in Paul Cohen and John Schrecker, eds., *Reform in Nineteenth Century China* (Cambridge, Mass., 1976), p. 146.
7. Hao Chang, *Liang Ch'i-ch'ao,* p. 26.
8. Benjamin Schwartz, *In Search of Wealth and Power* (Cambridge, Mass., 1964), p. 239, uses the phrase "Faustian energy."

9. Hao Chang, *Liang Ch'i-ch'ao*, pp. 28–31.
10. On capital appeals and Chia-ch'ing's opening of the *yen-lu*, see Jonathan Ocko, "Justice on Appeal: The Capital Appeals System in Ch'ing China," in Brian McKnight, ed., *Law and the State in Traditional East Asia* (forthcoming from University of Hawaii Press).
11. *CFTL*, 1:1.
12. Quoted in Polachek, "Literati Politics," p. 449.
13. *Kuang-hsu Tung-hua lu*, p. 589; Polachek, "Literati Politics," pp. 84–86.
14. On the role of Mu-ch'ang-a, see Philip Kuhn and Susan Mann Jones, "Dynastic Decline and the Roots of Rebellion" in John K. Fairbank, ed., *The Cambridge History of China* (New York, 1978), 10, 145–146.
15. See pp. 148–151.
16. Throughout this study, the terms "gentry" and "local elite" are generally used interchangeably. Also see pp. 135–144.
17. Hilary J. Beattie, *Land and Lineage in China* (Cambridge, England, 1979), p. 129.
18. Cf. Parts II and III of Joseph Levenson's *The Problem of Monarchical Decay*, in which Levenson argues that the challenge of Taiping ideology resolved the tension between Confucian literati and the monarch; Joseph Levenson, *Confucian China and Its Modern Fate: A Trilogy* (Berkeley, 1968), pp. 25–116.
19. See Wright, pp. 21–42, for a discussion of the Cooperative Policy, and Jonathan Ocko, "Defensive Diplomacy, A Case Study in Ch'ing Foreign Relations: Ting Jih-ch'ang as Shanghai taotai" (unpublished manuscript) for description of the Ch'ing's holding operation against foreigners during the 1860s.
20. G. William Skinner, "Regional Urbanization in Nineteenth Century China," in G. William Skinner, ed., *The City in Late Imperial China* (Stanford, 1977), p. 247.
21. For the views of some of Ting's colleagues, see Wang K'ai-t'ai (late T'ung-chih Governor of Fukien) in *IWSM:TC*, 99:77b; Chang Yao-tung (Ting's successor as governor of Kiangsu) in *CP* (Chü-heng), TC 8/4/6; Kuo Sung-tao in *Yang-chih shu-wu ch'üan-chi* (1872), 13:5b.
22. Daniel Bays, *China Enters the Twentieth Century: Chang Chih-tung and the Issues of a New Age, 1895–1909* (Ann Arbor, 1978), p. 3.

2. THE MAN AND THE PROVINCE

1. See p. 270, note 15.
2. Ting Ch'iao-yin, "Hsien-tsu k'ao chung-ch'eng Ting-kung hui Jih-ch'ang shih-lueh," handwritten manuscript. (I should like to thank Lü Shih-

ch'iang of the Academia Sinica, Taipei, for supplying me with a copy of this document.) Wen Chou-ming, "Kwangtung hsin t'ung-chih lieh-chuan kao Ting Jih-ch'ang," *Kuo-li Chung-shan ta-hsueh wen-shih-hsueh yen-chiu-so yueh-k'an,* 2:5 (1934), p. 115. The "bread and water" phrase is from *PLSK,* 1:5.

3. *PLSK,* 1:12, 15, 18b–19; Wen Chou-ming, p. 115. On Chang Na-t'ai, see *Feng-shun hsien-chih,* 4:4–4b.
4. *Feng-shun hsien-chih,* 6:17.
5. *PLSK,* 1:12, 2:22.
6. On *mu-yu,* see T'ung-tsu Ch'ü, *Local Government in China Under the Ch'ing* (Cambridge, Mass., 1962), pp. 93–115.
7. Watt remarks on the plethora of handbooks available to aid novice magistrates, but these guides seem to have been more widely read among *mu-yu* than officials; John R. Watt, *The District Magistrate in Late Imperial China* (New York, 1972), pp. 57–58, pp. 267–268 n. 56, 57.
8. *PLSK,* 1:4b, 23; *Feng-shun hsien-chih,* 2:5; Jao Tsung-i, *Ch'ao-chou-chih hui-pien* (Hong Kong, 1965), p. 674.
9. *Wan-an hsien-chih* (1877), 9:17; *PLSK,* 4:7–8; *PLSK* ts'z, p. 6.
10. Wen Chou-ming, p. 115.
11. *Ch'ing-shih lieh-chuan,* 55: 17b; Wen Chou-ming, p. 115.
12. On Li's service in Tseng's *mu-fu*, see Kwang-ching Liu, "The Confucian as Patriot and Pragmatist: Li Hung-chang's Formative Years, 1823–1866," *Harvard Journal of Asiatic Studies,* 30 (1970), pp. 10–11.
13. The quotation is drawn from Kwang-ching Liu, "The Confucian as Patriot," p. 45. Cf. Wang Erh-min who argues that Ting's political views and conduct were always consistent with Li's; *Huai-chün chih* (Taipei, 1967), p. 386.
14. Chao Lieh-wen, *Neng-ching-chü jih-chi,* TC 6/9/4, 6/9/17; Lü Shih-ch'iang, *Ting Jih-ch'ang yü tzu-ch'iang yun-tung* (Taipei, 1972), p. 377. Wang Erh-min suggests that Tseng's hostility to Ting was engendered by Ting's role as a financial agent for Li Hung-chang; *Huai-chün chih,* p. 257.
15. On Ting in Tseng's *mu-fu,* see Wang Ting-an, *Ch'iu-ch'ueh chai ti-tzu chi* (1876 preface), 28:34.
16. Tseng Kuo-fan, *Tseng Wen-cheng kung ch'üan-chi Tsou-kao*, Shih-chieh shu-chü, ed., 2, 485; Li Hung-chang, *Peng-liao han-kao,* 2:17, 3:3, 4b. Thomas Kennedy notes that Tseng gathered skilled engineers at Anking to work on armaments; Thomas Kennedy, *Arms of Kiangnan: Modernization of the Chinese Ordnance Industry, 1860–1895* (Boulder, Westview Press, 1978), pp. 35–36.
17. Wen Chou-ming, p. 116. On Ting's promotion, see *Ch'ing-shih lieh-chuan,* 55:17b.

18. *IWSM:TC,* 20:13b–14b; Li Hung-chang, *Peng-liao han-kao,* 4:15. Tseng also made an effort to have Ting assigned to his own staff; Tseng Kuo-fan, *Tsou-kao,* p. 603. Wang Erh-min in his study of the Huai Army emphasized Ting's importance to Li as a weapons and procurement specialist; *Huai-chün chih,* p. 313.
19. *Ch'ing-shih lieh-chuan,* 55:17b.
20. See Jonathan K. Ocko, "Ting Jih-ch'ang and Restoration Kiangsu, 1864–1870: Rhetoric and Reality" (PhD dissertation, Yale University, 1975), pp. 228–244, esp. 238–244.
21. *IWSM:TC,* 43:23b.
22. On Gordon and the role of the EVA in the suppression of the Taiping, see Richard J. Smith, *Mercenaries and Mandarins* (Millwood, N.Y., 1979).
23. *IWSM:TC,* 24:29, 25:25.
24. British Museum, Gordon-Bell Collection, 52–387, May 17, 1864, Hart to Gordon; 52–389, June 2, 1864, Gordon to Mother; 52–389, July 20, 1864, Gordon to Freddy.
25. *TCCCS:HHKT,* 1:2–2b; Wen Chou-ming, p. 116.
26. *TCCCS:FWTK,* 1:1b.
27. Ting's collection was catalogued by Mu Yu-chih, *Ch'ih-ching-chai shu-mu* (1870), and by Chiang Piao, *Feng-shun Ting-shih Ch'ih-ching chai shu-mu* (1898). On the history of the collection, see Hu Tao-ching, "Ch'ing tai ti Shanghai ts'ang-shu chia," in Shanghai T'ung-she, comp., *Shang-hai yen-chiu tzu-liao* (Shanghai, 1936), p. 180; also see Hsu Shao-ch'i, *Kwangtung ts'ang-shu chi-shih shih* (Hong Kong, 1963), pp. 20–22.

    On Ting's circle of acquaintances, see *PLSK,* 5:15; Chin Liang, *Chin-shih jen-wu chih* (Taipei, 1955), p. 216; Feng Kuei-fen, *Meng-nai shih-kao* (Soochow, 1877), p. 36b. Through his cataloger, Mu Yu-chih, Ting had contact with other scholar-officials, such as Wu Ta-ch'eng; Ku T'ing-ling, *Wu K'o-chai hsien-sheng nien-p'u* (Peiping, 1935), p. 26.
28. See pp. 36, 37, 54–55, 126, 140, 142–143.
29. Herman Ooms, *Charismatic Bureaucrat: A Political Biography of Matsudaira Sadanobu* (Chicago, 1975), pp. 33, 129–133.
30. Tetsuo Najita, *Japan: The Intellectual Foundations of Modern Japanese Politics* (University of Chicago Press, 1980), p. 38.
31. *PLSK,* 5:62.
32. Skinner, "Regional Urbanization," pp. 212–215.
33. Ibid., p. 217.
34. *HTSL,* 24:1, 5b, 6–6b; H. S. Brunnert and V. V. Hagelstrom, *Present Day Political Organization of China* (Taipei reprint), pp. 405, 406.
35. Access from the Yangtze to the Grand Canal, the main north-south line

of communication, was hampered by Taiping control of the approaches to the Canal; Yu-wen Jen, *The Taiping Revolutionary Movement* (New Haven, 1973), pp. 377–389.

36. *SL:TC,* 123:11b.
37. Tseng Kuo-fan periodically evaluated both the senior and local officials serving under him in Kiangsu, but there does not seem to have been a formal *ta-chi* until 1870. For the senior officials, see Tseng Kuo-fan, *Hsiang-hsiang Tseng-shih wen-hsien* (Taipei, 1965). Some local officials are rated in Tseng, *Tsou-kao,* pp. 815–816. For the court's response to Tseng's recommendations and for material on the *ta-chi,* see *SL:TC,* 213:27, 249:5, 259:9.
38. See pp. 75–76, 85–86, 160–161.
39. Upon becoming Governor, Ting reported to the court that he had toured the province; *TCCCS:FWTK,* 1:6–6b. But he must not have gone to Kiangpei, for he subsequently admitted to Tseng Kuo-fan that he was ignorant of conditions there; *FWKT,* 30:13.
40. Kung-chuan Hsiao, *Rural China: Imperial Control in the Nineteenth Century* (Seattle, 1967), pp. 373–374.
41. See, for example, *FWKT,* 30:13.
42. Ping-ti Ho, "The Salt Merchants of Yang-chou: A Study of Commercial Capitalism in Eighteenth-century China," *Harvard Journal of Asiatic Studies,* 17:130–168 (1954).
43. Li Chang-fu, *Chiang-su* (n.p., 1936), p. 13.
44. Ping-ti Ho, *Ladder of Success,* p. 232.
45. Ibid.; Yeh-chien Wang, *Land Taxation in Imperial China* (Cambridge, Mass., 1973), p. 75.
46. P'an Kuang-tan, "Chin-tai Su-chou ti jen-ts'ai," *She-hui k'o-hsueh,* 1.1:49–98 (October 1935).
47. Colin P. Mackerras, *The Rise of the Peking Opera 1770–1870: Social Aspects of the Theater in Manchu China* (London, 1972), pp. 118, 120, 136.
48. P'an Kuang-tan, p. 70.
49. Ibid., pp. 97–98.
50. Ocko, "Justice on Appeal"; see also pp. 88–89, 139.
51. *CT:KCW,* 3:1, p. 5025, Document 619.
52. Wright, pp. 128–129.
53. Yuji Muramatsu, "A Documentary Study of Chinese Landlordism in late Ch'ing and early Republican Kiangnan," *Bulletin of the School of Oriental and African Studies,* 29 (1966), 595.
54. Yeh-chien Wang, "The Impact of the Taiping Rebellion on Population in Southern Kiangsu," *Papers on China,* 19 (1965), p. 149.
55. See pp. 96–99.

56. Wang Yeh-chien, "Impact of the Taiping," p. 148.
57. Yu-wen Jen, pp. 495–510.
58. *TCCCS:FWTK,* 4:11.
59. *TCCCS:FanWKT,* 11:1b–4b; *FWKT,* 5:5–5b, 10:1b; *Hong Kong Daily Press,* January 4, 1864; FO 17/496/68, Alcock to Stanley, March 24, 1868.
60. *FWKT,* 46:5.
61. *TCCCS:FWTK,* 2:2–6b.
62. The northwest was pacified in 1873 as a result of Tso Tsung-t'ang's strenuous efforts; Wright, p. 113.
63. *TCCCS:FWTK,* 5:30.
64. *SL:TC,* 240:23.

3. Rectifying Society

1. Philip A. Kuhn, *Rebellion and Its Enemies in Late Imperial China* (Cambridge, Mass., 1970), especially pp. 189–225.
2. The misuse of *t'uan-lien* was prevalent throughout Kiangpei; see *Huai-an fu-chih* (1884), 2:4b. For an ongoing case of *t'uan-lien* difficulties, see *SL:TC,* 120:9–10, 121:23–23b, 123:11b–12. For specific evidence of bandit penetration of *t'uan-lien,* see *P'ei-hsien chih* (1918), 2:30 and *Ch'ing-shih kao,* 434:7.
3. *FWKT,* 8:10. For an example of a former Taiping official who transformed himself into a putatively upright citizen, see *CP* (Chü-heng), TC 7/5/27. The evidence for a rebellion was a wooden seal; *FWKT,* 5:26–26b. According to the *North China Daily News* (*NCDN*), the daily edition of the *North China Herald* (*NCH*), there were several thousand people involved in the original plot (June 16, 1869) and thousands more junkmen and coolies willing to join once it began (June 24, 1869). Ting's assessment was far less alarmist.
4. *SL:TC,* 132:24. Also see court order to Kuo Sung-tao and Mao Hung-pin to control the returned veterans plundering Fatshan near Canton; *SL:TC,* 109:3b.
5. Tseng Kuo-fan, *Tsou-kao* (Shih-chieh shu-chü edition), pp. 661–662.
6. *FWKT,* 19:2b.
7. Ting feared that the men would be a pool of potential recruits for any rebellion; see *FWKT,* 28:10b–11, 37:13b–14.
8. *NCH,* March 18, 1865. Ting spared no expense in offering rewards and hiring police. By his own reckoning, Ting punished more than 100 and forced more than 8,000 to return to their native places; *TCCCS:HHKT,* 5:12b.
9. On Tseng's measures, see *NCH,* July 3, 1868.

10. *FWKT,* 19:2b–3. Throughout the manuscript I have replicated Ting's emphasis.
11. See memorials by Ting, *CP* (Chü-heng), TC 8/10/28; Ma Hsin-i, *SL:TC,* 260:18b; and on seizure of Pao-shan, *NCH,* March 22, 1870.
12. *TCCCS:FWTK,* 3:3b–4. On Feng and P'an, see Arthur Hummel, *Eminent Chinese of the Ch'ing Period* (Taipei, 1967), pp. 241–242, 607–608. For a discussion of the role played by this gentry nexus, see James Polachek, "Gentry Hegemony: Soochow in the T'ung-chih Restoration," in Frederic Wakeman and Carolyn Grant, eds., *Conflict and Control in Late Imperial China* (Berkeley, 1975), pp. 211–256.
13. See, for example, *Kuang-hsu Tung-hua lu* (Taipei reprint), pp. 408 (KH 3/6), 1192–1193 (KH 7/9), 1207–1208 (KH 7/10), 1219–1220 (KH 7/11), 1231–1237 (KH 7/12); Ting Pao-chen, *Tsou-kao* (Taipei reprint), pp. 2507–2512, 2639–2646.
14. *FWKT,* 18:4–4b; *CP* (Chü-heng), TC 8/10/28. Also see p. 243, note 44. Ting maintained his support for summary execution of serious bandits, *yu-yung* or not, on the ground that the old regulations permitted local officials to be perfunctory in their handling of armed robberies and banditry; *Kuang-hsu Tung-hua lu* (KH 3/6) p. 408.
15. Lin Tse-hsu once wrote that, though times might still be hard after flood relief was distributed and tax exemptions approved, there was no longer any excuse for criminal activity; Lin Tse-hsu, *Lin Wen-ch'ung-kung cheng-shu* (Taipei reprint), p. 201.
16. *FWKT,* 27:2b. Coastal pirates, particularly in T'ung-chou near the mouth of the Yangtze River, were also a problem; *FWKT,* 2:1, 44: 4b–5.
17. *CP* (Chü-heng), TC 7/1/4–5. Kuo's official biography takes particular note of his efforts to control the pirates; *Ch'ing-shih kao,* 432:11.
18. *FWKT,* 19:1b, 21:14.
19. *FWKT,* 20:3b.
20. *FWKT,* 27:1. Tu Wen-lan may have been influenced by Feng Kuei-fen's proposal that village directors be elected to handle minor civil litigation; see p. 261, note 59. On Ting's attitude toward directors and their role in sub-district government, see pp. 142–143.
21. *FWKT,* 23:12; cf. Ting's use of bullying but able runners, p. 135.
22. For the regulations, see *FWKT,* 27:1b–5; *Kiangsu Sheng-li,* "Nieh," TC 7, pp. 20–24b. For Ting's memorial and the court's approving response, see *TCCCS:FWTK,* 3:2–2b and *SL:TC,* 242:4b–5.
23. The prices were: (1) 800 cash per fowling piece (*niao-ch'iang*); (2) 1,400 cash per two-man gingal (*t'ai-ch'iang*); (3) 30 cash per sword or spear; (4) 80 cash per catty of copper shot; and (5) 30 cash per catty of iron shot; *FWKT,* 27:3.

24. Ting's gun-control policy parallels one implemented in Shantung in the late 1840s; see *THTKTI,* 2.823.
25. Violators of this provision were to be punished according to the penalties for the private manufacture of military weapons. One who cast such weapons, or, presumably, one who built such a boat, was to be decapitated. His family was to be enslaved and all cognizant neighbors who had not reported him to the authorities were to be strangled; *TCLL,* p. 1633.
26. The warrants had been farmed out to the boat-owners themselves for serving. Lictors also impounded boats for use in serving warrants and then exacted payments as high as 3,000 cash to exempt the boat-owner; *FWKT,* 36:4b–5.
27. On the policy of encouraging agriculture as an element in bandit-suppression campaigns, see *MLSCY,* 9:19b.
28. Wright, p. 137.
29. Ibid.; *CP* (Chü-heng), TC 6/7/18. Even in the wake of the Rebellion, official laxness allowed the very "weed people" (*yu-min*) that the *pao-chia* was supposed to control to serve as *pao-chia* heads (*chia-chang*); *SL:TC,* 140:18–18b.
30. *CP* (Chü-heng), TC 6/7/18.
31. *Chiao-hui hsin-pao* 2:65 (December 11, 1869).
32. Ting Jih-ch'ang, comp., *Pao-chia shu chi-yao* (Taipei, 1968; fascimile reproduction of 1870 edition), pp. 22–23, 25–26, 97–100.
33. Ting in *CP* (Chü-heng), TC 8/10/28; Ma Hsin-i in *SL:TC,* 260:18b. Tightening up *pao-chia* regulations obviously was also a theme in other discussions of bandit suppression; see *MLSCY,* 9:19b, 30–34b.
34. *FWKT,* 32:2.
35. *FWKT,* 43:13. For a fuller discussion of Ting's attitude toward the gentry, see pp. 142–144, 175–177.
36. *TCCCS:FWTK,* 3:2–2b.
37. *HCCSWP,* 68:4.
38. *CP* (Chü-heng), TC 8/10/17. A summary of this memorial is in *SL:TC,* 269:3b–4. Ting was, in fact, punished with a one-grade demotion for failing to take adequately strict precautions in advance, but was allowed to remain in office and make monetary compensation (*ti-hsiao*).
39. *CP* (Chü-heng), TC 8/10/28. (This memorial is not in the *Shih-lu.*) *CP* (Chü-heng), TC 8/11/24; *SL:TC,* 271:9–10.
40. Ma Hsin-i, *Ma Tuan-min kung tsou-i,* 8:36–40b. The speculation was fueled by the fact that Ting's son, Hui-heng, devised an absence from the province during the investigation and trial. Although Hui-heng was proven innocent, his father, nonetheless, asked for his dismissal. Hui-heng's subsequent promotions (*Feng-shun hsien-chih,* 6:17b), and recep-

tion by Weng T'ung-ho and Chin Liang (*Chin-shih jen-wu chih,* p. 216) suggest that his reputation was untarnished by the whole incident. His biography in *Ch'ing-shih lieh-chuan,* 55:21, offers, however, a more negative assessment of Hui-heng's behavior. Ting's clansman and nephew were dismissed but pardoned from a beating. Only the servants and brothel-owner, commoners all, actually received corporal punishment; Ma Hsin-i, 8:39–40.

41. *NCDN,* August 11, 1869, August 19, 1869, October 18, 1869, December 8, 1869; *NCH,* January 1, 1870. The court dismissed as baseless Wang Chia-pi's charge that Ma Hsin-i had been killed to prevent him from trying Hui-heng's case. It pointed out that the trial had been concluded in Hui-heng's favor before the assassination; *SL:TC,* 299:3b–4. On Wang's hostility to Ting, see Lü Shih-ch'iang, *Ting Jih-ch'ang,* pp. 363-365. The *NCDN* of August 19 suggested that some of the false rumors about the case had been planted by Chinese opponents to Ting's support of Yung Wing's Chinese Educational Mission.
42. See pp. 60–61.
43. *FWKT,* 41:14b. Ying Pao-shih probably was the man to whom this remark was addressed. Ying had preceded and then succeeded Ting as Shanghai Taotai, and had just finished serving as Acting Financial Commissioner; *Su-chou fu-chih,* 22:23, 35b.
44. Chao Lieh-wen, *Neng-ching-chü jih-chi,* TC 6/6/12. Although Chao had made this criticism in private, it is likely that he expressed similar views to a broader audience, for he was extremely hostile to Ting; see Lü Shih-ch'iang, *Ting Jih-ch'ang,* pp. 365–370.
45. Feng Kuei-fen, *Meng-nai shih-kao,* pp. 36–36b; see also p. 163.
46. *FWKT,* 33:12b.
47. *FWKT,* 33:3.
48. *FWKT,* 33:12b.
49. *FWKT,* 33:12b.
50. *FWKT,* 36:3.
51. The *Chiao-hui hsin-pao* 2:65 (December 11, 1869), reported that, in Soochow alone, 3,700 dens were closed. The American Consul in Shanghai also made favorable observations on the effectiveness of Ting's measures; United States Department of State, *Despatches from United States Consuls in Shanghai,* Jenkins to Fish, July 11, 1870. Since the Convention of Peking in 1860 had legalized importation of opium, the Chinese had been confronted with how to deal with the dens. In 1861, a Censor's suggestion not to punish the building-owner had been rejected, and, in 1862, the court determined to hold building-owners responsible for dens in their buildings according to the laws on places of gambling; see *Fen-fa t'iao-li,* TC 1 "Yin-ch'ieh wen-ni hou chün liu ko-fan chi k'ai-

she yen-kuan," and TC 2 "Ssu-hou ch'iang-tao tzu-shou, jen-min k'ai-she yen-kuan, fu-nü fan-mou."

52. For the proclamation, see *TCCCS:FanWKT,* 10:9b–10b. On the law, see *TCLL,* pp. 1507–1509. Hsu Ch'ien-hsueh, who coined the epithet "greatest crime" was a Kiangsu native, Vice President of the Board of Rites, and nephew of Ku Yen-wu, also urged that men who delayed burial of their parents be forbidden to take the examinations; *HCCSWP,* 63:1. Ting noted that such a bar was an ancient regulation found in the *Li-chi* (Book of rites), *TCCCS:FanWKT,* 10:9b–10b; also see *HCCSWP,* 63:2b–3.
53. Cf. *HCCSWP,* 63:13b; Emily Ahern, *The Cult of the Dead in a Chinese Village* (Stanford, 1971), p. 181. Ahern notes that in Ch'inan, Taiwan, it is believed that the ancestor himself rather than the land is the source of geomantic benefits. The determining factor, however, is not the deceased's virtue, but the comfortableness of the grave. Although Ting himself searched for a good site for his mother's grave, he may have done so only with prodding; see letter to him from Li Hung-chang *P'eng-liao han-kao,* 13:7b. *Feng-shui* was also attacked on the ground that belief in it served only selfish ends; *HCCSWP,* 63:18.
54. Lao-tzu was a potent example, since much of the theory and practice of *feng-shui* were, and still are, based on Taoist concepts; see Stephen Feutchwang, "The Cosmology of Feng-shui" (PhD dissertation, University of London, 1969).
55. *TCCCS:FanWKT,* 11:7b; *Su-chou fu-chih* (1883), Chapter 24; *Wu-chiang hsien-chih* (1879), 2:7; also see discussion on pp. 43–44.
56. See *SL:TC,* 254:19 for a court order to provide public funds in order to equalize differences between rich and poor hsiens' *shan-t'ang.*
57. On the effective work by magistrates, see *CP* (Chü-heng), TC 8/8/23; *FWKT,* 37:15b. On the persistence of the custom, see *Kiangsu Sheng-li Hsu-pien,* "Fan" Kuang-hsu 17, "T'ung-ch'ih li-tsang pao-lu shih-kuan"; *Ch'ung-ming hsien-chih* (1881), 4:4; *Ch'uan-sha hsien-chih* (1935), 14:5–5b; *FWKT,* 28:13, 36:7b–8. At least in Feng hsien, the custom was observed by scholars as well as commoners; *Feng hsien-chih* (1877), 19:2.
58. The bones were washed and then placed in the jar. In Hai-men ting, the jars were placed on the ridgepole of the house to ward off floods; *FWKT,* 36:7b–8. For the relations of this practice to *feng-shui,* see Maurice Freedman, *Chinese Lineage and Society: Fukien and Kwangtung* (London, 1966), pp. 122–123.
59. *HCCSWP,* 63:9–11.
60. Ting's prohibition is in *FWKT,* 27:9 and *Kiangsu Sheng-li,* "Nieh," TC 7, pp. 25–25b. For full legal provisions on meddling with graves and

coffins, see *TCLL,* p. 2242. The crime was less serious if the coffin had not yet been buried; *TCLL,* p. 2259.

61. The *Ch'ung-ming hsien-chih,* 4:4, reports that, although the custom of cremation was gradually eliminated, coffins were still left exposed.
62. Barbara E. Ward, "Varieties of the Conscious Model: The Fishermen of South China," in Michael Banton, ed., *The Relevance of Models for Social Anthropology* (New York, 1965), pp. 113–138.
63. Alex Woodside, "Family Education in Eighteenth Century China," paper presented to the Harvard New England China Seminar, April 1974 (cited with permission of the author); Jonathan Spence, *The Death of Woman Wang* (New York, 1979), pp. 71–76; Arthur P. Wolf and Chieh-shang Huang, *Marriage and Adoption in China* (Stanford, 1980), pp. 227–228.
64. For the legal penalties and a discussion of the discrepancies in possible sentences, see *TCLL,* pp. 1029–1038 and *TLTI,* pp. 295–297 (105–01); also *TCCCS:FanWKT,* 4:6; *Ch'ung-ming hsien-chih,* 4:3b. For a discussion of widowhood as a source of family dissension, see Jonathan Ocko, "Family Disharmony as Seen in Ch'ing Legal Cases," paper prepared for ACLS-NEH Conference on "Orthodoxy and Heterodoxy in Late Imperial China," Montecito, California, August 1981.
65. *TCCCS:FanWKT,* 4:7–8.
66. "Proper" women did remarry willingly. This is explicitly stated in *Nan-hui hsien-chih,* (1878), 20:6b, and is implied in the provisions of the Penal Code; also see Wolf and Huang, *Marriage and Adoption,* p. 228.
67. Prince Kung once wrote that such attitudes were dangerous. "Those who would destroy the state must first eliminate these principles of social usage (*li*)"; Wright, p. 62. There is no indication that Ting ever inflicted the harsh sentences the Penal Code stipulated for those found guilty of forcing remarriage or of kidnapping, but in 1880 Shen Pao-chen, then Liang-kiang Governor-General, approved the summary execution of two men found guilty of kidnapping widows; *Kiangsu Sheng-li San-pien,* "Fan," KH 6, p. 4.
68. *TCCCS:FanWKT,* 4:8. Equally important, of course, was the honoring and protection of unmarried women of virtue. Ting impeached and dismissed an official who failed to catch a rapist; *FWKT,* 14:8; *CP* (Shantung), TC 8/2/9–10. On fault of directors, *Kiangsu Sheng-li San-pien,* "Nieh," KH 2, p. 14b; on plays, *Shen Pao* (Taipei reprint), p. 21087. For the role of *t'u-tung* in sub-county government, see pp. 137–138.
69. Kuang-hsu provincial regulations required the bureau in charge of the lecture system (*hsiang-yueh*) to certify the commitment of those widows who expressed a desire to remain chaste and to investigate any

rumors or accusations about their conduct or about attempts on their chastity; *Kiangsu Sheng-li San-pien,* "Fan," KH 6, pp. 1–3b.

70. On Chia-ting, *FWKT,* 30:14; on Ch'ung-ming, *Ch'ung-ming hsien-chih,* 4:3b; on Tan-yang, *FWKT,* 43:15b; on Nan-hui, *FWKT,* 36:12b and *Nan-hui hsien-chih* (1878), 20:6b.
71. Kiangsu *ch'ing-chieh t'ang* gave women support allowances of 350 cash per month; Wu Yun (Yü Chih), comp., *Te-i lu* (Shanghai, 1869; Taipei reprint), p. 222. A woman under 30 with young children could obtain an additional 100 cash per child.
72. C. K. Yang, *Religion in Chinese Society* (Berkeley, 1967), pp. 85–86.
73. Ibid., p. 86; *TCLL,* p. 1407. The same constraints applied to the plays which accompanied the festivals. Thanking the spirits was legitimate, but romances were not; see *HTSL,* 400:4b; also, pp. 47–48.
74. *Su-chou fu-chih,* 3:1b, 11–11b, 37. Their belief in spirits was so strong that they entrusted their illnesses to the care of shamans who "chased a ghost or invited a spirit"; *Su-chou fu-chih,* 3:37; *Ch'uan-sha hsien-chih* (1935), 14:4b.
75. *Ch'uan-sha hsien-chih* (1935), 14:4b; *TCLL,* p. 1407; *FWKT,* 36:8–8b. Ya Erh-t'u, who was Governor of Honan from 1739–1743, complained about the exactions levied to support the processions; *Ya-kung hsin cheng-lu,* 1741 preface, "Yao-shih," 2:75.
76. If the procession honored spirits other than the communal ones of the soil, the instigator was to be punished with 100 strokes of the heavy bamboo and the responsible official with a 6-month salary fine; *TCLL,* p. 1407. Ya Erh-t'u, Governor of Honan in the early 1740s, in a public notice warned that those who persisted in the custom would be punished with the even more severe sentence of the cangue; *Ya-kung-hsin cheng-lu,* "Yao-shih," 2:75.
77. *FWKT,* 36:8–8b. For a more complete, and translated, version, see *NCDN,* August 8, 1869.
78. *NCDN,* August 14, 1869.
79. *HTSL,* 400:2; Kung-chuan Hsiao, pp. 229–231.
80. *FWKT,* 41:14–15.
81. *FWKT,* 5:23b–25b.
82. *FWKT,* 42:12; *Nan-hui hsien-chih,* 20:6b; *FWKT,* 45:15b. K'ang-hsi seemed even less credulous than Ting about spirits, for he mocked a Governor who spoke of spirits raising a river when in fact it had simply rained heavily in the mountains; Jonathan Spence, *Emperor of China* (New York, Alfred A. Knopf, 1974), p. 40.
83. *FWKT,* 11:1–3, 28:10b.
84. *CP* (Chü-heng), TC 6/7/18; *Nan-hui hsien-chih,* 8:12; *FWKT,* 41:9b.

85. The nunneries were in Wu-hsi, Chin-kuei, and on T'ung-ting tung-shan Island in Lake T'ai; *FWKT,* 30:1. There is no indication in the *Su-chou fu-chih's* sections on temples that there was any reduction in the number of temples on T'ung-ting-shan; nor is Ting's order mentioned in the gazetteer; cf., Silas Wu, *Passage to Power* (Cambridge, Harvard University Press, 1979), p. 91. See also pp. 53, 57 for more on Ting's attitude toward Buddhism.
86. For the prohibition against women entering temples to burn incense and for the subsequent imperial reiterations, see *HT,* 36:3; *HTSL,* 400:5b. T'ang Pin, an early Ch'ing Governor of Kiangsu, said that the monks who encouraged the practice should be made to wear cangues in front of their temples and that husbands who permitted their wives to go to the temples should also be punished; *Su-chou fu-chih,* 3:33; also see *CP* (Chü-heng), TC 6/7/18 and *Ya-kung-hsin cheng-lu,* "Yao-shih," 1:43–45.
87. *FWKT,* 8:8b–9. The claim about the location of tea shops was advanced by Ch'ien-lung in an edict, which among other things bemoaned the decadent customs of Kiangsu; *HTSL,* 399:1b.
88. C. K. Yang, p. 86. For the imperial view on the relation of gambling to fairs, see *HTSL,* 400:2b, 4, 4b. See *FWKT,* 27:5, on pirates, and *HTSL,* 399:8b, on rebels.
89. *Su-chou fu-chih,* 3:36; *TCCCS:HHKT,* 1:6; Edict in Yung-cheng 7/6/6, manuscript copy in the British Museum, Royal Mss. 16Bxxi, ff, 171.
90. *Su-chou fu-chih,* 3:36.
91. Laws against gambling changed over time; penalties for gamblers were reduced, but penalties for owners of dens were made more severe. This latter group could receive up to 3 years' penal servitude. Makers of gambling materials were also singled out as responsible for the custom and consequently were included in the code; *TCLL,* pp. 3275–3292.
92. See Li Hsing-yuan, *Li Wen-kung kung tsou-i,* 9:53, in *Li Wen-kung kung ch'üan-chi,* n.d.; *FWKT,* 35:14.
93. *FWKT,* 45:18–18b; *TCCCS:HHKT,* 1:6–6b.
94. FO 228/388/1, Parkes to Wade, January 21, 1865; *NCH,* December 3, 1864. Foreigners also felt that taxation could not only regulate gambling but also produce revenue.
95. When importation of opium was legal, the Chinese did levy a likin tax on it but, when afforded the opportunity, they attempted to suppress its cultivation and use; Jonathan Spence, "Opium Smoking in Ch'ing China," in Wakeman and Grant, eds., *Conflict and Control,* pp. 143–173.
96. FO 227/388/6; *NCH,* December 3, 1864; *TCCCS:HHKT,* 5:11b, 12b.
97. *NCH,* December 3, 1864.

98. *Hong Kong Daily Press,* November 30, 1864. It was necessary in 1871 for the Shanghai Taotai again to prohibit gambling and lotteries; *Chiao-hui hsin-pao* 4:103, (September 16, 1871).
99. *Wu-Yang chih-yü* (1888), 6:20b.
100. Mackerras, p. 40.
101. The only specific prohibition in the Penal Code deals with the portrayal of historical and contemporary imperial personages; *TCLL,* p. 3325. The rest of the controls were established gradually, often on what seems to have been an ad hoc basis; *HTSL,* 400:1, 2b, 4, 4b, 5b. For local and provincial documentation, see Wu Yun, *Te-i lu,* pp. 787–828; also see Mackerras, pp. 34–39, 211–218; cf. Donald Shively, "Bakufu versus Kabuki," in John Hall and Marius Jansen, eds., *Studies in the Institutional History of Early Modern Japan* (Princeton University Press, 1968), pp. 231–261.
102. Wu Yun, *Te-i lu,* pp. 797, 798.
103. *Shen Pao,* p. 21087.
104. Wu Yun, *Te-i lu,* pp. 837–828; *FWKT,* 2:3b–4.
105. Wang Jen-k'an, *Wang Su-chou i-shu* (Taipei reprint, 1934), pp. 393–396.
106. *HTSL,* 400:1, 4b, 5b; Mackerras, pp. 211–218.
107. The term "lewd" (*yin-ssu*) was not defined either in the Penal Code, which only prohibits ownership and sale of "lewd" books (*TCLL,* p. 1897) or by the Ch'ien-lung Literary Inquisition; L. Carrington Goodrich, *The Literary Inquisition of Ch'ien-lung* (New York, 1966). Lü Shih-ch'iang suggests that works of unusual phrasing, romances, stories of secret societies and brigand heroes, and hard-core pornography were considered "lewd"; *Ting Jih-ch'ang,* pp. 142–143. The breadth of the term is indicated by the fact that pettifoggers' handbooks were comprised in the provision on "lewd" works; *TLTI,* p. 1021 (340–07).
108. *TCCCS:FWTK,* 1:4. For a listing of the proscribed books, see *Kiangsu Sheng-li,* "Fan," TC 7, pp. 15–19b; Wang Hsiao-ch'uan, ed., *Yuan Ming Ch'ing san-tai chin-hui hsiao-shuo chü-ch'ü shih-liao* (Peking, 1958), pp. 121–130.
109. For a list of the works proscribed during the Literary Inquisition, see Wang Hsiao-ch'uan, pp. 23–50. Officials who printed the books were to be dismissed from office (*ko-chih*). Commoners or soldiers who published such works were to receive 100 strokes with the heavy bamboo and a 3,000-*li* exile. Sellers of the books would receive a sentence of 3 years' penal servitude, while buyers and owners would receive 100 strokes with the heavy bamboo; *TCLL,* pp. 1897–1898. Hsueh Yun-sheng in *TLTI,* p. 598, notes the unusual discrepancy between the light punishment for officials and the heavier one for commoners, but offers no explanation for it.

110. *HCCSWP,* 68:58.
111. *FWKT,* 1:7. Advanced by another writer was the similar claim that even farmers and laborers had copies of these novels; *HCCSWP,* 68:58. Given Rawski's findings on levels of literacy, it is not an implausible claim; Evelyn G. Rawski, *Education and Popular Literacy in Ch'ing China* (Ann Arbor, 1979).
112. *FWKT,* 1:7. Also *HCCSWP,* 68:58; Wu Yun, *Te-i lu,* pp. 779–780, where it is asserted that while only 10–20% of the people had a general knowledge of the Classics, 80–90% knew the novels well.
113. *FWKT,* 1:7
114. Wang Hsiao-ch'uan, p. 122.
115. *FWKT,* 15:11 for Ch'ung-ming; *FWKT,* 15:11b for Lou hsien.
116. *HTSL,* 400:5b.
117. For Tao-kuang documents, see Wu Yun *Te-i lu,* pp. 765–778, and Wang Hsiao-ch'uan, pp. 113–116.
118. For Magistrates, see *FWKT,* 7:8, 15:11b. For Censor's memorial, see *HTSL,* 400:5b.
119. Lü Shih-ch'iang, *Ting Jih-ch'ang,* p. 143.
120. *NCH,* June 27, 1868.
121. Of the 2,665 books proscribed in whole or in part, only 476 survived (approximately 18%); Goodrich, p. 61.
122. Lü Shih-ch'iang, *Ting Jih-ch'ang,* pp. 137, 143–144.
123. Wu Yun, *Te-i lu,* pp. 760, 761. Authors have repeatedly noted that no less a rebellious character than Mao Tse-tung was attracted to the bandits of *Shui-hu chuan* and that the work had an impact on the structure as well as the style of various rebellious groups; Edgar Snow, *Red Star Over China* (New York, Grove Press, 1961), p. 127; Jean Chesneaux, "The Modern Relevance of *Shui-hu chuan:* Its Influence on Rebel Movements in Nineteenth and Twentieth Century China," *Papers on Far Eastern History,* 3 (March 1971), pp. 1–25. For the ongoing concern with the correct interpretation of *Hung-lou meng,* see Merle Goldman, *Literary Dissent in Communist China* (Cambridge, Mass., 1967), p. 116.
124. "In helping the poor, nothing is more urgent than this," said Ting of his efforts to establish more pawnshops and lower interest rates; *FWKT,* 18:10b; also see *FWKT,* 31:8b–9. For his efforts to guard against phony shops which disappeared as soon as they had built up their capital, see *FWKT,* 31:1–3.
125. *FWKT,* 1:7; Chao Lieh-wen, *Neng-ching-chü jih-chi,* TC 6/6/12. Chao claimed that this was Ting's first action upon becoming Financial Commissioner. The price Ting set was one cash less than that which prevailed in 1849, before the Hsien-feng inflation; see *Chinese Miscellany*

(Shanghai, 1849), p. 20. Of course, Ting subsequently made the tea shops less inviting by excluding women from them; see p. 46.

126. Woodside, "Family Education."
127. *Su-chou fu-chih,* Chapter 24; *Wu-chiang hsien-chih,* 2:7; *SL:TC,* 254:19; *Kiangsu Sheng-li hsu-pien,* "Fan," TC7, "Ch'ing-li shan-t'ang t'ien-ch'an" for provincial regulations on fiscal management. Also see Chao Lieh-wen, TC 6/9/15, for charges that Ting ignored influential gentry's serious mishandling of *shan-t'ang* funds.
128. *TCLL,* p. 923. This provision dates from Ming times; see *TLTI,* p. 260 (089–00).
129. *Wu-chiang hsien-chih* (1879), 2:4b–6b. One Censor, however, charged that the decay of the institutions was a result of the lassitude of local officials; *SL:TC,* 174:10b–11.
130. Ting fixed the number of indigent in Soochow at 1,150, a mere .23% of Soochow's estimated population of 500,000. I have made this very rough estimate of Soochow's size, which if anything is too large, on the basis of *Wu-hsien chih* (1933), 49:3, 4–4b. On infanticide as a severe problem, see *FWKT,* 24:7b; *Wu-chiang hsien-chih,* 2:4b.
131. Wu Yun, *Te-i lu,* pp. 106, 120.
132. Ibid., pp. 106, 133.
133. Ibid., pp. 185–186.
134. The penalty for unreasonably killing one's own child was 60 strokes with the heavy bamboo and 1 year of penal servitude; *TCLL,* p. 2817. If an adulterous mother killed one of her children in order to prevent him/her from reporting her behavior, the sentence was increased to strangulation after the assizes; *TCLL,* p. 2827; Derk Bodde and Clarence Morris, *Law in Imperial China* (Cambridge, Mass., 1967), p. 394. Compare these with a 3,000-*li* exile for publishing, and 3 years' penal servitude for selling, "lewd" novels; *TCLL,* pp. 1897–1898; see note 107 above. Although there was no punishment for abandoning a child, there was one for failing to report to officials "lost" children, that is, anyone over the age of 3 who knew his name, his parents' names, and their address; *TCLL,* p. 889.
135. See Wu Yun, *Te-i lu,* pp. 96–97, 115, on exhortations; p. 115, on the effectiveness of financial support. The Wu-chin *pao-ying hui* claimed that, within a 20-mile radius, there was no infanticide.
136. On the adult nature of the *yang-ch'i yuan,* see *HTSL,* 269:1; Wu Yun, *Te-i lu,* p. 266. On children with mothers, see *FWKT,* 26:2b.
137. See Wu Yun, *Te-i lu* pp. 193–217, for *yü-ying t'ang* regulations; and pp. 106-116, for *pao-ying hui* regulations.
138. Wu Yun, *Te-i lu,* p. 266. The Penal Code defined premeditated murder of a child as the killing of anyone under age 10; cf. Bodde and Morris,

Law in Imperial China, pp. 313-314. The punishment of immediate decapitation was far more serious than that stipulated for a parent who unreasonably killed his own child; see note 134 above. See T'ung-tsu Ch'ü, *Law and Society in Traditional China* (Paris, 1965), pp. 20–53, for a discussion of parent-child relations. For culprits, the "legal" definition of *adult* coincided with the "fiscal" one as anyone over 16. Also see Rawski, p. 32, on the age at which career decisions were made.

139. Wu Yun, *Te-i lu*, p. 105.
140. *FWKT*, 24:7b, 42:14, 26:2.
141. *FWKT*, 14:6b. Ting seemed to feel that land would provide a more permanent source of income.
142. *FWKT*, 26:2 on Yangchow, 41:9b on Buddhism. In his poems, too, Ting compared himself to Han Yü; see, for example, *PLSK*, 5:16b–17.
143. Wu Yun, *Te-i lu*, pp. 105–116.
144. *FWKT*, 24:8. Similar concerns about nurses can also be found in Wu Yun, *Te-i lu*, pp. 196–197, and *MLSCY*, 6:11b. The moral qualities of nurses were also important, for it was believed that a licentious nurse could adversely affect even the newest infant; Woodside, "Family Education."
145. Wu Yun, *Te-i lu*, p. 112. Children whose mothers had died in childbirth could be supported until age 3. In some areas, the monthly payments to such children were as high as 500 cash per month; ibid., p. 109. Matsudaira Sadanobu, the famed Tokugawa administrator, implemented a similar program of birth allowances in the mid-eighteenth century; Ooms, *Charismatic Bureaucrat*, p. 57.
146. Wu Yun, *Te-i lu*, p. 185.
147. *FWKT*, 26:3. Kung-chuan Hsiao's statement that the terms *i-hsueh* and *she-hsueh* were used interchangeably, seems to hold true for T'ung-chih Kiangsu; Hsiao, *Rural China*, pp. 238–239. Rawski, pp. 35–36, confirms this conclusion.
148. *FWKT*, 9:1–2. Huang Liu-hung, in *FHCS*, 25:12, 13, also established the same ratio as ideal, while T'ang Pin, the early Ch'ing Governor of Kiangsu, suggested that one school be established for every village (*ts'un*) or market town (*chen*) of more than 200 families; *Su-chou fu-chih*, 3:26–26b; Wu Yun, *Te-i lu*, p. 707.
149. *Su-chou fu-chih*, 27:15b–17b; *Wu-chiang hsien-chih*, 3:7b; *Chiang-yin hsien-chih* (1878), 5:32.
150. *FWKT*, 9:2; Wu Yun, *Te-i lu*, p. 689; *Su-chou fu-chih*, 3:27. These same works were also standard fare in many clan curricula; Rawski, p. 29. On the *Primer*, see Wing-tsit Ch'an, *Reflections on Things at Hand: The Neo-Confucian Anthology* (New York, Columbia University Press, 1967), p. xli note 132. Watt, pp. 82–83, 270 note 11, discusses the *Hsiao-ching*.

151. Wu Yun, *Te-i lu,* p. 739; also, pp. 685, 689, 712, 723, 728, 731, 732, 735.
152. Rawski, p. 49.
153. Wu Yun, *Te-i lu,* p. 709.
154. *FWKT,* 9:1.
155. *FWKT,* 9:1.
156. *TCCCS:FWTK,* 1:20b–21. Traditionally, said Ting, the financial commissioners had assessed each hsien for these amounts, but the practice had been stopped in 1858. Significantly, Ting claimed that most of the Kiangsu men going to Peking for the metropolitan examination were poor; cf., Ping-ti Ho, *Ladder of Success,* pp. 232–234.
157. The following discussion of school regulations, unless otherwise noted, is from *FWKT,* 9:2; cf. Rawski, pp. 38–40.
158. *FWKT,* 47:16; *HTSL,* 396:2. These are in line with the figures for other provinces and schools cited by Rawski, pp. 54–61.
159. *FWKT,* 16:10.
160. *FWKT,* 9:1b.
161. See *FWKT* 46:16 on pawnshops, 14:7 on illegal exactions, 11:3b–4 on land. Rawski, pp. 66–80, shows that, for most schools, landed income was the basic source of support. Wang Jen-k'an, Educational Commissioner in the 1880s in Shansi, suggested that, instead of heavy exactions for religious processions, villagers should levy a 40 cash per-*mou* fee, of which half would be used for *i-hsueh* and half for thanking the spirits (*pao-chi*); Wang Jen-k'an, p. 396.
162. Kuei Chao-wan, *Huan-yu chi-lueh* (Taipei reprint), p. 214.
163. *FWKT* 28:5b for Yangchow, and 41:9b for Chiang-yin.
164. See, for example, Edward Rhoads, *China's Republican Revolution* (Cambridge, Harvard University Press, 1975), p. 76. Moreover, the monks of Ting's day had neither of the alternatives of the early-twentieth-century monks. They could not start their own modern schools, and they could not link themselves to the Japanese for protection; see Holmes Welch, *The Buddhist Revival* (Cambridge, Harvard University Press, 1968), pp. 10–12.
165. *FWKT,* 19:4–4b.
166. *FWKT,* 11:3b. Rawski, p. 37, notes that some schools discriminated against the children of such groups as prostitutes, actors, and lictors.
167. *FWKT,* 27:8.
168. *FWKT,* 32:5 for Wu-chiang, 27:15b for Tan-yang, 27:16 for I-hsing. On Shen Hsi-hua, see p. 117, p. 254 note 121, p. 259 note 25.
169. *FWKT,* 46:15. For a fuller discussion of the financial pressures on officials, see pp. 89, 110, 156–159.
170. This Magistrate's impact was short-lived. Hsu-hai remained a difficult

place to govern into the twentieth century; see Wang P'ei-t'ang, *Chiang-su hsiang-t'u chih*, p. 370.

171. *Chiang-yin hsien-chih*, 5:29; *Wu-hsi chin-kuei hsien-chih* (1881), 6:21; *Nan-hui hsien-chih* (1878), 7:30b. Rawski, pp. 91–92, takes particular note of the expansion of charitable schools in Kiangsu.
172. For a survey of the lecture system, see Kung-chuan Hsiao, pp. 184–205.
173. *TCCCS:FanWKT*, 4:2.
174. Chao Lieh-wen, TC 6/6/12.
175. Kung-chuan Hsiao, p. 193.
176. *Nan-hui hsien-chih*, 7:30b.
177. Cf. Huang Liu-hung, *FHCS*, 25:8; Kung-chuan Hsiao, pp. 185, 617 note 9.
178. Kung-chuan Hsiao, p. 186; *CP* (Chü-heng), TC 8/3/24.
179. *TCCCS:FanWKT*, 4:2.
180. *FWKT*, 34:6.
181. *TCCCS:FWTK*, 4:38b.
182. With this remark Ting identified himself with the group of conservative Sung scholar-officials, led by Ssu-ma Kuang and Ou-yang Hsiu, which opposed the reforms of Wang An-shih. Actually, Ting shared much of Wang's outlook, in particular his belief in the need for an activist government and in the possibility of creating moral order through regulations and systems. Moreover, like Wang's policies, Ting's required more clerks. On Wang, see James T. C. Liu, *Reform in Sung China* (Cambridge, Mass., 1968), pp. 40–58, 112–113. On Ting and clerks, see pp. 133–134, 176–177.
183. *TCCCS:FWTK*, 4:39. For the large number of *i-hsueh* built in Chiang-yin, see *Chiang-yin hsien-chih*, 5:29; cf. Paul Cohen, *China and Christianity* (Cambridge, Mass. 1963), p. 84.
184. See pp. 152, 156–160.
185. *FHCS*, 25:2.
186. *TCCCS:FWTK*, 4:37. Ting stressed this theme from the very beginning of his official career; see *PLSK*, 3:17b.
187. *TCCCS:FWTK*, 4:37. For Ch'ien-lung, see *HTSL*, 299:1. Data compiled by Li Kuo-chi, *Chung-kuo ti-fang chih yen-chiu: Ch'ing-tai chi-ts'eng ti-fang kuan jen-shih shan-ti hsien-hsiang chih liang-hua fen-hsi*, (Taipei, 1975), pp. 1290–1291, seem to contradict the premise that work in cultural and educational (*wen-chiao*) matters was unimportant to an official's career, for it shows that 24% of prefects and nearly 20% of magistrates received their promotions or upward transfers on the basis of such work. However, since the category that accounted for the largest percentage of promotions, improvement of education, encompasses temple reconstruction as well as building of charitable schools, it is

difficult to tell how much of a direct impact the officials' labors had upon the people. And, significantly, few officials received promotions for improving the people's customs. For definitions of the categories, see Li, p. 20.

4. *JUDICIAL ADMINISTRATION AND REFORM*

1. Especially common in Kiangsu was the practice of implicating someone in a suicide case; *Kiangsu Sheng-li,* "Nieh," TC 7, 10–10b.
2. Kung-chuan Hsiao, p. 187; Watt, pp. 214–215; Susan Naquin, "The Accused," in Susan Naquin and Jonathan Ocko, "Two Sides of the Law," paper prepared for the American Historical Association, December 1977; Wei-jen Chang, "The Traditional Chinese Fear of Litigation: Its Causes and Effects," Conference on the History of Chinese Law, Lake Como, Italy, August 1969, p. 19. Litigation, and fear of it, caused numerous suicides. Chang states, p. 1, that, of the 569 suicide cases in the 3 editions of the *Hsing-an hui-lan,* 72, or 12%, were so caused.
3. *FWKT,* 20:1b.
4. David Buxbaum, "Some Aspects of Civil Procedure and Practice at the Trial Level in Tanshui and Hsinchu from 1789 to 1895," *Journal of Asian Studies,* 30.2:255–280 (February 1971); Ocko, "Justice on Appeal"; Ocko, "Family Disharmony."
5. Cited in Ts'ai Shen-chih, *Ch'ing-tai chou-hsien ku-shih* (Hong Kong, 1968), p. 33.
6. *FWKT,* 3:1b.
7. Kuei Chao-wan, 5:44.
8. The days were the 3rd, 8th, 13th, 18th, 23rd, and 28th. This interval was known as 3,8; Sheng K'ang, *HCCSWHP,* 102:3b; Chang Wei-jen, and Yu Yu-chan, "Ch'ing-chi ti-fang ssu-fa: Ch'en T'ien-hsi hsien-sheng fang-wen chi," (Late Ching judicial administration: an interview with Mr. Ch'en T'ien-hsi) *Shih-huo yueh-k'an,* 1:6 (September 1971), p. 325. Another less common pattern was 3,6,9; *FHCS,* 11:5b. There were also seasonal restrictions on the submission of civil suits; *TLTI,* pp. 991 (334–01), 993 (334–06), (334–07). On petitions in serious criminal cases, see T'ung-tsu Ch'ü, *Local Government,* p. 119; *FHCS,* 11:5b. Liu Heng, an especially able early-nineteenth-century Magistrate, allowed people to make shouted petitions or to beat a gong hung outside his yamen in the instance of serious cases; Sheng K'ang, *HCCSWHP,* 102:3.
9. *FHCS,* 11:5b; Sheng K'ang, *HCCSWHP,* 102:3.
10. *TCCCS:FanWKT,* 7:2; *FWKT,* 3:1. Magistrates were often unaware of the initial petition and subsequent jailing. The warrants often did not have the official seal; indeed, in *niu-chiao* a warrant was never even

issued. The person was arrested and jailed before the magistrate was notified. For the 1866 ban by Li Hung-chang, see *Kiangsu Sheng-li,* "Nieh," TC 5, p. 1.

11. A "chair petition" could be construed as "by-passing in submitting a plaint or in litigation" (*yueh-sung* or *yueh-k'ung*). This entailed going over the head of a local official directly to the prefect or higher officials; *TLTI,* pp. 977 (332–00), 992 (332–14). Chair petitions were punished only if the accusation was false. Indeed, one Magistrate urged his colleagues to encourage the practice in order to get at the truth; Sheng K'ang, *HCCSWHP,* 25:4.
12. *TCCCS:FanWKT,* 7:2; *FWKT,* 3:3b.
13. *FWKT,* 29:17–18b. For an instance of backsliding, see *FWKT,* 36:9b.
14. In one case involving robbery from a boat, the runners demanded 100,000 cash from the owner before they would let him press his charges. The man declined to pay and the case was never tried; *FWKT*, 10:13b–14.
15. According to a late Ch'ing *mu-yu*, out of the 400–600 petitions a month in his judicially busy county, there were 4–5 special ones, for which there was a charge of 4,000–5,000 cash apiece; Wei-jen Chang, "Late Ch'ing Judicial Administration," p. 325.
16. *TCLL,* p. 3205.
17. *Chih-che ch'eng-kuei* 8:34b.
18. In one instance, a landlord, whose only connection to a case was that the involved parties were both his tenants, expended more than 10,000 taels in less than a year in order to extricate himself from that case; *FWKT,* 20:15b.
19. According to Ting, the decision whether or not to jail the parties to a case should be made on a case-by-case basis, depending on the seriousness of the charge and the personal integrity and reputation of the people involved; *FWKT,* 45:15. In the instance of the brothel brawl involving Ting's family (see p. 38), everyone in the case was held in custody throughout the trial with the exception of Ting Hui-heng. Before being imprisoned, those with official titles had been deprived of them; Ma Hsin-i, 8:39b–40. This was supposed to be the procedure for even imperial relatives, *HTSL,* 1021:3b.
20. Lin Tse-hsu, *Lin Tse-hsu chi kung-tu,* "Ting-ch'i fang-kao fen-fa chuang-shih kao-shih" (Peking, 1963), p. 19; also see complaint forms in *Tang-hsin tang-an* (Tan-hsin legal archive), microfilm copy at Harvard Yenching Institute.
21. *MLSCY,* 7:27, 19:20; *Chih-che ch'eng-kuei,* 8:34; Edict by Chia-ch'ing, in Bodde and Morris, pp. 416–417.
22. Watt, pp. 222–223; Bodde and Morris, pp. 416–417. Ya Erh-t'u, Governor of Honan in the 1740s, issued a proclamation announcing that he

would give leniency to those who confessed and pointed out pettifoggers; "Yao-shih," 5:50. If the magistrate was duped by the trickster, he was fined one year's salary. If he knew the petition was from a trickster but did not report it, he was demoted and transferred; *TCLL*, p. 3208. Imperial commissioners who were sent out to try appeals were supposed to discover pettifogger influence and recommend for discipline the provincial officials who had either concealed or failed to see it; *TLTI*, p. 1021 (340–08).

23. *MLSCY*, 7:27. Others also made the points about using simple colloquial language and making accurate references to the Penal Code; see *MLSCY*, 6:21, 7:2–2b; *FWKT*, 16:4b.
24. *FWKT*, 30:8.
25. *TCCCS:FanWKT*, 7:11b.
26. *FWKT*, 7:9b, 23:11b, 36:10, 48:13b.
27. *TCCCS:FanWKT*, 7:11b.
28. *TCLL*, pp. 3031–3032. Still more startling, local officials in Peking never even selected official scribes, but simply allowed anyone to prepare petitions; *TLTI*, p. 1022 (340–10).
29. *FWKT*, 30:2b.
30. *FWKT*, 30:2.
31. Juan Pen-yen, *CMCY*, pp. 144, 224; also *Chih-che ch'eng-kuei*, 8:35.
32. *MLSCY*, 7:8b–9; editorial comment by Ting. When an inquest was over, the pen was thrown away and the writing table kicked over in order to break any symbolic connection between the inquest record and the register at the gate of Hell; Ts'ai Shen-chih, p. 30. On the use of spirits as a disciplinary tool, see pp. 168–169.
33. *CFTL*, 43:1–3; *TCLL*, 3685–3689.
34. *MLSCY*, 8:3b–4; Lin Tse-hsu, *Lin Tse-hsu chi kung-tu*, TK 4, "T'ung-chih ko-shu hsuan-lien wu-tso cha," pp. 11–12.
35. *FWKT*, 8:5–5b. Just a decade before, the Board of Civil Office (Li-pu) had approved a request to increase the punishment for magistrates who did not personally conduct the inquest. *Fen-fa t'iao-li*, HF 6, "Ssu-hou ko chih-sheng chou-hsien-kuan yü min-jen ch'eng-pao tou-shang chung-an." N.B. Brian McKnight's translation of *Hsi-yuan-lu, The Washing Away of Wrongs* (Ann Arbor, 1981).
36. *FWKT*, 2:2b.
37. *FWKT*, 30:3, 5:10–11b. In Kiangpei, troublemakers in one county, in order to grab some property, falsely claimed that their women relatives had married into the deceased's family. To discourage the practice, the Magistrate announced that he would hold the family member who reported the suicide in custody; Juan Pen-yen, *CMCY*, p. 143.
38. *TCLL*, p. 3692; *TLTI*, p. 1269 (412–04).

39. *FWKT,* 30:3.
40. Metzger, *Internal Organization,* pp. 127, 190.
41. Wei-jen Chang, "Late Ch'ing Judicial Administration," pp. 327–328. This same article contains sample warrants.
42. *FWKT,* 19:6. Punishment could be avoided only if the suspect confessed before the crime became known to the authorities. In this instance, Mr. Ch'en's punishment would have been reduced; *TCLL,* p. 455.
43. If a false accusation resulted in the accused's execution, the accuser would be put to death and his family forced to make monetary restitution to the falsely accused; *TCLL,* p. 2952. Police who falsely accused good people were to be demoted 3 grades and transferred; *CFTL,* 42:6.
44. *FWKT,* 17:2b. In an 1864 edict, the court had said that such officials should not be punished, since their intentions were often good (i.e., they wanted to stamp out rebellion or brigandry) and since discipline would set a negative example, discouraging officials from taking swift action on important business; *CP* (Shantung), TC 4/1/29–30. Five years later, another edict seemed to order a complete halt to summary executions and a return to normal procedures (*SL:TC,* 253:8b–9), but the practice continued unabated with Ting among its supporters; see p. 227, note 14.
45. On the application of classical Confucian ideas to Ch'ing administration, see Watt, pp. 90–98. For changing ideas on the meaning of "closeness," see Watt, p. 232.
46. *FWKT,* 44:16b.
47. *Chih-che ch'eng-kuei,* 8:34b; *FWKT,* 44:16b.
48. Sheng K'ang, *HCCSWHP,* 102:28b.
49. *FWKT,* 43:9.
50. *FWKT,* 7:1b–2, 10:6b–7, 14:1b–2, 32:3–3b; *FHCS,* 11:13.
51. *FWKT,* 7:1b–2.
52. *FWKT,* 43:9b.
53. *TCCCS:FanWKT,* 7:2; *FWKT,* 3:1; *Fen-fa t'iao-li,* HF 5, "Yen-hsing ch'a-chin pao-tien teng ming-mu ping-ting shih-ch'a ch'u-fen."
54. *FWKT,* 28:12b, 17:13b, 11:1b, 31:1. Similar problems existed elsewhere; see *THTKTI,* 4.1701; *Kuang-hsu Tung-hua lu* (KH 7/1), p. 1017; *Fen-fa t'iao-li,* HF 5, "Yen-hsing . . . ch'u-fen."
55. Derk Bodde, "Prison Life in Eighteenth Century Peking," *Journal of the American Oriental Society,* 89 (1969), p. 320.
56. *FHCS,* 11:18–19b.
57. *FWKT,* 31:1–1b. In the late 1870s, Juan Pen-yen, Magistrate of Funing, reported that the county continued to implement the registers on regulations, but that it had just established a formal place of custody and was still looking for funds for it; *CMCY,* p. 118.

58. Bodde, "Prison Life," p. 317.
59. See pp. 71, 74, 78.
60. Bodde, "Prison Life," pp. 321–322.
61. Ibid., p. 320; Watt, p. 214.
62. The Penal Code contained numerous provisions dealing with the treatment of prisoners: extortion or oppression of witnesses or suspects by either clerks or officials were to be severely punished; establishment of private lockups was forbidden; maltreatment through beatings or shortchanging on provisions—whether provided by the jailer or the family—were both punishable as capital crimes, even if death did not result; and officials who through oversight or negligence failed to uncover any of these abuses were subject to both administrative discipline and criminal penalties; *TCLL*, pp. 3507–3508, 3517–3518, 3526–3527, 3533; *CFTL*, 49:1b, 2b–3, 8b.
63. *TCCCS:FanWKT*, 6:11b.
64. For Magistrates' compliance with these orders, see Appendix C–1. For the reissuance of the order and for the form, see *TCCCS:FanWKT*, 7:5b–6; *Kiangsu Sheng-li*, "Fan," TC 6, pp. 20–24.
65. *FWKT*, 2:6b–11b; *TCCCS:FWTK*, 2:19–19b; *Kiangsu Sheng-li*, "Fan," TC 7, pp. 6–11.
66. In 1659, local officials were instructed to provide their superiors with registers on long-imprisoned people and with detailed explanations of the cases and the reasons for delay; *HTSL*, 840:1b. In 1833, regulations for registers similar to Ting's were incorporated into the Penal Code. These registers were to go monthly to the Taotai and tri-monthly to the Governor, unlike Ting's which were to be sent directly to the Governor each month; *TCLL*, p. 3526.
67. The best account in English of the obligatory review system is Shuzo Shiga, "Criminal Procedure in the Ch'ing Dynasty," *Memoirs of the Toyo Bunko*, 34 (1976), pp. 16–26.
68. The characterization "on a a high shelf" comes from *Chih-che ch'eng-kuei*, 2:20. On the registers, see Pao Shih-ch'en, *An-wu ssu-chung* (Taipei reprint), pp. 2154, 2185–2186.
69. Han Wen-ch'i, *Kung-shou-t'ang tsou-i*, 2:9–18, 67–73, 6:17–24, 10:31–36.
70. *TCCCS:FWTK*, 3:12b.
71. Ibid., 5:1b.
72. Ibid., 3:12–13b, 5:1b; *SL:TC*, 246:12–13b; *CP* (Chü-heng). TC 8/3/22.
73. *TCCCS:FWTK*, 1:4b–5.
74. For court approval, see *CP* (Chü-heng), TC 7/11/8; *SL:TC*, 246:12–13b. For the extension of the procedures, see *FWKT*, 3:14b, and for the Tao-kuang precedent, see Han Wen-ch'i, 2:50–53.

75. *TCCCS:FWTK,* 1:4b–5.
76. *FWKT,* 18:9. The cost of sending prisoners to Soochow could be as high as 10 taels a person.
77. *FWKT,* 27:6b–7, 29:6b–7; cf. *Hsing-tseng HAHL,* 50:6–7, where the Board of Punishment rejected a request for a blanket exemption from discipline of all officials who corrected their own judicial errors in homicide cases.
78. *FWKT,* 32:10b.
79. Ibid., 11:5b.
80. Ibid., 16:14b; also see *MLSCY,* 6:21, 7:20b, 27.
81. *FWKT,* 29:5.
82. Ibid., 15:2.
83. Ibid., 41:6, 24:1, 14:12. Despite the supposed respect for age in China, Ting frequently used such metaphors derisively; see, for example, p. 163.
84. *FWKT,* 14:6.
85. Ibid., 14:12, 20:3b, 16:5.
86. Ibid., 24:1.
87. Ibid., 1:1b.
88. Ibid., 3:6.
89. *TCLL,* pp. 3507–3533; *TLTI,* pp. 1206–1211; *CFTL,* 49:1b–8b; *HTSL,* 839:2b–3b, 840:6.
90. *TCCCS:FanWKT,* 9:8–8b.
91. *CFTL,* 49:2, 2b; *HTSL,* 839:3b; *TCLL,* p. 3526.
92. *CP* (Chü-heng), TC 7/5/28.
93. See above, note 66.
94. *FWKT,* 31:5b–6.
95. Ibid., 34:9b. As we know, Ting was not speaking rhetorically, for he knew how hard it was to obtain status.
96. *TCCCS:FanWKT,* 11:7b–9b. The fellow had been imprisoned for more than a year when Ting entered the case. Nearly another year passed between that time and the man's death. Ting asked for a major demerit for himself as a warning to his colleagues.
97. Ibid., 5:1b–2; *SL:TC,* 246:12–13b.
98. On Tseng, see Sheng K'ang, *HCCSWHP,* 102:9. On Shansi, see *Chincheng chi-yao,* 34:14b, 22b, 25. Although Tseng's order was nearly a verbatim duplicate of Ting's, Tseng referred not to Ting but rather to Chihli precedents. About a year later, a Censor submitted a memorial requesting the court to instruct all officials to prepare biweekly reports on the nature and progress of all litigation and criminal cases in their jurisdictions; *CP* (Chü-heng), TC 8/3/24. In this instance, too, no reference was made to Ting's procedures, though they had been established by the court as a model and given wide publicity in the *Peking Gazette.*

99. *Kiangsu Sheng-li ssu-pien,* "Nieh," KH 15, p. 1. They also continued to be used in some of the most litigious hsien; Juan Pen-yen, *CMCY,* p. 118.
100. *Kuang-hsu Tung-hua-lu* (KH 7/1), p. 1017, on lockups and prisoners; *Kiangsu Sheng-li Ssu-pien,* "Nieh," KH 17, p. 1, on auxiliary court. Although in Kiangsu the witness hostel at Soochow was maintained by funds from the provincial government, *Kiangsu Ts'ai-cheng shuo-ming shu,* "Sui-ch'u pu," Hsu-pien, pp. 6–8, in Shansi it was supported by "contributions" extracted from the head prefect's supplementary salary; *Chin-cheng chi-yao,* 34:14b. It would appear that in Kiangsu magistrates themselves had to seek out funds to build witness hostels; Juan Pen-yen, *CMCY,* p. 118.
101. Ocko, "Justice on Appeal."
102. Customary fees (*lou-kuei*) alone could sometimes amount to 40–50 taels, while the escort costs were about 6 taels; *FWKT,* 8:1. Out of sheer annoyance, local officials immediately recommended that plaintiffs in capital appeals be punished for by-passing in litigation (*yueh-sung*), regardless of the legitimacy of the appeal; *FWKT,* 28:6–6b.
103. *FWKT,* 8:2. Ting's only reaction to this exchange was to comment to the Soochow Financial Commissioner that it showed how a case could break the homes of the common people and to instruct magistrates to pay the traveling and escort fees. For the impact that his order had on the magistrates, see pp. 156, 158. Eventually, Ting instructed the provincial government to absorb the escort costs; 19:2–2b.
104. *FWKT,* 45:12b–13b; *Kiangsu Sheng-li,* "Nieh," TC 8, pp. 1–6; *Kiangsu Sheng-li Ssu-pien,* "Nih," KH 17, pp. 1–3; *CP* (Chü-heng), TC 8/3/24.
105. *FWKT,* 41:12.
106. Ibid., 47:4–6b; Bodde and Morris, pp. 115–116.
107. *FWKT,* 1:1b.
108. Ibid., 6:2; *MLSCY,* 7:7, 15–23b, 32b–33, 8:7b–8; *THTKTI,* 1:218–219.
109. *FWKT,* 4:5, 5:1b.
110. Ibid., 49:5b, 43:14, 30:14b–15b, 5:1b, 44:13b.
111. *TLTI,* pp. 781 (284–00), 928 (315–00).
112. See p. 42.
113. *FWKT,* 38:10b, 29:16–16b.
114. Ibid., 7:3–4b, 12:9, 23:17–17b.
115. Ibid., 10:2–4, 19:10–10b, 19:10b.
116. These skills are described in *MLSCY,* 7:15–19b.
117. *FWKT,* 37:12.
118. *TCCCS:FanWKT,* 6:10b.

5. FISCAL AFFAIRS

1. Wu Pao-san et al., eds., *Chung-kuo chin-tai ching-chi ssu-hsiang yü ching-chi cheng-ts'e tzu-liao hsuan-chi* (Peking, 1959), 1, 1.
2. Yeh-chien Wang, *Land Taxation,* pp. 10, 80.
3. *SL:TC,* 252:8b.
4. Yeh-chien Wang, *Land Taxation,* p. 27, states that, in the last 150 years of the Ch'ing, 4/5 of newly cultivated land was unregistered; also see Ping-ti Ho, *Studies on the Population of China, 1368–1953* (Cambridge, Mass., 1959), pp. 101–123.
5. When Ting spoke of the "people," he was referring only to the land-owning taxpayers, who constituted between 40–50% of the population. The remainder were tenants; see Frank Arno Lojewski, "Confucian Reformers and Local Vested Interests: The Su-Sung-T'ai Tax Reduction of 1863 and its Aftermath" (PhD dissertation, University of California, Davis, 1973), pp. 3–4, 270–272, notes 4, 5, 6. For Ting's views on problems of tenancy, see p. 112.
6. An interim tax remission was approved in conjunction with the tax reduction in the summer of 1863; Hsia Nai, "T'ai-p'ing t'ien-kuo ch'ien-hou Ch'ang-chiang ko-sheng chih t'ien-fu wen-ti'i," *Ch'ing-hua hsueh-pao,* 10.2 (1935), p. 460. But the first formal general remission of all land, grain, and miscellaneous taxes and wastage fees for areas damaged by the Rebellion was not issued by the court until late August 1864; *SL:TC,* 100:7. Yet, a month later, a British consular official traveling between Shanghai and Soochow reported that farmhouses were already repaired and "yards [were] full of rice and fowls"; FO 17/423/17, Wade to Russell, February 17, 1865.
7. Lojewski, p. 157; Hsia Nai, pp. 429–460; Chu Ch'ing-yung, "T'ung-chih erh-nien Su-Sung erh-fu chien-fu chih yuan-yin," *Cheng-chih ching-chi hsueh-pao,* 3.3:510–529 (1935).
8. *Hsu-hsiu Chiang-ning fu-chih* (1880), 2:1.
9. Unless otherwise indicated, the following discussion is taken from *FWKT,* 37:7b–10.
10. On land ownership policy, see Wright, p. 159.
11. In 1865, the Governor of Shensi had suggested that, if the original owners of a piece of abandoned land had not returned within 3 years after an attack, then the guest people should be given deeds to that land. If they met the land-tax quotas, the deeds were to be confirmed; *THTKTI,* Vol. 5, p. 1944.
12. Ma Hsin-i, 7:51b–52b. Officials had on the books a law that enabled them to sentence land-seizing bullies to military exile. The bullies, moreover, should have needed more than simply a deed to have proven long-

term ownership of land, but, in the absence of other records, it was difficult to convict anyone; see *TLTI*, p. 267 (090–00). In a study of Vietnamese peasants, Samuel Popkin has suggested that peasants may be deprived of land they have recently reclaimed in order to force them into tenantry; Samuel L. Popkin, *The Rational Peasant* (Berkeley, University of California Press, 1979), p. 180.

13. *FWKT*, 37:10.
14. Ibid. On infanticide, see p. 52.
15. This is probably a reference to the phrase *shih-nien sheng-chü*, which means to build population and increase resources; see James Legge, *Tso Chuan, The Chinese Classics*, 5, 794.
16. *HTSL*, Chapter 166.
17. Ma Hsin-i, 7:53. Ma asked local officials to "exhort natives not to cheat and insult outsiders and outsiders not to oppress and harass natives." In Ching-chi and I-hsing, a decline in the quality of customs and local disorders was attributed to the presence of immigrants; Yeh-chien Wang, "Impact of the Taiping Rebellion," p. 131.
18. *Hsu-hsiu Chiang-ning fu-chih*, 2:1b.
19. Yeh-chien Wang, *Land Taxation*, p. 21, has pointed out that a Board of Revenue regulation on land reclamation provided that "no punishment should be imposed on people who did not immediately report newly reclaimed land to the government or on the local official who failed to detect it, and that tax assessment began from the year when the land was reported, not when it was reclaimed."
20. *FWKT*, 9:1b; cf., Lojewski, p. 57. For the legal provisions, see *TLTI*, p. 269 (091–00).
21. *FWKT*, 41:3b–4. For the law, see *TLTI*, p. 269 (091–00). On the problem in the late Ch'ing, see *TCSMS*, Ning-shu, chia-p'ien, p. 85.
22. *FWKT*, 35:4b; Juan Pen-yen, *CMCY* (Taiwan reprint), p. 216.
23. *TCCCS:FanWKT*, 2:5b; *TCCCS:FWTK*, 4:9b–10.
24. Ting's references to gentry directors are inconsistent: in some instances he uses the generic term *shen-tung;* in other cases he writes that *t'u-cheng* were to compile registers under the supervision of *hsiang-tung; TCCCS:FanWKT*, 2:6b, 3:5b. On gentry directors, see pp. 135–140.
25. *TCCCS:FanWKT*, 3:1b–2.
26. Ibid., 12:11.
27. Ibid., 3:11b.
28. Juan Pen-yen, *CMCY*, 187 ff.
29. *HTSL*, 165:5.
30. Ch'en Teng-yuan, *Chung-kuo t'ien-fu shih* (Taipei, 1970), p. 209. Yeh-chien Wang essentially concurs and notes that the Ch'ing conducted no surveys for three reasons: (1) they considered the Ming records adequate;

(2) the surveys were politically undesirable; and (3) the surveys were too expensive; *Land Taxation,* p. 27.

31. Yeh-chien Wang, *Land Taxation,* p. 20.
32. On problems with the surveys, see *FHCS,* 8:10, 10:1b; Feng Kuei-fen, *HCTK,* 5:53b; Liu Hsun-kao, comp., *Kiangsu chien-fu ch'üan-an* (preface, 1866), 2:39b–20; *HCCSWHP,* 31:44–47b; Ping-ti Ho, *Studies on Population,* pp. 101–123. The Board of Revenue itself was against surveys for making supplements to the Fish-Scale Registers; *Chih-che ch'eng-kuei,* n.d., 1:29–30b.
33. Feng Kuei-fen, *HCTK,* 5:19b.
34. *TCCCS:FanWKT,* 12:4–4b.
35. *FWKT,* 44:7.
36. Ibid., 50:10b–11.
37. Ibid., 44:7.
38. Ibid., 47:9b–10. On the land quota, see *K'un-hsin liang-hsien hsu-hsiu ho-chih* (1880), 7:16b. The Magistrate, Chang Chin, was a *chu-jen* who had served previously as Magistrate of I-hsing. He had made an excellent initial impression on Ting (*FWKT,* 13:4b, 7), but then had experienced chronic difficulties with fiscal affairs; *FWKT,* 14:1, 16:3, 20:12, 29:17. He had, however, been able to implement properly Ting's order on tax-rate notices; *FWKT,* 33:7, 8; also see pp. 117–122 and Appendix C-2.
39. *FWKT,* 50:11.
40. Ibid., 47:10. According to the *Ch'u-fen tse-li,* a magistrate's delay of land surveys and submission of unclear reports were considered private crimes (*ssu-tsui*) punishable by a 1-year salary fine. A supervising prefect's failure to detect such behavior was considered a public crime (*kung-tsui*) and was punishable by a 6-month salary fine; *CFTL,* 19:2b.
41. *K'un-hsin ho-chih,* 7:19b.
42. *FWKT,* 38:4–4b.
43. Ibid., 50:14. Ting fixed the total land quota at 1,120,000 *mou.* The *Li-yang hsien-chih* (1881) 4:1b, gives a figure of 1,667,000 *mou* for the quota and reports, 4:9b, that the 1869 (TC 8) survey ultimately recorded 916,000 *mou* of taxable land.
44. The Magistrate of Chen-ts'e had chronic difficulties with police work; *FWKT,* 21:14, 26:13b, 39:15, 47:16b, 49:7. But he had prepared good tax-rate notices; *FWKT,* 12:6, 33:7; Appendix C. Chou Pan-ch'ing, a *chien-sheng* who served as Li-yang Magistrate from mid-1868 to late 1870, made a good start by beginning regular taxation again and thereby reducing his hsien's dependence on likin for administrative expenses. But subsequently he demonstrated a laxness in his supervision of fiscal affairs; *FWKT,* 37:7, 47:9, 48:20.
45. *FWKT,* 50:5b.

46. Metzger, *Internal Organization,* p. 265.
47. Yeh-chien Wang, *Land Taxation,* pp. 20–29.
48. *HTSL,* 165:5b, 6, 6b, 7; *Ch'ung-ming hsien-chih,* (1881), 6:17b–25b.
49. *HTSL,* 165:5b, 7.
50. *TCCCS:FWTK,* 3:8–9; *FWKT,* 49–4. On gentry directors, see pp. 135–140.
51. *TCCCS:FWTK,* 9:8–8b; *FWKT,* 21:13.
52. Ying stated that he "obstructed" (*tsu*) Ting's effort, but he did not elaborate; Wu Yun, *Liang-lei-hsuan ch'ih-tu* (1884 preface), 5:28b.
53. *TCCCS:FWTK,* 9:8–8b; *FWKT,* 21:13.
54. *FWKT,* 21:13.
55. Ibid., 17:11b. On the problem of different size acres (*mou*), see Ping-ti Ho, *Studies on Population,* pp. 104–121.
56. *TCCCS:FWTK,* 3:10.
57. According to T'ao Chu, there were old precedents in the *Lü-k'o ch'uan-shu* (Complete book on alluvial grassland taxes) for *shui-ying* and *kuang-t'an,* but he too opposed such devices and ordered that land could not be taxed until it had actually produced some grass; *T'ao Wen-i kung chi,* 10:9. T'ao also forbade what was the then common practice of local bullies forcing payment of taxes to be held against future shortages in case the land reappeared (*liu-liang tai-pu*); ibid., 10:2. For Ting's prohibition of such practices, see Kiangsu sheng po-wu-kuan, comp., *Chiang-su-sheng Ming-Ch'ing i-lai p'ei-k'o tzu-liao hsuan-chi* (Peking, 1959; reprinted Tokyo, 1967), p. 262.
58. *TCCCS:FWTK,* 3:7b.
59. The regulations can be found in *FWKT,* 21:9–10.
60. Cf., *Ch'ung-ming hsien-chih,* 6:17b and Lin Tse-hsu, *Lin Wen-ch'ung kung cheng-shu,* continuous pagination, pp. 123, 128. Both these sources offer different rules for handling such land. In general, local officials found rentals of alluvial land an ongoing source of difficulties; Juan Pen-yen, *CMCY,* pp. 257–258.
61. In the original regulations, back payments on land were not forgiven. When Ting found that most of the old records had been destroyed and that many of the people occupying the land were not the same ones who had contracted for it before the Rebellion, he changed the regulations to exempt present occupants from old debts; *FWKT,* 27:10–11.
62. *FWKT,* 17:12b. On Ting's attitude toward "outsiders," see FO 682/1798B.
63. *TCCCS:FWTK,* 3:9b–10.
64. *T'ao Chu,* 10:2.
65. *FWKT,* 1:8b–9; *TCCCS:FWTK,* 3:8, 9b. In Fu-ning, the Magistrate had

to employ troops to enforce an alluvial survey; Juan Pen-yen, *CMCY*, pp. 257–258.

66. *HTSL*, 165:8b.
67. *FWKT*, 35:3. One particularly troublesome clerk had the paradoxical name Huang Shou-ch'en, "Protect the official Huang."
68. Ibid., 40:7. The director, Wang Te-huai, collected 700 taels while his accomplice, a clerk who was found to be in unauthorized possession of seals and warrants, collected 290 taels. Yet, much to Ting's annoyance, the Magistrate recommended a far heavier sentence for the clerk than for Wang. Ting noted that they both had committed the same crime and should be punished accordingly; *FWKT*, 47:7b. Interestingly, the Magistrate, a Chinese bannerman *fu-kung* named Sung T'ing, had only just been praised by Ting for eliminating his old bad habits and for being tough in carrying out his duties; *FWKT*, 13:5b. Sung had served in Chiang-tu previously. In 1869, he was promoted in recognition of his diligence in judicial administration; *CP* (Chü-heng), TC 8/3/22.
69. The two hsien were Wu-chin and Yang-hu; Kiangsu-sheng po-wu-kuan, *P'ei-k'o tzu-liao*, p. 262.
70. *FWKT*, 42:5–5b.
71. *HTSL*, 165:8.
72. Chu Chih-chen, *Ch'ang-ch'ieh-chai wen-chi* (Taiwan reprint), continuous pagination, pp. 195–196.
73. Ibid. On Chu, see *Ch'ing-shih kao*, 434:7b. Chu's father, Chu Shan-chang had been Hsu-hai Taotai and had been successful enough against the Nien to earn the shadow privilege for his son. Chu Chih-chen's biography characterizes him as honest and upright and a key adviser to senior officials.
74. Chu Chih-chen, p. 195. There is nothing in Chu's biography (above, note 73) to suggest that he would have had an ulterior motive for his criticism. In 1882, Tso Tsung-t'ang, then Liang-kiang Governor-General, submitted a memorial on the survey which endorsed Chu's assessment of the deficiencies in the 1868 survey; Ko Shih-chün, *HCCSWHP*, 32:12.
75. Ting's experience also confirms Yeh-chin Wang's contention that land registration was the weakest link in the administration of the land tax; *Land Taxation*, p. 47.
76. Beattie, pp. 16–17, Chapter 2, esp. pp. 73–75, 78–81.
77. Juan Pen-yen, *CMCY*, p. 188.
78. *HTSL*, 172:4b–9. The terms *ta-hu* and *hsiao-hu* might be more accurately translated as "influential" and "non-influential households" since one's category depended upon the extent one could influence the rate at which one's taxes were collected. Thus, rich commoners as well as

office-holders might be *ta-hu*, while lower degree-holders without office might well be *hsiao-hu*. Han Wen-ch'i, Governor of Kiangsu in the early 1820s, noted that in Fu-ning hsien anyone with less than 50 *mou* was considered a *hsiao-hu* (*Kung-shou-t'ang tsou-i* 2:56), while Pao Shih-ch'en, who served as a *mu-yu* in Kiangsu in the 1820s suggested that, for *pao-chia* registers, any household with 6 or more *mou* per person be considered a "top household" (*shang-hu*) and those with 2 *mou* per person a "lower household" (*hsia-hu*); Pao Shih-ch'en, p. 1920. However, since Ting seems to have identified *ta-hu* with gentry (*shen*) and *hsiao-hu* with commoners (*min*), I have generally followed his terminology. On Ting's usage, see *FWKT,* 1:9b, 32:9; *TCCCS:FWTK,* 1: 13b; cf., Lojewski, "Confucian Reformers," pp. 52–53, 294 note 23.

79. *FWKT,* 5:6; 23:12b.
80. Ibid., 20:4b–5.
81. Ibid., 22:1b, 45–44; *CP* (Chü-heng), TC 8/12/25. However, the problem of gentry *pao-lan,* which hurt the state more than the commoners, appears to have concerned Ting less than the impact upon the people of the clerks' abuses and the gentry tax-rate advantage.
82. On direct payment and equity of payment, see Lin Tse-hsu, *Lin Wen-ch'ung,* p. 933; Hu Lin-i, *Hu Wen-chung kung i-chi* (comp. 1867, Taiwan reprint), 85:14; Li Hung-chang, *Li Wen-chung,* 3:65, 8:61b; *MLSCY,* 3:60; *Su-chou fu-chih,* 13:26b; Wang Ping-hsieh, *Wu-tzu ch'i-shih wen-chi* (1885 preface, Taiwan reprint), continuous pagination, p. 210; Feng Kuei-fen, *HCTK,* 10:1b, 3b; *FHCS,* 6:4. On beatings, see Ch'en Hung-mou in *MLSCY,* 3:62, who advocated their use only if the actual defaulter and not a substitute were being beaten. Also on beatings, see T'ung-tsu Ch'ü, *Local Government in China,* p. 139.
83. *MLSCY,* 3:59b; Wang Ping-hsieh, p. 209; Lin Tse-hsü, *Li Wen-chung,* p. 943; Feng Kuei-fen, *HCTK,* 10:4b–5.
84. For the common use of precedents in official proposals, see Metzger, *Internal Organization,* pp. 127, 190–192.
85. Hu Lin-i, 85:14b, recommended bonded constables; *Su-chou fu-chih,* 13:23. Late Ch'ing fiscal reformers again favored substantial, honest families to man the chests; *Kiangsu Ts'ai-cheng shuo-ming shu,* Su-shu, sui-ju-pu, chia-p'ien, p. 18.
86. Feng Kuei-fen, *HCTK,* 10:6.
87. *MLSCY,* 3:62.
88. Ibid., 3:62.
89. Ibid., 3:71 b. Wang Ping-hsieh wrote that, immediately after the Taiping Rebellion, it cost approximately 20 foreign dollars to obtain a post as precinct (*t'u*) revenue clerk, the clerk who made up the tax registers. For the doorkeeper (*men-ting*) and the chief grain clerks (*ts'ao-shu*) in the

Soochow Prefect's office, that meant an annual take of 36,000 dollars (i.e., 20 dollars × 200 *t'u*/hsien = 4,000 dollars/hsien × 9 hsien/Soochow prefecture = 36,000 dollars).

90. See pp. 133–134.
91. The following two paragraphs, unless otherwise indicated, are based on T'ao Chu, 7:5; Lin Tse-hsu, *Lin Wen-ch'ung,* pp. 326–347; Li Hung-chang, *Tsou-kao,* 3:64–65; *THTKTI,* 1, 11–12.
92. Susan Mann Jones, "Hung Liang-chi (1746–1890): The Perception and Articulation of Political Problems . . ." (PhD dissertation, Stanford University, 1972), p. 176.
93. Cf., Metzger, *Internal Organization,* p. 321 n. 75.
94. Kuhn and Jones, "Dynastic Decline," p. 130.
95. Polachek, "Literati Groups," Chapters 3, 4.
96. Kuei Chao-wan, p. 281.
97. Lojewski, "Confucian Reformers," p. 157.
98. On Feng's dissatisfaction with the nature and extent of the reduction, see ibid., p. 178.
99. Wright, pp. 165–167.
100. Cf. Cole, pp. 116–129. On rent reductions, see Feng Kuei-fen, *HCTK,* 4:12; Hsia Nai, p. 472; and Frank A. Lojewski, "The Soochow Bursaries: Rent Management During the Late Ch'ing," *Ch'ing-shih wen-t'i,* 4:3 (June 1980), pp. 54–55.
101. *TCCCS:FanWKT,* 2:1b; *Kiangsu Sheng-li,* "Nieh," TC 7, p. 35; cf. Murmatsu Yuji, pp. 566–599. On rent reports, see *FWKT,* 50:3b.
102. Li Hung-chang, *Tsou-kao,* 8:61–62; Liu Chin-tsao, ed., *Ch'ing-ch'ao hsu wen-hsien t'ung-k'ao* (Shanghai, 1935), pp. 7523–7524; Liu Hsun-kao, comp., *Kiangsu chien-fu ch'üan-an,* 1:506, 2:29–32b.
103. *Tsou-kao,* 7:43–44b; *FWKT,* 22:6; *SL:TC,* 121:3–4; *MLSCY,* 10:48b–50.
104. *Tsou-kao,* 10:31b.
105. *Kiangsu Sheng-li,* "Fan," TC 6, pp. 19, 32; "Fan," TC 7, p. 3; "Fan," TC 8, p. 8.
106. *TCCCS:FWTK,* 1:11b; *FWKT,* 36:13, 39:4.
107. *FWKT,* 35:13b; *Kiangsu Sheng-li,* "Fan," TC 7, pp. 54–54b.
108. *FWKT,* 1:9b; *TCCCS:FanWKT,* 12:7b; *TCCCS: FWTK,* 1:11b.
109. Yeh-chien Wang, *Land Taxation,* p. 41; T'ung-tsu Ch'ü, *Local Government,* pp. 133–134.
110. *TCCCS:FanWKT,* 2:4b. On the relation of the *Yellow* and *Fish-Scale Registers,* see Kung-chuan Hsiao, pp. 85–88 and Wei Ch'ing-yuan, *Ming-tai huang-ts'e chih-tu* (Peking, 1961), pp. 72–79.
111. Wan Wei-han, "Mu-hsueh chü-yao," in Chang T'ing-hsiang, ed., *Ju-mu hsu-chih wu-chung* (1890 preface; Taiwan reprint), continuous pagination, p. 55; *MLSCY,* 3:40b, 3:42: *Su-chou fu-chih,* 13:27.

112. *TCCCS:FanWKT,* 2:4–4b. On using both methods of urging, see Wan Wei-han, pp. 55–56.
113. *TCCCS:FanWKT,* 3:7, 12:4b–5.
114. *Su-chou fu-chih,* 13:28b; *TCCCS:FanWKT,* 12:1b.
115. The above account is drawn from *Su-chou fu-chih,* 13:30b; Yeh Meng-chu, *Yueh-shih pien,* 6:17b–19, in Shanghai T'ung-she, comp., *Shanghai chang-ku ts'ung-shu* (Shanghai, 1936); Chiang Chen-wu, "Shanghai hsien tsai Ch'ing-tai," *Shanghai t'ung-chih kuan ch'i-k'an,* 2:2 (September 1935), p. 496; Kuribayashi Nobuo, *Rikōsei no kenkyu* (Tokyo, 1971), pp. 318–345; Jerry Dennerline, "Fiscal Reform and Local Control," in Wakeman and Grant, eds., *Conflict and Control in Late Imperial China* (Berkeley, 1975), pp. 106–109.
116. *TCCCS:FanWKT,* 2:4b–5. Indeed, for this very reason the Ming began to use the Fish-Scale Register. Wei Ch'ing-yuan, p. 76.
117. *FWKT,* 45:16b; also T'ung-tsu Ch'ü, *Local Government,* pp. 137–138 and Kung-chuan Hsiao, pp. 96, 102.
118. *K'un-hsin ho-chih,* 7:19b.
119. Wang Ch'ing-yun, *Shih-ch'ü yu-chi* (alternate title, *Hsi-ch'ao chi-cheng,* 1890 preface), 3:16b. For the first use of *yu-tan* in Kiangsu in 1674, see *Su-chou fu-chih,* 13:26b.
120. Lin Tse-hsu, *Lin Wen-ch'ung,* p. 943. Feng Kuei-fen had fruitlessly proposed reinstituting the *yu-tan; HCTK,* 9:3b, 4b–5; cf., Wang Ping-hsieh, p. 209. On the number of rates in Kiangsu, see *TCCCS:FWTK,* 2:10.
121. Shen had served previously as Acting Magistrate of the head county, Wu-hsien. Chao Lieh-wen, TC 6/9/15, charged that Ting had accepted a bribe from Shen to quash an impeachment, but Lü Shih-ch'iang has effectively disputed this accusation; Lü, *Ting Jih-ch'ang,* pp. 367–370.
122. *Wu-chiang hsien-chih* (1879), 10:25–25b; *TCCCS:FanWKT,* 2:8–8b. Rawski has shown that peasants possessed this level of literacy.
123. *TCCCS:FanWKT,* 2:8–8b.
124. *TCCCS:FanWKT,* 2:9b–10. The number of rates remained the same; *K'un-shan ho-chih,* 6:17b–19. It was the amount charged per acre at each rate that was reduced; Lojewski, "Confucian Reformers," pp. 191–194.
125. For Ting's order, see *TCCCS:FanWKT,* 2:10b.
126. Han Wen-ch'i, 1:69–72b.
127. *TCCCS:FWTK,* 1:10b–11, 4:12–13b. On the governor's control of the rate of collection, see Yeh-chien Wang, *Land Taxation,* pp. 36–37; also see ibid., pp. 60–61, 110–128, on the relation of prices to the rate of collection and to the burden of taxation.
128. Lin had issued a proclamation announcing the date on which the *yu-tan* were to be issued. If the taxpayer had not received his within 5 days of

that date, he could make an accusation against the chief grain clerk (*ching-tsao*); Lin Tse-hsu, *Lin Wen-ch'ung,* p. 943.

129. For the tax regulations that were issued by Ting at the end of 1867, see *TCCCS:FanWKT,* 12:5b–7; *Kiangsu Sheng-li,* "Fan," TC 6, p. 38. For the extension of these procedures to Kiangpei, see *FWKT,* 5:4b–5b.
130. *TCCCS:FWTK,* 2:10b.
131. *FWKT,* 5:4–4b.
132. The Magistrate of Tang-shan, a *chin-shih* named Kuo Chin-lai, was impeached and dismissed for failing to post the notices, and for various other deficiencies; *TCCCS:FWTK,* 2:19b; *FWKT,* 19:15b; below, p. 267 note 151. The Magistrates of Fu-ning, Ch'ing-ho, and T'an-yuan were all given demerits for failing to post a sufficient number of the notices; *FWKT,* 32:8. Ting's memorial on the rate sheets, which included the specific request for court approval of the practice as a permanent institution, appeared in the *Peking Gazette* without an imperial rescript; *CP* (Shantung), TC 7/7/13. But its prominent position in that day's issue suggests that his idea was supported by the court. On the importance of the placement of documents in the *Peking Gazette,* see Jonathan Ocko, "The British Museum's *Peking Gazettes,*" *Ch'ing-shih wen-t'i,* 2.9:45–46 (January 1973).
133. *FWKT,* 5:4b.
134. For Magistrates' compliance, see Appendix C-2.
135. *FWKT,* 13:1.
136. Ibid., 33:10b–11.
137. Ibid., 24:12.
138. Ibid., 33:8b.
139. Ibid., 32:1b.
140. Ibid., 37:4b. Ting was commenting on a Magistrate who had misappropriated money contributed to buy emergency grain.
141. Ibid., 35:6b.
142. Ibid., 41:6.
143. Ibid., 35:6b. The excess fees averaged 1,000 cash. Tung-t'ai had the same problem. There a grain-shop owner and several taxpayers complained of surcharges 500 cash over the fixed rate. Moreover, one complainant charged that he had never seen any rate notices out in the countryside. The Magistrate was not punished; ibid., 35:5.
144. Ibid., 35:14b.
145. Ibid., 35:7; Metzger, *Internal Organization,* pp. 310–311.
146. Commoner rates were from 9–18 times higher than gentry ones; *FWKT,* 20:4b.
147. Ibid., 32:9b.
148. See, for example, Kiangsu Governor T'an Chun-p'ei's 1880 proclamation

against the use of different size grain measures for gentry and commoners in Kiangsu-sheng po-wu-kuan, *P'ei-k'o tzu-liao,* pp. 262–263; and Soochow Financial Commissioner Ying Pao-shih's 1874 circular order prohibiting rate discrimination in *Kiangsu Sheng-li Hsu-pien,* "Fan," TC 13, p. 25b.

149. On the *i-t'u,* see Wan Kuo-ting et al., *Chiang-su Wu-chin Nan-t'ung t'ien-fu tiao-ch'a pao-kao* (1934), p. 84; *TCSMS,* "Su-shu, sui-ju-pu, chia-pien," p. 18; cf., David Faure, "Local Political Disturbances in Kiangsu Province, China, 1870–1911" (PhD dissertation, Princeton University, 1976), p. 219. For litigation arising out of *i-t'u,* see Han Wen-ch'i, 8:61–66b, 10:56–60b (on concern for *pao-lan*), 10:61–66. On the concept of the bursary as a protective mechanism, see Lojewski, "The Li Kung-jen Bursary." Kuhn suggests such bursaries were exempt from suspicions of *pao-lan;* "Local Self-Government Under the Republic," in Wakeman and Grant, eds., *Conflict and Control in Late Imperial China* (Berkeley, 1975), p. 268, 268n. 17.
150. Cited in Li Wen-chih, comp., *Chung-kuo chin-tai nung-yeh shih tzu-liao,* 1840–1911, (Peking, 1957), 1. 345.
151. See pp. 157–158. Feng Kuei-fen, *HCTK,* 5:7b, estimated that, while the official received at best 30–40% of the illegal fees, he was, nonetheless, held responsible for the entire amount.
152. The phrase is Feng Kuei-fen's; *HCTK,* 9:26. And, though he used it to describe commoners, it seems equally appropriate for the gentry.
153. Ibid., 9:26. Elsewhere, Ibid., 5:7b, Feng commented that, while the people of Soochow were timid, they were also cunning and would take advantage of any shortcut. In a similar vein, Juan Pen-yen, Magistrate of Fu-ning in the 1870s, reminded people that the legal machinations of tricksters would not free them from the risks of farming; Juan Pen-yen, *CMCY,* p. 235.
154. *FWKT,* 37:4b. The complaint had been made by some village elders and gentry who had stopped Ting's chair on his way to Shanghai.
155. *CFTL,* 19:4b; *TCLL,* p. 931.
156. *TCLL,* p. 1139; *TLTI,* p. 328 (122–00, 01); *HAHL,* 9:22b.
157. Metzger, *Internal Organization,* pp. 284–285; *TLTI,* p. 341 (127–00).
158. *TLTI,* pp. 321 (119–00, 01), 324 (119–06); *TCLL,* pp. 1115–1119.
159. *CFTL,* 19:4b.
160. *FWKT,* 29:18; also see p. 152.
161. Although embezzlers (*ch'in-ch'i, ch'in-k'uei*) could escape criminal punishment by making restitution, they could not be restored to office; *CFTL,* 27:3b. Juggling of funds (*no-i ch'ien-liang*) was classified in the *CFTL* as a private offense (*ssu-tsui*), but, if an official guilty of this offense made restitution within a specified time limit, he could be re-

stored to office; *CFTL,* 27:4b. The Penal Code, however, considered *no-i* a public offense (*kung-tsui*). The Penal Code also correlated the punishment to the amount juggled: 20,000 taels was a watershed; if an official juggled more than that, even complete restitution could not get him restored to office; *TCLL,* pp. 1117–1118; *TLTI,* p. 342 (127–02). Officials seem to have been punished under the terms of the Penal Code; see Han Wen-ch'i, 8:1–6b and *HAHL,* 9:23–27 for relevant cases. For a discussion of the problems in distinguishing juggling from embezzlement, see Metzger, *Internal Organization,* p. 284; also see case in *Kung-chung-tang Kuang-hsu ch'ao tsou-che* (Taipei, 1973), 3. 902. Although officials were forbidden to remain in office while they made restitution, for fear they would extract the cost from the people, there does not seem to have been an awareness that the same situation might arise with a restored official; *CFTL,* 27:3b–4.

162. See exchange between the Literary Chancellor, Hsin Ts'un-i, and the Governor of Kiangsu, T'ao Chu, on whether or not *sheng-yuan* and *chien-sheng* were being singled out for punishment for *pao-lan,* while the clerks were shielding themselves behind the officials. For Hsin, see *THTKTI,* 1, 173–175; for T'ao, *T'ao Wen-i kung-chi,* 7:19b–25. The Tao-kuang Emperor shared the concern of Hsin; *Chin-ting t'ai kuei,* 14:39. But one of T'ao's immediate predecessors, Han Wen-ch'i, an able and honest official, had found most of the charges made against clerks to be untrue; 1:69–72b, 8:61–66b, 10:56–66. The Literary Chancellor's concern for his charges, the *sheng-yuan,* belies Feng Kuei-fen's assertion that literary chancellors and magistrates enjoyed humiliating *sheng-yuan* and *chien-sheng;* Feng, *HCTK,* 9:25. For the general political context of the struggle between T'ao Chu and Hsin Ts'un-i, see Polachek, "Literati Groups and Literati Politics," pp. 310–322.
163. The phrase is Chia-ch'ing's. According to T'ao Chu, the *chien-sheng* simply continued in their old ways; *T'ao Wen-i kung chi,* 7:7.
164. Hsueh Yun-sheng in *TLTI,* pp. 321–322 (119–01). Ting's experiences show this already to be true in the mid-nineteenth century. The number of land-tax cases in *HAHL* and its later editions is too small either to corroborate or to dispute Hsueh's assertion. Compare with the much larger number of cases relating to violation of salt-monopoly regulations.
165. The first and only time the Ch'ing state strictly enforced its tax laws was under the Oboi Regency when the Manchu Princes decided to make an example out of Kiangnan gentry tax evaders. For the political history of this Kiangnan Tax Case, see Robert B. Oxnam, "Policies and Institutions of the Oboi Regency 1661–1669," *Journal of Asian Studies,* 31.2: 265–286 (February 1973).
166. Moral economists see landlords as paternally concerned with the needs

of their tenants. In particular, landlords demonstrate their concern by guaranteeing their tenants socially accepted fundamental subsistence rights. By contrast, political economists argue that the landlord will work not to improve the subsistence of his tenants but to reinforce his own position; see James C. Scott, *The Moral Economy of the Peasant* (Yale University Press, 1976); Samuel Popkin, *The Rational Peasant: The Political Economy of Rural Society in Vietnam* (Berkeley, University of California Press, 1979). In particular, see Polachek, "Gentry Hegemony," pp. 216–217.

167. Cf., Polachek, "Gentry Hegemony," pp. 211–256 and Lojewski, "The Li Kung-jen Bursary." Ping-ti Ho, in a review of Vol. 10, *Late Ch'ing*, of the *Cambridge History of China* argues that, in any case, all the attention on land-tax reform is misplaced and that the truly significant economic history concerns the immigration and resettlement discussed above, pp. 96–99; Ping-ti Ho, *Journal of Asian Studies* 39:1 (November 1979), p. 136.
168. Dennerline, p. 96; Polachek, "Gentry Hegemony," p. 221.
169. See memorials and edicts on the case in Tung-hsiang, Szechuan; Chang Chih-tung in Sheng K'ang, *HCCSWHP*, 4453–61; Li Tsung-hsi in *Kuang-hsu Tung-hua lu* KH 4/4.17; and edict in *SL:KH*, 93:2–2b (continuous pagination, p. 847).
170. *FWKT*, 37:7b–8, 29:1–1b; Tseng Kuo-fan, *Tsou-kao*, 241:17; Polachek, "Gentry Hegemony," pp. 244–245, 254–255.
171. *FWKT*, 50:2; Polachek, "Gentry Hegemony," pp. 255–256.
172. On Magistrates' length of service, see Appendix B.
173. Li Kuo-ch'i, "T'ung-chih chung-hsing shih-ch'i Liu K'un-i tsai Kiangsi hsun-fu jen-nei ti piao-hsien," *Kuo-li T'ai-wan shih-fan ta-hsueh li-shih hsueh-pao* 1 (1973), pp. 248, 260.
174. *FWKT*, 50:13.

6. *Personnel*

1. *TCCCS:HHKT*, 1:2b.
2. Watt, pp. 225–233.
3. *HCCSWP*, 16:11. Wang Chih-i was a *chu-jen* of 1771 who rose to be Min-che Governor-General.
4. Metzger, *Internal Organization*, pp. 260–261.
5. Thomas A. Metzger, "Some Legal Aspects of Bureaucratic Organization in China under the Ch'ing" (PhD dissertation, Harvard University, 1967), p. 229.
6. G. William Skinner, "Cities and the Hierarchy of Local Systems," in *The City in Late Imperial China* (Stanford, 1977), has argued that, in

the peripheral counties, parapolitical structures were weaker and that county-level yamens consequently had to shoulder more responsibilities of governance, while, in the core counties, responsibility for social management was allowed to be assumed by the informal parapolitical structures; pp. 308, 338–339.

7. T'ung-tsu Ch'ü, *Local Government,* pp. 36, 39, 58–60.
8. On these duties and wages, see ibid., pp. 41–43, 44–49, 60–61, 64–67.
9. Feng Kuei-fen, *CPLKI,* 1:15; *CP* (Chü-heng), TC 7/11/27.
10. *TCCCS:FWTK,* 5:18b–21.
11. *Kiangsu Sheng-li,* "Fan," TC 6, p. 25.
12. *FWKT,* Preface, p. 2.
13. Chao Lieh-wen, TC 6/9/7; Cf., Lü Shih-ch'iang, *Ting Jih-ch'ang,* p. 375. Lü feels that Ting's measures were successful.
14. Liang Chang-chü, *T'ui-an sui-pi,* 5:4b–5. Another Ch'ing administrative writer asserted that many of the clerks were from good families, sons who failed the examinations; *HCCSWP,* 214:8.
15. Sheng K'ang, *HCCSWHP,* 28:1, 4–5.
16. Feng Kuei-fen, *CPLKI,* 1:6–7; Wright, pp. 90–91.
17. Feng Kuei-fen, *CPLKI,* 1:16. Feng said that, once his proposal to reduce and simplify the precedents was implemented, officials could consolidate clerical work in the hands of their *mu-yu,* who would then become part of the official hierarchy. Those *mu-yu* who had served 9 years could be tested and selected to serve as subordinate officials. But Feng urged that, in order to distinguish this route from the regular one, a former *mu-yu* be prohibited from entering the Hanlin Academy or serving as a Grand Secretary.
18. *FWKT,* 7:5–5b. As Financial Commissioner, Ting had received permission to draw up to 100,000 cash from ready cash accounts to pay for additional clerks. When he became Governor and extended his procedures to the entire province, he found that he would require another 100,000 a month.
19. *IWSM:TC,* 55:17–20.
20. *IWSM:TC,* 55:18; cf., Wright, p. 94.
21. *TCCCS:FWTK,* 5:29b.
22. *MLSCY,* 2:27.
23. Feng Kuei-fen, *CPLKI,* 1:16.
24. *HT,* 12:13b–14; T'ung-tsu Ch'ü, *Local Government,* p. 44.
25. Shen Hsi-hua served as Acting Wu hsien Magistrate in 1861 (in Shanghai), Acting Yuan-ho Magistrate for 5 months in 1863, and as Magistrate of Wu-chiang from 1862 to 1868 and 1869 to 1870. Li Ko-chin served as Magistrate of Yuan-ho (in Shanghai) from late 1861 to early 1862, of Ch'ing-p'u from 1863 to 1864, and of T'an-yuan from 1868 to

1870. In the last post, Li succeeded the egregiously incompetent Tseng Hui; see pp. 163–166.

26. Wei-jen Chang, "Late Ch'ing Judicial Administration," p. 331.
27. *FWKT,* 2:1b.
28. Ts'ai Shen-chih, p. 13. One writer, referring to these responsibilites, observed that, while runners were less literate than clerks, they were far more awe-inspiring; Sheng K'ang, *HCCSWHP,* 28:51.
29. See p. 158.
30. *FWKT,* 2:1b–2b.
31. *FWKT,* 20:9b–10.
32. Chao Lieh-wen, TC 6/9/4.
33. A late Ch'ing *mu-yu* described the gentry (*shih-shen*) as a group with great economic and political influence upon which the local official relied for assistance in handling local affairs; Wei-jen Chang, "Late Ch'ing Judicial Administration," p. 338.
34. Runners in Chekiang forced substantial landowners to serve as local constables (*ti-pao*) and well-off *sheng-chien* to assume onerous tax-prompting responsibilities; *Chih-che ch'eng-kuei,* 2:56–57b. On underling harassment of lower degree-holders over taxes, see p. 257 note 162; Kuei Chao-wan, p. 255; Pao Shih-ch'en, pp. 2045–2046. Also, runners apparently imprisoned even elite in their unauthorized lockups; *FWKT,* 18:1.
35. *Kiangsu Sheng-li san-pien,* "Nieh," KH 2, pp. 12–14b.
36. *FWKT,* 49:6.
37. For a discussion of the historical decay of the *li-chia* system and the atrophy of these districts, see Obata Tatsuo "Kōnan ni okeru rikō no hensei ni tsuite," *Shirin* 39.2:1–35 (March 1956).
38. See, for example, Ma Hsin-i, 8:10, on the stockade chiefs.
39. *FWKT,* 47:7b and pp. 136–137, 251 note 68.
40. *FWKT,* 43:14; *Kiangsu Sheng-li san-pien,* "Nieh," KH 2, p. 12b.
41. *Chih-che ch'eng-kuei,* 2:56–57b; Mary Rankin, "Late Ch'ing Chekiang Elite Activisits," paper delivered at New England China Seminar, Harvard University, October 1978 (cited with permission of the author).
42. Juan Pen-yen, *CMCY,* pp. 82, 216.
43. Ibid., pp. 196–198, 213, 224–225.
44. Ocko, "Justice on Appeal."
45. See p. 257, note 163; *Fen-fa t'iao-li* HF 9, "Ssu-hou sheng-chien tzu-shih chiao-kuan pu-neng chen yueh-shu."
46. *FWKT,* 27:1.
47. *FWKT,* 47:18b. Philip Kuhn has drawn precisely the opposite conclusion, arguing that clerks could be effectively disciplined neither by bureaucratic accountability (since they were not part of the formal

system) nor "by an intimate and regular relationship to the natural units of local society"; "Local Self-Government," p. 262.

48. *FWKT,* 29:2b.
49. See p. 26 for an example of the type of politically powerful group that might coalesce around an issue of concern to them.
50. Juan Pen-yen, *CMCY,* pp. 54–55, 127.
51. Pao Shih-ch'en, pp. 2045–2046, noted that local officials could also invoke the support of their superiors, who, in order to protect themselves, often sided with their subordinates against the local elite.
52. Ya Erh-t'u, "Yao-shih," 4:40.
53. *MLSCY,* 6:25.
54. Kuhn, *Rebellion and Its Enemies,* pp. 9–10, 58–59, 62–63.
55. On tribute-grain tax riots, see *FWKT,* 43:10b; on salt smuggling, see *SL:TC,* 295:11–12, 269:12–13; on collusion with criminals, see *FWKT,* 48:6, and Ma Hsin-i, 8:10.
56. See p. 37; T'ung-tsu Ch'ü, *Local Government,* p. 192; Polachek, "Gentry Hegemony," especially pp. 228–249, 254–256.
57. Frequently holders of purchased titles, the *hsun-chien* were endowed with the lowest rank and commensurately paltry salaries; *FWKT,* 8:4; also, *FWKT,* 28:8; *TCCCS:FanWKT,* 2:1b. On landlords' use of government personnel, see Muramatsu Yuji, pp. 568–569, 590–594.
58. *CFTL,* 47:8–8b. The magistrate was punished for failing to uncover such activity or for delegating such authority to *tso-tsa.*
59. Feng Kuei-fen, *CPLKI,* 1:13b–14. Feng called for triennial elections to select *fu-tung* (assistant directors) for every 100 families and *cheng-tung* (chief directors) for every 1,000 families. Civil litigation would be initiated at a court held by the former and appealed up through the latter. If people by-passed these men, they would be punished according to the provisions for by-passing in litigation; see p. 241, note 11. Feng also proposed the establishment of additional *hsun-chien* and the new post of vice-magistrate (*ch'eng-po*); also see Lojewski, "Confucian Reformers," pp. 139–146; Kuhn, "Local Self-government," p. 266.
60. See *TCCCS:FanWKT,* 1:1b for the initial proclamation. See *TCCCS:FanWKT,* 2:1b and *FWKT,* 8:3 for later difficulties.
61. *FWKT,* 28:7b–8, 8:4. Ting's argument parallels that of the writer who criticized all the official layers above the magistrate (see p. 132), but Ting himself seemed unaware of the analogy.
62. *FWKT,* 2:2–2b, 8:6.
63. *FWKT,* 26:10. In the instance of the street-cleaning organizations that Ting instituted, however, he exempted the gentry households from serving a turn and ordered that the rubble in front of their houses be cleaned up for them; *TCCCS:FanWKT,* 11:4.

64. Gentry were supposed to be registered in but not to lead *pao-chia*. The principle, however, was not always observed; Kung-chuan Hsiao, pp. 68–72. Indeed, one able Magistrate wrote that, while it was improper for *sheng-yuan* to urge taxes, they ought to serve as constables in order to avoid unfairly burdening commoners; Kuei Chao-wan, pp. 197–203. In any case, in difficult times the *pao-chia* was supplanted by the elite-led *t'uan-lien* as the force of order; Kuhn, *Rebellion and Its Enemies*, pp. 61–62.
65. *FWKT*, 43:13, 27:1.
66. Cf., Wright, pp. 128–129; and Kuhn, *Rebellion and Its Enemies*, p. 214. Kuhn argues that the officials encouraged this shift of power from the "relatively uncontrollable" clerks and runners to the "relatively sympathetic and predictable" elite. While in his later work, "Local Self-Government," he maintains his arguments about the accountability of the elite, he refines his point to distinguish between the upper elite, such as Feng Kuei-fen, and the lower elite of rural gentry managers. It was in the interest of both the state and upper elite, he states, to suppress the activities of the gentry directors. My own work and Polachek's, "Gentry Hegemony" emphasize the tension and conflict that pervaded all elite-state relationships. For a stimulating discussion of the political ties between the Restoration local elite, *ch'ing-i* opponents of self-strengthening, and the reformers of 1898, see Schrecker, "The Reform Movement of 1898."
67. Wright, p. 77. For her discussion of leading Restoration officials, see pp. 73-77.
68. *SL:TC*, 254-20; *TCCCS:FWTK*, 5:16.
69. *TCCCS:FWTK*, 5:16.
70. Ibid., 30:8.
71. Ibid., 27:6b.
72. Ibid., 5:3.
73. Ibid., 28:1b.
74. Ibid., 28:2b.
75. *MLSCY*, 2:35; editorial comment by Ting.
76. This list of expectations was derived from Ting's comments to magistrates; see *FWKT*, 28:2, 13:4b, 13:7, 30:7, 4:3.
77. *FWKT*, 5:3.
78. Feng Kuei-fen, *CPLKI*, 1:12b, expressed doubt that the magistrate could visit each of the "several hundred thousand" households in his district. Hence, how could the magistrate "have a thorough knowledge of its goodness, its energy, or its physical condition?"
79. *TCCCS:FWTK*, 5:15b–16.
80. *IWSM:TC*, 55:19–19b. Wang T'ao and Feng Kuei-fen, both of whom

were in regular contact with Ting, were thinking along similar lines. On Wang, see Paul Cohen, *Between Tradition and Modernity: Wang T'ao and Reform in Late Ch'ing China* (Cambridge, Mass., 1974), pp. 164–168. For Feng's views, see *CPLKI,* 2:67–70.

81. For a stimulating discussion of the significance of the post designations, see Skinner, "Cities and the Hierarchy of Local Systems," pp. 314–336.
82. On the appointments process, see Watt, pp. 45–58; also Robert N. Weiss, "Flexibility in Provincial Government on the Eve of the Taiping Rebellion," *Ch'ing-shih wen-t'i* 4.3:5–14 (June 1980).
83. Candidates for preferment posts had to have served for 5 years, be acting or probationary magistrates under the governor's authority, or be officials due for promotion. Candidates for transfer posts had to have served 3 years in another substantive position of the same rank; Watt, p. 46.
84. The Board's rejections usually involved "irregular" appointments; see pp. 155–156.
85. Kwang-ching Liu, "The Ch'ing Restoration," pp., 441, 443.
86. Li Kuo-ch'i, *Chung-kuo ti-fang chih yen-chiu,* p. 28, has a chart that graphically demonstrates the rise.
87. See p. 259, note 25.
88. *SL:TC,* 254:20 on the need for good magistrates.
89. Such modifications usually involved the downgrading of another post; Han Wen-ch'i, 11:50–52. After the outbreak of revolt in Hunan, changes in the status of counties had been made; Weiss, p. 6.
90. Wu Ta-ch'eng, head of Soochow's Tzu-yang shu-yuan in the late 1860s, made this charge; Ku T'ing-lung, p. 17.
91. Skinner, "Cities and the Hierarchy of Local Systems," p. 323. Wu, Yuan-ho, and Ch'ang-chou were the only hsien which did not set time limits for runners' service of warrants; *FWKT,* 45:9. These 3 also delayed preparing for the ceremonial rites in honor of Confucius and sought to evade this responsibility; *FWKT,* 28:3b; also see *FWKT,* 39: 12, 28:7b–8, 27:8, 45:10b; *TCCCS:FanWKT,* 2:7b. The Prefect of Soochow, the Magistrates' immediate supervisor, also had his troubles with judicial affairs; *FWKT,* 32:2b, 11b. Perhaps he was too involved with fiscal administration.
92. *Fen-fa t'iao-li,* TC 3, "Ssu-hou shou-fu-hsien ch'ueh-ch'u ying-ling kao tu-fu yu t'ung-sheng cheng-t'u."
93. Weiss, pp. 5–14; see also p. 265, note 115.
94. Kwang-ching Liu, "The Ch'ing Restoration," p. 440.
95. The following section is drawn from Board of Civil Office materials in *Fen-fa t'iao-li* between the dates TC 1 and TC 12.
96. Originally, purchasers could obtain only the ranks of petty officials,

but, beginning in Tao-kuang, they seem to have been allowed to buy substantive offices; see Hsu Ta-ling, *Ch'ing-tai chüan-na chih-tu* (Peking, 1950), pp. 58–59, 169.

97. Wright, pp. 85–87.
98. *THTKTI,* 4.1675; *Fen-fa t'iao-li,* TC 12, "Cheng-t'u jen-yuan yung-chi ch'ing chuo-ho pao-chü."
99. Wright, p. 86; *CP* (Shantung), TC 4/12/16–17.
100. On sale of office at discount, see Hsu Ta-ling, pp. 109–111; *NCH,* May 23, 1867.
101. *TCCCS:FWTK,* 5:16b–18. The system of sale of office was never discontinued. See Hsu Ta-ling, pp. 166–170.
102. *TCCCS:FWTK,* 5:17b. In the 1820s, Kiangsu Governor Han Wen-ch'i, citing similar requests from other provinces, had asked the court to stop sending petty officials (*tso-tsa*) to Kiangsu as alternates because they were overwhelming the quota of positions. Some men were waiting 10–20 years for opportunities to serve; *Kung-shou-t'ang tsou-i,* 3:33–35; also Weiss, pp. 11–12.
103. *FWKT,* 29:18.
104. Watt, p. 42; *FWKT,* 24:5; *TCCCS:FanWKT,* 1:3b; Ts'ai Shen-chih, p. 63.
105. *TCCCS:FWTK,* 5:17b–18.
106. *NCH,* May 23, 1867, Hupei, Hunan, Kiangsi, Anhwei, and Shantung all also examined those who had earned their candidacy for office through contributions or military merit in order to weed out the unlettered; *Fen-fa t'iao-li,* TC 3, "Ssu-hou shou-fu shou-hsien ch'ueh-ch'u ying-ling kai tu-fu yu t'ung-sheng cheng-t'u."
107. Watt, pp. 52–53.
108. *THTKTI,* 2.463. Alternate officials who performed well were to be recommended for substantive appointments. See, for example, Ting's regulations for alternate officials assigned to the judicial commissioner's auxiliary court; *FWKT,* 41:3.
109. *FWKT,* 8:7–7b.
110. *MLSCY,* 1:36; editorial comment by Ting.
111. Metzger, *Internal Organization,* p. 262.
112. The Censor Ch'en Wen-chu (1839) said that, although alternate officials were interviewed by the superior officials on 3,6,9 days, there were so many alternates that they just milled about trying to get noticed while the superior officials barely saw an individual face, much less conducted an actual interview; *THTKTI,* 2.463.
113. *FWKT,* 29:7b. Some Magistrates never appeared for their examinations; *FWKT,* 43:11.
114. *TCCCS:FanWKT,* 1:3, 9–10. One Magistrate, transferred to Soochow

for supervision and seasoning, not only took 2 years to familiarize himself with the local situation but also never demonstrated he was capable enough to handle the more difficult post to which he was originally appointed; *CP* (Chü-heng), TC 8/9/7.

115. For Tao-kuang cases, see Li Hsing-yuan, 10:62–64, 11:37–39; Weiss, p. 9. For T'ung-chih appointments, see *SL:TC,* 114:16b–17, *CP* (Shantung), TC 4/12/14–15. For the court's approval of the compromise measures, see *SL:TC,* 183:8–8b. The court's objection in most cases was that the official had not had an audience. Aware of the court's feelings on this matter, Ting phrased his recommendations in strong language; *TCCCS:FWTK,* 3:11–11b.

116. The court refused to promote the Shan-yang Magistrate who had been especially successful at suppressing the Nien to the rank of independent department magistrate (*chih-li chou chih-chou*). *CP* (Chü-heng), TC 8/9/7.

117. The court responded by instructing governors to examine carefully all newly arrived taotais, prefects, and magistrates, regardless of how they had obtained their appointments, and by reminding senior provincial officials that they should distinguish between easy and difficult posts and recommend only the best candidates; *SL:TC,* 300:7b–8. The court also repeatedly warned senior officials against allowing personal feelings and questions of face to influence their recommendations; *SL:TC,* 254: 19, 260:9b–10.

118. *THTKTI,* 3.1329, 4.1706.

119. On officials, see p. 86; on clerks, see *FWKT,* 29:18.

120. Acting magistrates, of whom there were many during Ting's tenure, received only half the stipulated *yang-lien; TCSMS,* "Su-shu ch'ing-li ts'ai-cheng chü fu-pien fu chou ting hsien ju-k'uan," p. 5. Chung-li Chang, *The Income of the Chinese Gentry* (Seattle, 1962), p. 31, asserts that, on the average, a magistrate's real income totaled nearly 30,000 taels. On *mu-yu* salaries, see T'ung-tsu Ch'ü, *Local Government,* p. 112.

121. The situation occurred because of deficits in the meltage fees which were used to pay for the *yang-lien,* as well as in salt-monopoly fees which were to have been substituted for the meltage fees. Ting drew the precedent for conversion of back pay into rank from the military; *TCCCS:FWTK,* 2:17b–18. *Yang-lien* payments were not subject to disciplinary fines but could be garnished to make up deficits in one's own, or even one's grandfather's, accounts and to pay assigned contributions (*t'an-chüan*); Metzger, *Internal Organization,* p. 321.

122. *TCCCS:FWTK,* 5:19.

123. Ibid., 5:19.

124. T'ung-tsu Ch'ü, *Local Government,* pp. 218, note 64, 219, note 68; Polachek, "Literati Politics," pp. 46–47.
125. *TCCCS:FWTK,* 5:19; *FWKT,* 22:5. Feng Kuei-fen also proposed to increase salaries, in the magistrate's case up to 10,000 taels. The additional funds were to come from the monies saved by the elimination of all sinecures and the cessation of tribute rice transport; Lojewski, "Confucian Reformers," pp. 149–150. In the late 1870s, officials were still trying to convert *lou-kuei* into rationalized fees; *Kuang-hsu Tung-hua lu,* p. 589.
126. *THTKTI,* 1.11.
127. *TCCCS:FanWKT,* 10:3; *FWKT,* 13:4b. According to Ting, everyone obeyed his order except for one sub-district Magistrate in Ch'ung-ming, to whom he gave a major demerit; *FWKT,* 13:4. Chao Lieh-wen charged that Ting himself was an ambitious flatterer; *Neng-ching-chü jih-chi,* TC 6/9/17.
128. *FWKT,* 23:9.
129. Ibid., 20:13.
130. Ibid., 23:9b.
131. On juggling of funds, see p. 256, note 161.
132. For the case of the Kiangnan Arsenal, see *TCCCS:HHKT,* 3:5–6.
133. In December 1864, the court had approved Li Hung-chang's request for a remission of all pre-1860 assigned contributions still in arrears, but it had declined to end the practice completely; *Tsou-kao,* 7:43–44b; *SL: TC,* 121:3–4.
134. *FWKT,* 6:3b–4.
135. *TCCCS:FanWKT,* 10:3b–4b.
136. *FWKT,* 23:1–6.
137. Ting, for instance, used surveying officers (*ch'ing-chang wei-yuan*) to check on the accuracy of correspondence registers in Kiangning (Nanking) prefecture; *FWKT,* 6:7.
138. *FWKT,* 15:9b.
139. Ibid., 37:2b–3, 17:3b, 15:9b.
140. T'ung-tsu Ch'ü, *Local Government,* p. 154; *FHCS,* 30:7b–8; *HT,* 51:1. For a complete listing of Kiangsu's courier stations and the distances between them, see *HTSL,* Chapter 666.
141. *FHCS,* 30:7–8b.
142. *FWKT,* 12:5b, 13:13.
143. *TCCCS:FanWKT,* 1:1b–2b.
144. Ibid., 5:2b, 5–6b. Liang Chang-chü, a Tao-kuang Governor of Kiangsu, complained that buck-passing was endemic in the bureaucracy. Officials

never posted notices, so the people had no way of knowing what to do. Yet, when queried on a matter, the officials said either it could not be done or that the people were unwilling to do it; *T'ui-an sui-pi,* 5:1.

145. *TCCCS:FanWKT,* 5:10. For a summary of the Magistrates' compliance, see Appendix C.

146. For the office regulations of the commissioners, see *FWKT,* 10:8–12b. For Kiangpei, *FWKT,* 3:3b–4.

147. Ibid., 20:5.

148. Ibid., 20:3b. Ting called one Kiangpei hsien, Kao-yu, a "fount of corruption" (*t'an-ch'üan*); ibid., 35:11b.

149. Ibid., 14:1. This same Magistrate, a *chin-shih* who had also made a request for an individual exemption from *t'an-chüan* (ibid., 8:11b), was awarded a promotion in 1869 for diligence in eliminating backlogged litigation; *CP* (Chü-heng), TC 8/3/22. He had previously served as Magistrate of Wu hsien (1857–1858) and of P'ei chou (1862–1864).

150. *FWKT,* 24:13.

151. Ibid., 16:9. This Magistrate, Kuo Chin-lai, was eventually dismissed for gross incompetence. Because he was not "evil" and was a *chin-shih,* the Nanking Financial Commissioner recommended that he be transferred to a teaching post, provided that he had not been at his post for more than 6 months. Had his tenure already exceeded 6 months, Kuo would have been forced to retire but would have been allowed to retain his rank; Ibid., 29:6–6b. See *HTSL,* 82:1b for the appropriate regulations.

152. *FWKT,* 21:6–6b.

153. Ibid., 30:3b. Ying Pao-shih made almost the identical comment in a letter to Liu K'un-i; Lü Shih-ch'iang, *Ting Jih-ch'ang,* p. 150.

154. Metzger, *Internal Organization,* pp. 299–300.

155. Wu Chih-hsiang, for example, had his button removed for failing to hang out the board listing witnesses in custody and had it returned for energetic work in the establishment of charitable schools; *CP* (Chü-heng), TC 7/5/28, 8/8/23. Without the shame, Ting commented, officials would not change; and he ordered that disobediant officials be impeached; *FWKT,* 8:11.

156. Li Kuo-ch'i, *Chung-kuo ti-fang chih yen-chiu,* p. 1437.

157. These two officials had been charged with overcollection of the per-acre contributions which were being collected in lieu of taxes. The court had overruled Tseng Kuo-fan's recommendation for leniency; *Tsou-kao,* pp. 815–816. *SL:TC.* 213:27; also see p. 267, note 151.

158. *FWKT,* 27:6.

159. Ibid., 15:3b–4.
160. Hu Lin-i, *Hu Wen-chung kung i-chi,* Chapters 8–10; also Tseng Kuo-fan, *Tseng kuo-fan p'i-tu* (1876 preface, Taipei reprint, 1969).
161. *TCCCS:FanWKT,* 7:10b–11.
162. *FWKT,* 17:15.
163. For example, Ting wrote to Tseng Kuo-fan that, in reviewing a case of drowning, the Judicial Commissioner had written *juo* (weak) instead of *ni* (drown) (the two characters are similar) and had thus made it seem that Ch'ung-ming had a "Juo River (*juo-shui*)." Ting sarcastically asked Tseng: "Is it something we're ever likely to see?"; *FWKT,* 16:9b; also, see Ting's comment about Tseng's inability to empathize with the plight of a lowly Magistrate, p. 159.
164. *FWKT,* 15:2b.
165. Ibid., 28:15.
166. Ibid., 5:2, 7:7, 12:2b–3b, 19:5b; *TCCCS:FWTK,* 2:19b.
167. See pp. 13–21, 87.
168. *FWKT,* 28:4. Ting warned the newly appointed Magistrate of Wu-chiang that, if his deeds fell short of his words, it would cause him (Ting) and the Financial Commissioner "to be left with a bad reputation of not being able to judge men." The man did prove to be a disappointment; ibid., 32:5. And at least in some circles Ting did have a reputation for impulsively employing people without giving it too much thought; Hsu K'o, comp., *Ch'ing-pai lei-ch'ao,* 26. 48–49.
169. *TCCCS:FWTK,* 3:11–11b; *CP* (Chü-heng), TC 6/9/9, 7/5/23, 7/5/24, 8/4/2, 8/9/7; *SL:TC,* 243:33.
170. Kwang-ching Liu, "The Ch'ing Restoration," p. 490.
171. See, for example, the case of one Chin Hung-pao, the Magistrate of Tan-yang. Li Hung-chang felt that he could not be dismissed because of his local connections and special expertise in likin; Kwang-ching Liu, "The Confucian as Patriot," p. 23. But, after a critical report from Ting and further outrageous behavior, Tseng Kuo-fan had Chin removed from office; *TCCCS:FanWKT,* 6:2b; Tseng Kuo-fan, *Tsou-kao,* 22:6b.
172. *FWKT,* 24:5–6b. Ting's solution was to despatch the replacement secretly in advance.
173. *CP* (Chü-heng), TC 9/2/8. Three years earlier, the court had moved to end practices whereby reinstated officials were serving in their native provinces in violation of the rule of avoidance; *SL:TC,* 195:30. For a general discussion on the redemption of punishments through contributions and on the problems of reinstatement, see Metzger, *Internal Organization,* pp. 302–317.
174. While serving as Magistrate in Kan-yu, a one-character post, Chang Hung-sheng was deprived of his button and dismissed for failure to clear

up a backlog of litigation, some of which dated from as far back as Hsien-feng's reign; *TCCCS:FWTK,* 2:10; *FWKT,* 19:15b, 24:12–12b. Ting suspected that Chang's lethargy might have been a manifestation of opium addiction, but Chang, a *chu-jen,* was appointed to the two-character post of Yen-ch'eng Magistrate in 1873.

175. *PLSK* ts'z, p. 6.
176. Wei-jen Chang, "Late Ch'ing Judicial Procedure," p. 334. "Your salary is taken from the people. It is easy to oppress the people; it is difficult to deceive heaven."
177. Hu Shih, "Chuan-chi wen-hsueh," in Li Shao-t'ang, *Shen-ma shih chuan-chi hsueh* (Taipei, 1968), pp. 246–247.
178. *FWKT,* 15:3–3b. The Confucian reluctance is undoubtedly a function of Confucius' own evasion of questions about the spirits; Legge, *The Confucian Analects,* XI:II.

7. *CONCLUSION*

1. Wright, preface to Atheneum edition, p. vii, pp. 45, 94.
2. The argument that rampant provincial regionalism, epitomized by Li Hung-chang, undermined the center has been put to rest by this study and a number of others; see, for example, Daniel Bays, "The Nature of Provincial Political Authority in Late Ch'ing Times: Chang Chih-tung in Canton, 1884–1889," *Modern Asian Studies* 4.4:325–347 (1970); Kwang-ching Liu, "The Limits of Regional Power in the Late Ch'ing Period: A Reappraisal," *The Tsing Hua Journal of Chinese Studies* 10.2: 207–223 (1974); Stephen MacKinnon, "The Peiyang Army, Yuan Shih-k'ai, and the Origins of Modern Chinese Warlordism," *Journal of Asian Studies* 32.3:405–423 (May 1973).
3. Wright, p. 164.
4. The best known of the late Ch'ing "injustices" is the case of Yang Nai-wu and Hsiao Pai-ts'ai, which is the subject of an essay by William Alford, in McKnight, ed., *Law and the State in Traditional East Asia.* Cecilia Kuo-ying Hsu and I are preparing translations and analyses of three other similar "wrongs": Kiangnan San-p'ai lou, Tung-hsiang, and Wang Shu-wen.
5. Kwang-ching Liu, "The Ch'ing Restoration," pp. 435, 489–490.
6. Ibid., p. 409. Chang Chih-tung saw it somewhat differently. "Truly it was just as in the Sung when Han Ch'u and Ou-yang Hsiu said, 'We five or six scholars helped the Empress Dowager and the nation followed. How could the power of all the military officials accomplish this?'"; Shen K'ang, *HCCSWHP,* p. 4456.
7. See pp. 28–29 for discussion of the financial drain. By 1869, Kiangsu

was sending more than 1.5 million taels a year to Tso Tsung-t'ang in Shen-kan for the Moslem suppression campaign; *SL:TC,* 252:11. In 1868, the court had acknowledged that military affairs were distracting officials from administrative problems and instructed them not to slight the latter; *TCCCS:FWTK,* 5:14b. But, 2 years later, a Censor charged that the quality of governance was still declining as a result of over concentration on military affairs; *CP* (Chü-heng), TC 9/2/28.

8. *TCCCS:FWTK,* 5:14b. For a satirical view of the uninvigorated bureaucracy, see Li Pao-chia, *Kuan-ch'ang hsien-hsing chi* (1903 preface).
9. *TCCCS:FWTK,* 5:15.
10. Hao Chang drew this distinction in speaking of the contrast between the School of Sung Learning and the Statecraft School; *Liang Ch'i-ch'ao and Intellectual Transition,* p. 27.
11. Feng Kuei-fen, *CPKLI,* 1:13b–14.
12. Kuhn, "Local Self-Government," pp. 267–268.
13. Faure, pp. 178, 251–252.
14. Even Chang Chih-tung, whose personal background made him more palatable to local elite than Ting, shared this view; see Bays, "Nature of Provincial Political Authority," and Bays, *China Enters the Twentieth Century* (Ann Arbor, 1978), pp. 15–18, 216.
15. Feng Kuei-fen, *Meng-nai shih-kao,* p. 36b.
16. Feng Kuei-fen, *CPLKI.* 1:15b.
17. *FWKT,* 45:16b. On *ch'ing-i* emphasis on the people, see Lü Shih-ch'iang, *Ting Jih-ch'ang,* pp. 353–354.
18. *PLSK,* 5:7b.

Bibliography

Ahern, Emily. *The Cult of the Dead in a Chinese Village.* Stanford, Stanford University Press, 1971.

Bays, Daniel. "The Nature of Provincial Political Authority in Late Ch'ing Times: Chang Chih-tung in Canton, 1884–1889," *Modern Asian Studies,* 4.4:325–347 (1970).

——. *China Enters the Twentieth Century: Chang Chih-tung and the Issues of a New Age, 1895–1909.* Ann Arbor, University of Michigan Press, 1978.

Beattie, Hilary J. *Land and Lineage in China: A Study of T'ung-ch'eng County Anhwei in the Ming and Ch'ing Dynasties.* Cambridge, Cambridge University Press, 1979.

Bodde, Derk. "Prison Life in Eighteenth Century Peking," *Journal of the American Oriental Society,* 89:311–333 (1969).

—— and Clarence Morris. *Law in Imperial China: Exemplified by 190 Ch'ing Dynasty Cases.* Cambridge, Harvard University Press, 1967.

Boulais, Guy. *Manuel du Code Chinois.* Taipei, Ch'eng-wen, 1966.

Brunnert, H. S. and Hagelstrom, V. V. *Present Day Political Organization of China.* Taipei reprint.

Buxbaum, David C. "Some Aspects of Civil Procedure and Practice at the Trial Level in Tanshui and Hsinchu from 1789 to 1895," *Journal of Asian Studies,* 30.2:255–280 (February 1971).

CFTL. See *Ch'in-ting liu-pu ch'u-fen tse-li.*

Chang Chung-li. *The Chinese Gentry: Studies in Their Role in Nineteenth Century Chinese Society.* Seattle, University of Washington Press, 1955.

——. *The Income of the Chinese Gentry.* Seattle, University of Washington Press, 1962.

Chang Hao. *Liang Ch'i-ch'ao and Intellectual Transition in China, 1890–1907.* Cambridge, Harvard University Press, 1971.

Chang Hao. "The Intellectual Context of Reform," in Paul Cohen and John Schrecker, eds., *Reform in Nineteenth Century China*. Cambridge, Harvard East Asian Research Center, 1976.

Chang T'ing-hsiang. 張廷驤. *Ju-mu hsu-chih wu-chung* 入幕須知五種 (Five types of essential knowledge for becoming a *mu-yu*). 1890 preface, Taipei reprint.

Chang Wei-jen 張偉仁. "The Traditional Chinese Fear of Litigation: Its Causes and Effects." Conference on the History of Chinese Law, Lake Como, Italy, August 1969.

—— and Yu Yu-chen 俞瑜珍. "Ch'ing-chi ti-fang ssu-fa: Ch'en T'ien-hsi hsien-sheng fang-wen chi" 清季地方司法 陳天錫先生訪問記 (Local judicial administration in the late Ch'ing: an interview with Mr. Ch'en T'ien-hsi), *Shih-huo yueh-k'an* 食貨月刊 1.6:319–339 (September 1971); 1.7:388–397 (December 1971).

Chang Yueh-hsiang. 張耀翔. "Ch'ing-tai *chin-shih* chih ti-li fen-pu" 清代進士之地理分布 (The geographical distribution of *chin-shih* in the Ch'ing), *Hsin-li* 4.1:1–12 (March 1926).

Chao Lieh-wen 趙烈文. *Neng-ching-chü jih-chi* 能靜居日記 (Diary of one able to live in peace). Taipei, 1964.

Ch'en Teng-yuan 陳登原. *Chung-kuo t'ien-fu shih* 中國田賦史 (History of China's land taxation). Taipei, Commercial Press, 1970.

Ch'en Tso-lin 陳作霖. *Chiang-su ping-shih chi-lueh* 江蘇兵事紀略 (A brief record of military events in Kiangsu). 1920 postface.

Cheng-yang hsien T'ai-ts'ang chou ho-shih 鎮洋縣太倉州和志 (Joint gazetteer of Cheng-yang hsien and T'ai-ts'ang chou). 1918.

Chesneaux, Jean. "The Modern Relevance of *Shui-hu Chuan*: Its Influence on Rebel Movements in Nineteenth and Twentieth Century China," *Papers on Far Eastern History*, 3:1–25 (March 1971).

Chia-ting hsien-chih 嘉定縣志 (Gazetteer of Chia-ting hsien). 1880.

Chiao-hui hsin-pao 教會新報 (Church News). Shanghai, 1868–1871.

Chiang Piao 江標. *Feng-shun Ting-shih Ch'ih-ching chai shu-mu* 豐順丁氏持靜齋書目 (The catalog of Mr. Ting of Feng-shun's uphold tranquility book collection). 1898.

Chiang-yin hsien-chih 江陰縣志 (Gazetteer of Chiang-yin hsien). 1878.

Chih-che ch'eng-kuei 治浙成規 (Established regulations for administering Chekiang). n.d.

Chin-cheng chi-yao 晉政輯要 (Essentials for the governance of Shensi). n.d.

Chin Liang 金梁. *Chin-shih jen-wu chih* 近世人物志 (A record of contemporary people). Taipei, Kuo-min ch'u-pan she, 1955.

Chin-t'an hsien-chih 金壇縣志 (Gazetteer of Chin-t'an hsien). 1885.

Ch'in-ting liu-pu ch'u-fen tse-li 欽定六部處分則例 (Disciplinary regulations for the six boards). Taipei reprint..

Ch'in-ting Ta-Ch'ing hui-tien 欽定大清會典 (Statutes of The Great Ch'ing). 1899 ed.
Ch'in-ting Ta-Ch'ing hui-tien shih-li 欽定大清會典事例 (Statutes and precedents of the great Ch'ing). 1899 ed.
Ch'ing-ting t'ai-kuei 欽定臺軌 (Regulations of the Censorate). Peking, 1892 preface.
Ching-pao 京報 (Peking Gazette).
Ch'ing-p'u hsien-chih 青浦縣志 (Gazetteer of Ch'ing-pu hsien). 1879.
Ch'ing-shih kao 清史稿 (Draft history of the Ch'ing). 1927.
Ch'ing-shih kao hsing-fa chih chu-chieh 清史稿刑法志註解 (Notes and commentaries on the "Essay on Justice" in *Ch'ing-shih kao*). Peking, Fa-lü ch'u-pan she, 1957.
Ch'ing-shih lieh-chuan 清史列傳 (Biographies from the Ch'ing history). 1928.
Ch'ou-pan i-wu shih-mo 籌辦夷務始末 (The complete account of our management of barbarian affairs). Taipei reprint.
Chu Chih-chen 朱之榛. *Ch'ang-ch'ieh-chai wen-chi* 常慊齋文集 (Collected writings from the "always-happy" study). Taipei reprint.
Chu Ch'ing-yung 朱慶永. "T'ung-chih erh-nien Su-Sung erh-fu chien-fu chih yuan-yin" 同治二年蘇松減賦原因 (Causes of the 1863 tax reduction in Soochow and Sungchiang prefectures), *Cheng-chih ching-chi hsueh-pao* 政治經濟學報 3.3:510–529 (1935).
Chu K'o-pao 諸可寶. *Chiang-su ch'üan-sheng yi-t'u* 江蘇全省輿圖 (An atlas of Kiangsu province). Chiang-su shu-chü, 1895.
Ch'ü T'ung-tsu. *Local Government in China Under the Ch'ing.* Cambridge, Harvard University Press, 1962.
——. *Law and Society in Traditional China.* Paris, Mouton, 1965.
Ch'uan-sha hsien-chih 川沙縣志 (Gazetteer of Ch'uan-sha hsien). 1935.
Ch'uan-sha ting-chih 川沙廳志 (Gazetteer of Ch'uan-sha ting). 1879.
Chung-hsiu Ching-chiang hsien-chih 重修靖江縣志 (Newly revised gazetteer of Ching-chiang hsien). 1879.
Ch'ung-ming hsien-chih 崇明縣志 (Gazetteer of Ch'ung-ming hsien). 1881.
CMCY. See Juan Pen-yen, *Ch'iu-mu ch'u-yen.*
Cohen, Paul. *China and Christiantiy: The Missionary Movement and the Growth of Chinese Anti-Foreignism, 1860–1870.* Cambridge, Harvard University Press, 1963.
——. *Between Tradition and Modernity: Wang T'ao and Reform in Late Ch'ing China.* (Cambridge, Harvard University Press, 1974.
Cole, James H. "Shaohsing: Studies in Ch'ing Social History." PhD dissertation, Stanford University, 1975.
CPLKI. See Feng Kuei-fen, *Chiao-pin-lu k'ang-i.*
CT. See *Tsung-li ko-kuo shih-wu ya-men ch'ing-tang.*

Dennerline, Jerry. "Fiscal Reform and Local Control: The Gentry Bureaucratic Alliance Survives the Conquest," in Frederic Wakeman and Carolyn Grant, eds., *Conflict and Control in Late Imperial China*. Berkeley, University of California Press, 1975.

Faure, David. "Local Political Disturbances in Kiangsu Province, China, 1870–1911." PhD dissertation, Princeton University, 1976.

Fen-fa t'iao-li 分發條例 (Distributed rules and precedents). n.d.

Feng Kuei-fen 馮桂芬 *Hsien-chih-t'ang kao* 顯志堂稿 (Collected essays from the Hsien-chih hall). 1877.

——. *Meng-nai shih-kao* 夢奈詩稿 (Poetic drafts of Meng-nai). Soochow, 1877.

——. *Chiao-pin-lu k'ang-i* 校邠廬抗議 (Straightforward words from the Chiao-pin studio). 1897.

Feng hsien-chih 豐縣志 (Gazetteer of Feng county). 1877.

Feng-shun hsien-chih 豐順縣志 (Gazetteer of Feng-shun county). 1884.

FHCS. See Huang Liu-hung.

Freedman, Maurice. *Chinese Lineage and Society: Fukien and Kwangtung*. London, Athlone, 1966.

FWKT. See Ting Jih-ch'ang, *Fu-wu kung-tu*.

Goldman, Merle. *Literary Dissent in Communist China*. Cambridge, Harvard University Press, 1967.

Goodrich, Luther Carrington. *The Literary Inquisition of Ch'ien-lung*. New York, Paragon, 1966.

Great Britain, Foreign Office. *General Correspondence, China* FO 17.

——. *Embassy and Consular Archives, China* FO 228.

Great Britain War Office. *Monthly Returns, China Station* WO 17.

HAHL. See *Hsing-an hui-lan*.

Han Wen-ch'i 韓文綺. *Kung-shou-t'ang tsou-i* 恭壽堂奏議 (Memorials from the Hall of Reverence for Long Life). n.d.

Hao Yen-p'ing. *The Comprador in Nineteenth Century China: Bridge Between East and West*. Cambridge, Harvard University Press, 1970.

Harrison, Judy Feldman. "Wrongful Treatment of Prisoners: A Case Study of Ch'ing Legal Practice," *Journal of Asian Studies*, 23.2:227–244 (February 1964).

HCCSWP. See *Huang-ch'ao ching-shih wen-pien*.

HCTK. See Feng Kuei-fen. *Hsien-chih t'ang-kao*.

Ho Ping-ti. "The Salt Merchants of Yang-chou: A Study of Commercial Capitalism in Eighteenth-century China," *Harvard Journal of Asiatic Studies*, 17:130–168 (1954).

——. *Studies on the Population of China, 1368–1953*. Cambridge, Harvard University Press, 1959.

——. *The Ladder of Success in Imperial China, Aspects of Social Mobility 1368–1911.* Chicago, University of Chicago Press, 1964.

Hsia Nai 夏鼐. "T'ai-p'ing t'ien-kuo ch'ien-hou Ch'ang-chiang ko-sheng chih t'ien-fu wen-t'i" 太平天國前後長江各省之田賦問題 (The land tax in the Yangtze provinces before and after the Taiping Rebellion), *Ch'ing-hua hsueh-pao,* 清華學報 10.2:429–474 (1935).

Hsiao Kung-chuan. *Rural China: Imperial Control in the Nineteenth Century.* Seattle, University of Washington Press, 1967.

Hsing-an hui-lan 刑案滙覽 (Conspectus of penal cases). Compiled by Chu Ch'ing-chi 祝慶祺 and Pao Shu-yun 鮑書芸. 1834 preface.

Hsing-cheng yuan nung-ts'un fu-hsing wei-yuan hui 行政院農村復興委員會 (Administrative Yuan's Commission for the Rehabilitation of Rural Villages). *Chiang-su sheng nung-ts'un t'iao-ch'a* 江蘇省農村調查 (An investigation of Kiangsu's rural villages). Shanghai, Commerical Press, 1933.

Hsu-hsiu Chiang-ning fu-chih 續修江寧府志 (Supplementary revised Chiang-ning prefecture [Nanking] gazetteer). 1880.

Hsu, Immanuel. *China's Entrance into the Family of Nations.* Cambridge, Harvard University Press, 1960.

Hsu K'o 徐珂 comp. *Ch'ing-pai lei-ch'ao* 清稗類鈔(Anecdotes from the Ch'ing). 1928.

Hsu Shao-ch'i 徐紹棨. *Kwangtung ts'ang-shu chi-shih shih* 廣東藏書紀事詩 (A record of Kwangtung bibliophiles). Hong Kong, Commercial Press, 1963.

Hsu Ta-ling 許大齡. *Ch'ing-tai chüan-na chih-tu* 清代捐納制度 (The system of purchasing offices through contributions during the Ch'ing period). Peking, Harvard Yenching Institute, 1950.

Hsueh Fu-ch'eng 薛福成. *Ch'ou-yang ch'u-i* 籌洋芻議 (Proposals on the management of foreign affairs). 1885 preface.

Hsueh Yun-sheng 薛允升. *Tu-li ts'un-i* 讀例存疑(Questions on reading the penal regulations). Taipei, Chinese Materials and Research Aids Service Center. Typeset Edition. 1970.

HT. See *Ch'in-ting Ta-Ch'ing hui-tien.*

HTSL. See *Ch'in-ting Ta-Ch'ing hui-tien shih-li.*

Hu Lin-i 胡林翼. *Hu Wen-chung kung i-chi* 胡文忠公遺集 (Posthumous works of Hu Lin-i). Comp. 1867. Taipei reprint.

Huai-an fu-chih 淮安府志 (The gazetteer of Huai-an prefecture). 1884.

Huang-ch'ao ching-shih wen hsu-pien 皇朝經世文續編 (Supplementary collection of our august dynasty's writings on statecraft). Comp. Ko Shih-chün 葛士濬. 1888 preface. Taipei reprint.

Huang-ch'ao ching-shih wen hsu-pien 皇朝經世文續編 (Supplementary collection of our august dynasty's writings on statecraft). Comp. Sheng K'ang 盛康. 1897 preface. Taipei reprint.

Huang-ch'ao ching-shih wen-pien 皇朝經世文編 (Our august dynasty's writings on statecraft). Comp. Ho Ch'ang-ling 賀長齡. Taipei, Shih-chieh shu-chü, 1964.

Huang Liu-hung 黃六鴻. *Fu-hui ch'üan-shu* 福惠全書 (Complete book of good government). 1893 ed.

Hummel, Arthur. *Eminent Chinese of the Ch'ing Period.* Taipei, Ch'eng-wen, 1967.

I-hsing Ching-ch'i hsien-chih 宜興荊溪縣志 (Gazetteer of I-hsing and Ching-ch'i hsiens). 1882.

IWSM:TC. See *Ch'ou-pan i-wu shih-mo.*

Jao Tsung-i 饒宗頤. *Ch'ao-chou-chih hui-pien* 潮州志匯編 (A compendium of Ch'ao-chou prefecture gazetteers). Hong Kong, Lung-men shu-tien, 1965.

Jen Yu-wen. *The Taiping Revolutionary Movement.* New Haven, Yale University Press, 1973.

Jones, Susan Mann. "Hung Liang-chi: The Perception and Articulation of Political Problems in Late Eighteenth Century China." PhD dissertation, Stanford University, 1972.

Juan Pen-yen 阮本焱. *Ch'iu-mu ch'u-yen* 求牧芻言 (Plain talk on being a magistrate). Taipei reprint, 1887.

Kan-ch'üan hsien-chih 甘泉縣志 (Gazetteer of Kan-ch'üan hsien). 1885.

Kan-yü hsien-chih 贛榆縣志 (Gazetteer of Kan-yü hsien). 1888.

Kiangsu Sheng-li 江蘇省例 (Kiangsu provincial regulations) Nanking: Kiangsu shu-chu, 1866–1904).

Kiangsu Sheng-li Hsu-pien 江蘇省例續編 (Supplement to Kiangsu provincial regulations). Nanking, Kiangsu shu-chü, 1875.

Kiangsu Sheng-li San-pien 江蘇省例三編 (Third edition of Kiangsu provincial regulations). Nanking, Kiangsu shu-chü, 1883.

Kiangsu Sheng-li Ssu-pien 江蘇省例四編 (Fourth edition of Kiangsu provincial regulations). Nanking, Kiangsu shu-chü, 1890.

Kiangsu-sheng po-wu-kuan (Kiangsu Provincial Museum), comp. *Kiangsu-sheng Ming-Ch'ing i-lai p'ei-k'o tzu-liao hsuan-chi* 江蘇省明清以來碑刻資料選集 (A selection of materials from stone inscriptions in Kiangsu since Ming-Ch'ing). Tokyo, Ta-an, 1967.

Kiangsu Ts'ai-cheng shuo-ming shu 江蘇財政說明書 (Kiangsu financial reports). Ching-chi hsueh-hui, 1915.

Ku T'ing-ting 顧廷龍. *Wu K'o-chai hsien-sheng nien-p'u.* 吳客齋先生年譜 (A chronological biography of Wu Ta-ch'eng). Peiping, Harvard Yenching Institute, 1935.

K'uai Te-mo 蒯德模. *Wu-chung p'an-t'u* 吳中判牘 (Judicial decisions from Soochow), in *Hsiao-yuan ts'ung-shu* 嘯園叢書. 1878.

Kuang-hsu Tung-hua lu 光緒東華錄 (Kuang-hsu period records from the Tung-hua gate). Taipei reprint.

Kuei Chao-wan 桂超萬 *Huan-yu chi-lueh* 宦遊紀略 (Memoirs of an official life). Taipei reprint.

Kuhn, Philip A. *Rebellion and Its Enemies in Late Imperial China: Militarization and Social Structure, 1796–1864.* Cambridge, Harvard University Press, 1970.

——. "Local Self-Government Under the Republic," in Frederic Wakeman and Carolyn Grant, eds., *Conflict and Control in Late Imperial China.* Berkeley, University of California Press, 1975.

—— and Susan Mann Jones. "Dynastic Decline and the Roots of Rebellion," in John K. Fairbank, ed., *The Cambridge History of China,* Vol. 10, pt. 1, pp. 107–162. New York, Cambridge University Press, 1978.

K'un-hsin liang-hsien hsu-hsiu ho-chih 崑新兩縣續修合志 (Revised supplementary gazetteer of Kun-shan and Hsin-yang hsiens). 1880.

Kung-chung-tang Kuang-hsu ch'ao tsou-che 宮中檔光緒朝奏摺 (Palace memorials from the Kuang-hsu reign). Taipei, National Palace Museum, 1973.

Kuo Sung-tao 郭嵩燾. *Yang-chih shu-wu ch'üan-chi* 養知書屋全集 (Collected works of Kuo Sung-tao). 1892.

Kuribayashi Nobuo 栗林宣夫. *Rikōsei no kenkyu* 里甲制の研究 (A study of the *li-chia* system). Tokyo, Bunrishoin, 1971.

Levenson, Joseph. *Confucian China and Its Modern Fate: A Trilogy.* Berkeley, University of California Press, 1968.

Li Chang-fu 李長傅. *Chiang-su* 江蘇 (Kiangsu). 1936.

Li Ch'ing-yun 李慶雲. *Chiang-su shui-li ch'üan-an t'u-shuo* 江蘇水利全案圖說 (Complete illustrated record of Kiangsu waterworks). 1910.

Li Hsing-yuan 李星沅. *Li Wen-kung kung ch'üan-chi* 李文恭公全集 (Complete works of Li Hsing-yuan). 1865 preface. Taipei reprint.

Li Hung-chang 李鴻章. *Li Wen-ch'ung kung ch'üan-chi* 李文忠公全集 (Complete works of Li Hung-chang). 1908.

——. *Li Wen-ch'ung peng-liao han-kuo* 李文忠朋僚翰稿 (Draft letters to friends). Taipei, Wen-hai reprint, 1967.

Li Kuo-ch'i 李國祁. "T'ung-chih chung-hsing shih-ch'i Liu K'un-i tsai Kiangsi hsun-fu jen-nei ti piao-hsien," 同治中興時期劉坤一在江西巡撫任內的表現 (Liu K'un-i's performance as Governor of Kiangsi during the T'ung-chih Restoration), *Kuo-li T'ai-wan shih-fan ta-hsueh li-shih hsueh-pao,* 1 (1973).

Li Kuo-ch'i, Chou T'ien-sheng 周天生, and Hsu Hung-i 許弘義. *Chung-kuo ti-fang chih yen-chiu: Ch'ing-tai chi-ts'eng ti-fang kuan jen-shih shan-ti hsien-hsiang chih liang-hua fen-hsi* 中國地方志研究清代基層地方官人事嬗遞現象之量化分析 (Chinese gazetteer studies: A quantitative analysis of the careers of prefects and magistrates in the Ch'ing dynasty). 3 vols. Taipei, National Science Council, 1975.

Li Pao-chia 李寶嘉. *Kuan-ch'ang hsien-hsing chi* 官場現形記 (A record of present conditions in the official world). 1903 preface.

Li Wen-chih 李文治 comp. *Chung-kuo chin-tai nung-yeh shih tzu-liao 1840–1911* 中國近代农业史資料第一輯 (Source materials on China's modern agricultural history, 1840–1911). Peking, San-lien shu-tien, 1957.

Li-yang hsien-chih 溧陽縣志 (Gazetteer of Li-yang hsien). 1881.

Li-yang hsu hsien-chih 溧陽續縣志 (Supplementary gazetteer of Li-yang hsien). 1897.

Liang Chang-chü 梁章鉅. *T'ui-an sui-pi* 退庵隨筆 (Random notes written in retirement). Foreword by Ho Ch'ang-ling. n.d.

Lin Tse-hsu 林則徐. *Lin Wen-ch'ung-kung cheng-shu* 林文忠公政書 (Political papers of Lin Tse-hsu). 1885 preface. Taipei reprint.

——. *Lin Tse-hsu chi kung-tu* 林則徐集公牘 (Collected inter-office communications of Lin Tse-hsu). Peking, Chung-hua shu-chü, 1963.

Liu Chin-tsao 劉錦藻, ed. *Ch'ing-ch'ao hsu wen-hsien t'ung-k'ao* 清朝續文獻通考 (Encyclopedia of the historical records of the Ch'ing dynasty continued). Shanghai, Commerical Press, 1935.

Liu Hsun-kao 劉郇膏, comp. *Kiangsu chien-fu ch'üan-an* 江蘇減賦全案 (The complete record of the Kiangsu tax reduction). 1866 preface.

Liu, James T. C. *Reform in Sung China: Wang An-shih and his New Policies.* Cambridge, Harvard University Press, 1968.

Liu, Kwang-ching. "Nineteenth Century China: The Distintegration of the Old Order and the Impact of the West," in Ho Ping-ti and Tang Tsou, eds., *China in Crisis,* Vol. 1. Chicago, University of Chicago Press, 1968.

——. "The Confucian as Patriot and Pragmatist: Li Hung-chang's Formative Years, 1823–1866," *Harvard Journal of Asiatic Studies,* 30:5–45 (1970).

——. "The Limits of Regional Power in the Late Ch'ing Period: A Reappraisal," *The Tsing Hua Journal of Chinese Studies,* New Series, 10.2:207–223 (1974).

——. "The Ch'ing Restoration," in John K. Fairbank, ed., *The Cambridge History of China,* Vol. 10, pt. 1. New York, Cambridge University Press, 1978.

Lojewski, Frank Arno. "Confucian Reformers and Local Vested Interests: The Su-Sung-T'ai Tax Reduction of 1863 and its Aftermath." PhD dissertation, University of California, Davis, 1973.

——. "The Soochow Bursaries: Rent Management During the Late Ch'ing," *Ch'ing-shih wen-t'i*, 4.3:43–65 (June 1980).

Long Chin-hsiao 郎擎霄. "Ch'ing-tai yueh-tung hsieh-tou shih-shih" 清代粵東械鬥史實 (A history of "weapons fights" in Kwangtung during the Ch'ing dynasty), *Ling-nan hsueh-pao*, 4.2:103–151 (June 1935).

Lü Shih-ch'iang. 呂實強 "Feng Kuei-fen ti cheng-chih ssu-hsiang" 馮桂芬的政治思想 (Feng Kuei-fen's political thought), *Chung-hua wen-hua fu-hsing yueh-k'an*, 4.2:1–8 (February 1971).

——. *Ting Jih-ch'ang yü tzu-ch'iang yun-tung* 丁日昌與自強運動 (Ting Jih-ch'ang and the self-strengthening movement). Taipei, Academia Sinica, Institute of Modern History, 1972.

Ma Hsin-i 馬新貽. *Ma Tuan-min kung tsou-i* 馬端敏公奏議 (The memorials of Ma Hsin-i). Taipei reprint.

Mackerras, Colin P. *The Rise of the Peking Opera 1770–1870: Social Aspects of the Theater in Manchu China.* London, Oxford University Press, 1972.

McKinnon, Stephen. "The Peiyang Army, Yuan Shih-k'ai, and the Origins of Modern Chinese Warlordism," *Journal of Asian Studies* 32.3:405–423 (May 1973).

McKnight, Brian. *The Washing Away of Wrongs: Forensic Medicine in Thirteenth Century China.* Ann Arbor, Center for Chinese Studies, University of Michigan, 1981.

Metzger, Thomas A. "Ch'ing Commercial Policy," *Ch'ing-shih wen-t'i*, 1.3:4–10 (February 1966).

——. *The Internal Organization of Ch'ing Bureaucracy: Legal, Normative, and Communication Aspects.* Cambridge, Harvard University Press, 1973.

——. *Escape from Predicament: Neo-Confucianism and China's Evolving Political Culture.* New York, Columbia University Press, 1977.

MLSCY. See Ting Jih-ch'ang, comp., *Mu-ling shu chi-yao.*

Mu Han 穆翰. *Ming-hsing kuan-chien lu* 明刑管見錄 (On handling the law). 1845.

Mu Yu-chih 莫友芝. *Ch'ih-ching-chai shu-mu* 持靜齋書目 (A catalog of the [Ting Jih-ch'ang's] Ch'ih-ching chai book collection). 1870.

Muramatsu Yuji. "A Documentary Study of Chinese Landlordism in late Ch'ing and early Republican Kiangnan," *Bulletin of the School of Oriental and African Studies,* 29:566–599 (1966).

Nan-hui hsien-chih 南滙縣志. (The gazetteer of Nan-hui county). 1878 preface.

Naquin, Susan. "The Accused," in "Two Sides of the Law." Prepared with Jonathan Ocko for American Historical Association. December 1977.

North China Daily News. Shanghai.

North China Herald. Shanghai.

Obata Tatsuo 小畑龍雄. "Kōnan ni okeru rikō no hensei ni tsuite" 江南における里甲の編成について (The organization of the *li-chia* system in Kiangnan), *Shirin* 39.2:1–35 (March 1956).

Ocko, Jonathan K. "The British Museum's *Peking Gazettes,*" *Ch'ing-shih wen-t'i,* 2.9:35–49 (January 1973).

——. "Ting Jih-ch'ang and Restoration Kiangsu, 1864–1870: Rhetoric and Reality," PhD dissertation, Yale University, 1975.

——. "Family Disharmony as Seen in Ch'ing Legal Cases." Paper prepared for ACLS-NEH Conference on "Orthodoxy and Heterodoxy in Late Imperial China." Montecito, California, August 1981.

——. "Justice on Appeal: The Capital Appeals System in Ch'ing China," in Brian McKnight, ed., *Law and the State in Traditional East Asia.* University of Hawaii Press, forthcoming.

——. "Defensive Diplomacy, a Case Study in Ch'ing Foreign Relations: Tin Jih-ch'ang as Shanghai taotai." Unpublished manuscript.

Ooms, Herman. *Charismatic Bureaucrat: A Political Biography of Matsudaira Sadanobu*. Chicago, University of Chicago, 1975.

Oxnam, Robert B. "Policies and Institutions of the Oboi Regency 1661–1669," *Journal of Asian Studies,* 31.2:265–286 (February 1973).

P'an Kuang-tan 潘光旦. "Chin-tai Su-chou ti jen-ts'ai,"近代蘇州的人才 (Outstanding men from Soochow in recent times), *She-hui k'o-hsueh,* 1.1:49–98 (October 1935).

Pao Shih-ch'en 包世臣. *An-wu ssu-chung* 安吳四種 (Four kinds of writings from Mr. An-wu). 1872 preface. Taipei reprint.

P'ei hsien-chih 沛縣志 (Gazetter of P'ei hsien). 1918.

PLSK. See Ting Jih-ch'ang, *Pai-lan-shan-kuan ku-chin t'i-shih fu-tz'u.*

Polachek, James. "Gentry Hegemony: Soochow in the T'ung-chih Restoration," in Frederic Wakeman and Carolyn Grant, eds., *Conflict and Control in Late Imperial China.* Berkeley, University of California Press, 1975.

——. 'Literati Groups and Literati Politics in Nineteenth Century China." PhD dissertation, University of California, Berkeley, 1976.

Rankin, Mary. "Local Reform Currents in Chekiang before 1900," in Paul Cohen and John Schrecker, eds., *Reform in Nineteenth Century China.* Cambridge, Harvard East Asian Research Center, 1976.

——. "Late Ch'ing Chekian Elite Activists." Paper presented to Harvard New England China Seminar, October 1978.

——. "Gentry Leadership Groups in Chekiang, 1865–1900." Paper presented to Harvard New England China Seminar, November, 1978.

Rawski, Evelyn S. *Education and Popular Literacy in Ch'ing China.* Ann Arbor, University of Michigan Press, 1979.

Schrecker, John. "The Reform Movement of 1898 and the *Ch'ing-i:* Reform as Opposition," in Paul Cohen and John Schrecker, eds., *Reform in Nineteenth Century China.* Cambridge, Harvard East Asian Research Center, 1976.

Schwartz, Benjamin. *In Search of Wealth and Power: Yen Fu and the West.* Cambridge, Mass.; Belknap Press of Harvard University Press, 1964.

Shanghai t'ung-chih-kuan ch'i-k'an 上海通志館期刊 (Periodical of the Shanghai local history bureau). Shanghai, 1935.

Shanghai T'ung-she 上海通社 (Shanghai News Agency), comp. *Shanghai chang-ku ts'ung-shu* 上海掌故叢書 (Collected Shanghai historical documents). Shanghai, 1936.

——. *Shang-hai yen-chiu tzu-liao* 上海研究資料 (Research materials on Shanghai). Shanghai, 1936.

Shen Pao 申報. Shanghai. Taipei reprint.

Shiga Shuzo. "Criminal Procedure in the Ch'ing Dynasty," *Memoirs of the Toyo Bunko,* 34:1–44, 35:115–137 (1976).

Skinner, G. William. "Regional Urbanization in Nineteenth Century China," in G. William Skinner, ed., *The City in Late Imperial China.* Stanford, Stanford University Press, 1977.

——. "Cities and the Hierarchy of Local Systems," in G. William Skinner, ed., *The City in Late Imperial China.* Stanford, Stanford University Press, 1977.

SL:TC. See *Ta-Ch'ing Mu-tsung-i (T'ung-chih) huang-ti shih-lu.*

Smith, Richard J. *Mercenaries and Mandarins: The Ever Victorious Army in Nineteenth Century China.* Millwood, N.Y., KTO Press, 1979.

Spector, Stanley. *Li Hung-chang and the Huai Army: A Study in Nineteenth Century Chinese Regionalism.* Seattle, University of Washington Press, 1964.

Spence, Jonathan. "Chang Po-hsing and the K'ang-hsi Emperor," *Ch'ing-shih wen-t'i,* 1.8:3–9 (May 1968).

——. "Opium Smoking in Ch'ing China," in Frederic Wakeman and Carolyn Grant, eds., *Conflict and Control in Late Imperial China.* Berkeley, University of Califronia Press, 1975.

——. *The Death of Woman Wang.* New York, Penguin, 1979.

Su-chou fu-chih 蘇州府志 (Gazetteer of Su-chou [Soochow] prefecture). 1883.

Sun, E-tu Zen. *Ch'ing Administrative Terms.* Cambridge, Harvard University Press, 1961.

Sun K'ai-ti 孫楷第. *Chung-kuo t'ung-su hsiao-shu shu-mu* 中國通俗小說書目 (A catalog of popular Chinese novels). Peking, Tso-chia ch'u-pan she, 1957.

Ta-Ch'ing Chin-shen ch'üan-shu 大清搢紳全書 (The complete record of Ch'ing officials). 1864–1870.

Ta-Ch'ing Lü-li hui-t'ung hsin-pien 大清律例會通新纂 (Completely new edition of the Ch'ing Penal Code). Yao Yü-hsiang 姚雨薌 ed. 1873 preface. Taipei reprint, 1964.

Ta-Ch'ing Mu-tsung-i (T'ung-chih) huang-ti shih-lu 大清穆宗毅（同治）皇帝實錄 (Veritable records of the T'ung-chih Emperor's reign).

Taiping Tienkuo li-shih po-wu kuan 太平天國历史博物館 (Museum of Taiping History), ed. *T'ai-p'ing t'ien-kuo shih-liao ts'ung-pien chien-chi* 太平天國史料叢編簡輯 (Collection of historical materials on the Taiping kingdom), Vols. 1, 2. Peking, 1961.

Tan-t'u hsien-chih 丹徒縣志 (The gazetteer of Tan-t'u hsien). 1879.

Tan-yang hsien-chih 丹陽縣志 (The gazetteer of Tan-yang hsien). 1885.

T'ao Chu 陶澍. *T'ao Wen-i kung chi* 陶文毅公集 (The collected works of T'ao Chu). Taipei reprint.

T'ao Hsi-sheng 陶希聖. "Ch'ing-tai chou-hsien ya-men hsing-shih-shen-p'an chih-tu chi ch'eng-hsu" 清代州縣衙門刑事審判制度及程序 (The system and process of judicial administration in a Ch'ing district office), *Shih-huo yueh-k'an*, 1.1:2–14 (April 1971); 1.2:108–124 (May 1971); 1.3:160–172 (June 1971); 1.4:212–225 (July 1971); 1.5: 265–280 (August 1971).

Tao-hsien t'ung-kuang ssu-ch'ao tsou-i 道咸同光四朝奏議 (Memorials from the Tao-kuang, Hsien-feng, T'ung-chih, and Kuang-hsu reigns). Taipei, Commercial Press, 1970.

TCCCS. See Ting Jih-ch'ang, *Ting Chung-ch'eng cheng-shu*.

TCLL. See *Ta-Ch'ing Lü-li hui-t'ung hsin-pien*.

THTKTI. See *Tao hsien t'ung-kuang ssu-ch'ao tsou-i*.

Ting Ch'iao-yin 丁樵隱. "Hsien-tsu k'ao chung-ch'eng Ting-kung hui Jih-ch'ang shih-lueh" 先祖考中丞丁公諱日昌事略 (A brief biography of my late grandfather, Ting Jih-ch'ang). Handwritten manuscript.

Ting Jih-ch'ang 丁日昌. *Fu-wu kung-tu* 撫吳公牘 (Official papers from Ting Jih-ch'ang's governorship of Kiangsu). 1878 preface. Taipei, Hua-wen shu-chü reprint.

——, comp. *Mu-ling shu chi-yao* 牧令書輯要 (Important selections from Hsu Tung's [徐棟] magistrate's handbook). Soochow, Kiangsu shu-chü, 1868.

——. *Pai-lan-shan-kuan ku-chin t'i-shih fu-tz'u ying-lien* 白蘭山館古近體詩附詞楹聯 (Poetry and couplets from the 100-Orchid Pavilion).

——. *Pao-chia shu chi-yao* 保甲書輯要 (Important selections from Hsu Tung's handbook on *pao-chia*). 1870.

——. *Ting Chung-ch'eng cheng-shu* 丁中丞政書 (The political papers of Ting Jih-ch'ang), manuscript at Sterling Memorial Library, Yale University. The following sections of this work were used:

Fan-wu kung-tu 藩吳公牘 (Official papers of the Soochow Financial Commissioner).

Fu-wu tsou-kao 撫吳奏稿 (Memorials as Governor of Kiangsu).

Hsun-hu kung-tu 巡滬公牘 (Official papers as Shanghai Taotai).

TLTI. See Hsueh Yun-sheng, *Tu-li ts'un-i*.

Tsai-hsu Kao-yu chou-chih 再續高郵州志 (Again supplemented gazetteer of Kao-yu chou). 1883.

Ts'ai Shen-chih 蔡申之. *Ch'ing-tai chou-hsien ku-shih* 清代州縣故事 (The chou and hsien administration in Ch'ing times). Hong Kong, Lung-men shu-tien, 1968.

Tseng Kuo-fan 曾國藩. *Tseng Kuo-fan wei-k'an hsin-kao* 曾國藩未刊信稿 (Unpublished letters of Tseng Kuo-fan). Comp. Chiang Shih-jung 江世榮. Shanghai, Chung-hua shu-chü, 1959.

——. *Hsiang-hsiang Tseng-shih wen-hsien* 湘鄉曾氏文獻 (Documents of Mr. Tseng from Hsiang-hsiang). Taipei, 1965.

——. *Tseng Kuo-fan p'i-tu* 曾國藩批牘 (Tseng Kuo-fan's orders and comments to his subordinates). Taipei, 1969. Facsimile reproduction of 1876 edition.

——. *Tseng Wen-cheng kung ch'üan-chi, Tsou-kao* 曾文正公全集奏稿 (Tseng Kuo-fan's memorials). Shanghai, Shih-chieh shu-chü, 1937.

Tsung-li ko-kuo shih-wu ya-men ch'ing-tang 總理各國事務衙門清檔 (Archives ["clean copies"] of the Tsungli Yamen). (*CT*)

Chiao-wu pu 教務部 (Section on missionary affairs). *Kiangsu chiao-wu* 江蘇教務 (Missionary problems in Kiangsu). (*KCW*)

T'ung-chih Hsu-chou fu-chih 同治徐州府志 (The T'ung-chih period gazetteer of Hsu-chou prefecture). 1874.

T'ung-chih Shang-hai hsien-chih 同治上海縣志 (The T'ung-chih period gazetteer of Shanghai hsien). 1871.

T'ung-chou chih-li chou-chih 通州直隸州志 (The gazetteer for the independent department of T'ung-chou). 1876.

T'ung-shan hsien-chih 銅山縣志 (The gazetteer of T'ung-shan hsien). 1923.

Wakeman, Frederic. *Strangers at the Gate: Social Disorder in South China, 1839–1861*. Berkeley, University of California Press, 1966.

Wan-an hsien-chih 萬安縣志 (The gazetteer of Wan-an [Kiangsi] hsien). 1877.

Wan Kuo-ting 萬國鼎 et al., *Chiang-su Wu-chin Nan-t'ung t'ien-fu tiao-ch'a pao-kao* 江蘇武進南通田賦調查報告 (Report on the investigation of the land tax in Kiangsu's Wu-chin and Nan-t'ung hsien). 1934.

Wan Wei-han 萬維翰. "Mu-hsueh chü-yao" 幕學舉要 (Essentials for studying to be a *mu-yu*) in Chang T'ing-hsiang, ed., *Ju-mu hsu-chih wu-chung* (Five essential works for entering a *mu-fu*). 1890 preface. Taiwan reprint.

Wang Ch'ing-yun 王慶雲. *Hsi-ch'ao chi-cheng* 熙朝紀政 (A political record of our glorious dynasty). Alternate title, *Shih-ch'ü yü-chi* (Reminiscences of Mr. Shih-ch'ü). 1898.

Wang Erh-min 王爾敏. *Huai-chün chih* 淮軍志 (The Huai Army). Taipei, 1967.

Wang Hsiao-ch'uan 王曉傳 ed., *Yuan Ming Ch'ing san-tai chin-hui hsiao-shuo chü-ch'ü shih-liao* 元明清三代禁毀小說戲曲史料 (Historical materials on the proscription of novels and plays in the Yuan, Ming, and Ch'ing dynasties). Peking, Tso-chia ch'u-pan she, 1958.

Wang Jen-k'an 王仁堪. *Wang Su-chou i-shu* 王蘇州遺書 (Posthumous papers of Mr. Wang of Soochow). 1934 preface. Taipei reprint.

Wang P'ei-t'ang 王培堂. *Chiang-su sheng hsiang-t'u chih* 江蘇省鄉土志 (A gazetteer of Kiangsu province). Shanghai, Commercial Press, 1938.

Wang Ping-hsieh 王炳燮. *Wu-tzu ch'i-shih wen-chi* 毋自欺室文集 (Wang Ping-hsieh's collected writings). 1885 preface. Taipei reprint.

Wang Ting-an 王定安. *Ch'iu-ch'ueh chai ti-tzu chi* 求闕齋弟自記 (Notes from a disciple of Ch'iu-ch'ueh Study). 1876 preface.

Wang Yeh-chien. "The Impact of the Taiping Rebellion on Population in Southern Kiangsu," *Papers on China*, 19:120–158 (1965).

——. *Land Taxation in Imperial China, 1750–1911*. Cambridge, Harvard University Press, 1973.

Ward, Barbara. "Varieties of the Conscious Model: The Fishermen of South China," in Michael Banton, ed., *The Relevance of Models for Social Anthropology*. New York, Frederick A. Praeger, 1965.

Watt, John R. *The District Magistrate in Late Imperial China*. New York, Columbia University Press, 1972.

Wei Ch'ing-yuan 韦庆远. *Ming-tai huang-ts'e chih-tu* 明代黄册制度 (The Ming system of Yellow Registers). Shanghai, Chung-hua shu-chü, 1961.

Weiss, Robert N. "Flexibility in Provincial Government on the Eve of the Taiping Rebellion," *Ch'ing-shih wen-t'i*, 4.3:1–42 (June 1980).

Wen Chou-ming 温舟銘. "Kwangtung hsin t'ung-chih lieh-chuan kao Ting Jih-ch'ang" 廣東新通志例傳丁日昌 (Draft biography of Ting Jih-ch'ang for the new Kwangtung provincial gazetteer), *Kuo-li Chung-shan ta-hsueh wen-shih-hsueh yen-chiu-so yueh-k'an*, 2.5:115–128 (1934).

Wolf, Arthur, and Chieh-shan Huang. *Marriage and Adoption in China, 1845–1945*. Stanford, Stanford University Press, 1980.

Woodside, Alex. "Family Education in Eighteenth Century China," Harvard New England China Seminar, April 1974. Unpublished manuscript.

Wright, Mary C. *The Last Stand of Chinese Conservatism: The T'ung-chih Restoration, 1862–1874*. New York, Atheneum, 1966.

Wu-chiang hsien-chih 吳江縣志 (The gazetteer of Wu-chiang hsien). 1879.

Wu-hsi Chin-kuei hsien-chih 無錫金匱縣志 (Gazetteer of Wu-hsi and Chin-kuei hsiens). 1881.

Wu hsien-chih 吳縣志 (The gazetteer of Wu hsien). 1933.

Wu-Yang chih-yü 武陽志餘 (Supplement to the gazetteer of Wu-chin and Yang-hu). 1888.

Wu Pao-san 巫寶三 et al., eds., *Chung-kuo chin-tai ching-chi ssu-hsiang yü ching-chi cheng-ts'e tzu-liao hsuan-chi* 中國近代經濟思想與經濟政策資料 (Selected materials on China's economic thought and policy in modern times). Peking, 1959.

Wu Yun 吳雲. *Liang-lei-hsuan ch'ih-tu* 兩罍軒尺牘 (Letters from Two-Jar Pavilion). Taipei reprint. 1884.

——, comp. *Te-i lu* 得一錄 (Records of a purist). Shanghai, 1869. Taipei reprint.

Ya Erh-t'u 雅爾圖. *Ya-kung-hsin cheng-lu* 雅公心政錄 (The political records of Ya Erh-t'u). 1741.

Yang, C. K. *Religion in Chinese Society*. Berkeley, University of California Press, 1967.

Yeh Meng-chu 葉夢珠. *Yueh-shih pien* 閱世編 (A survey of the age), in Shanghai T'ung-she, comp., *Shanghai chang-ku ts'ung-shu* (A collectanea of historical materials of Shanghai). Shanghai, 1936.

Yuan Shou-ting 袁守定. *T'u-min lu* 圖民錄 (Planning for the people). 1836.

Glossary

Characters for people in Hummel, places in Playfair, or titles and ranks in Brunnert and Hagelstrom are not included.

an-chien 案件

ch'ai-i 差役
ch'ai-kuan 差館
ch'ai-tien 差墊
ch'ao-t'ing te-shih 朝廷得失
chen 鎮
cheng-tung 正董
ch'eng-po 丞簿
cheng-t'u 正徒
chi-o shu-shen 嫉惡殊甚
chi-shan yü-ch'ing 積善餘慶
chi pu-shan yü ts'an
積不善餘殃

chi ta-kuo 記大過
ch'i tzu t'ien-jen 起自田人
chia-chang 甲長
ch'iang-ch'uan 槍船
chiao 教
chiao-yang 教養
chiao-yü 教諭
chieh-ch'ang 節場
ch'ih-k'uei 吃虧
ch'ih-t'ang 赤堂
ch'ih-tzu 赤子
ch'in-ch'i 侵欺
ch'in-k'uei 侵虧
ch'in-min kuan 親民官
ching-k'ung 京控
ching-shih 經世
ching-tsao 經造
ch'ing-chieh t'ang 清節堂
ch'ing-i 清議
ch'ing-ming 清明
chiu-ti cheng-fa 就地政法

ch'iu chin-kung 求近功
ch'iu-ling hu 坵領户
chu-ming wan-hu 著名頑户
ch'u-fen 處分
ch'u-shen 出身
chü 聚
chü-piao 拘票
ch'uan-ch'eng 傳呈
ch'uan-piao 傳票
chüan-t'an 捐攤
chuang 莊
chuang-shou 莊首
chun 准
chün-t'ien chün-i 均田均役
ch'ung 衝

fa 法
fan 繁
fa-shen chü 發審局
fei-sai 飛灑
fei-wei liang-wu t'e-tung chi 非為兩無特腞計
fen-fa chih-fu 分發知府
feng-shui 風水
feng-tien 封典
fou-shou 浮收
fu 福
Fu-i ch'üan-shu 賦役全書
fu-mu kuan 父母官
fu-tung 副董
fu-tzu 撫字

han-ch'eng 喊呈
hou-pu 候補
Hsi-yuan lu 洗寃錄
hsia-hu 下户
hsiang 鄉
hsiang-kuei 鄉櫃
hsiang-tung 鄉董
hsiang-yueh 鄉約
Hsiao-ching 孝經
Hsiao-hsueh 小學
hsiao-hu 小户
hsiao-jen 肖人
hsieh-tou 械鬥
hsien 賢
hsien-liang 賢良
hsing 刑
hsing-fa 刑法
hsu-li hui 恤嫠會
hsun-chien 巡檢
Hu-ch'un pai-shih 呼春稗史
hu-ling ch'iu 户領坵
hua 化
huang-fei 荒費
Huang ts'e 黄册
hung-mien 紅棉

i 役
i-chih yu-tan 易知由單
i-hsueh 義學
i-kun 蟻棍

i li-hsueh wei tzu-ming 以理學為自名
i-t'u 義圖

jen-lun 人倫
jou-shih-che pi 肉食者鄙
juo-shui 弱水

k'ao-ch'eng 考成
k'ao-t'ien t'ien 靠天田
Kiangsu shu-chü 江蘇書局
ko-chih 革職
ko-k'ou 各口
k'o-jen 客人
kou-an 苟安
kuan ch'i k'ou 関其口
kuei-chi 詭寄
k'uei-lei 傀儡
k'uei-shen 鬼神
kung-chü ts'un-tung 公舉村董
kung-ming 功命
kung-tsui 公罪
kuo-chi 國計
kuo-pao 果報

lan-na 攬納
lao-tsai t'u 老災圖
li 禮
li-chia 里甲
li-chiao 禮教
lü-hsi chiao-ts'o 履舃交錯
li-hsueh chih-jen 理學之人
li-ts'ai 理財
liang-min 良民
liao-shu 僚屬
lieh-shen 劣紳
lieh-tung 劣董
liu-liang tai-pu 留糧代補
liu-min 流民
lou-kuei 陋規

ma-shih pai-hsing 蟊食百姓
men-ting 門丁
mi-yun pu-yü 密雲不雨
min 民
min chih yu tung pu-chih yu kuan 民知有董,不知有官
min-sheng 民生
mou 畝
mu-fu 幕府
mu-yu 幕友

nai fan-lao 耐煩勞
nan 難
nei-chien 內監

nei-luan 内亂
neng 能
ni 溺
niao-ch'iang 鳥槍
niu-chiao chih-chiao 扭交指交
no-i ch'ien-liang 挪移錢糧
no-tien 挪墊
nu 奴
nu-p'u 奴僕

pai-che pu hui 百折不回
pa-ku 八股
Pa-mei t'u 八美圖
pai ma-i 白螞蟻
pan-fang 班方
p'an-t'u 版圖
pao-chia 保甲
pao-lan 包攬
pao-ying hui 保嬰會
p'ao-fu 跑夫
pei 婢
p'i 痞
po 駁
pu-ch'eng ta-fu 不成大夫
pu-chih tsu 不知足
pu-liu jen yü-ti 不留人餘地
pu-chün t'ung-ling ya-men 步軍統領衙門
p'u 舖
p'u-ping 舖兵
p'u-ssu 舖司

sai 塞
sai-chu 塞主
sai-tung 塞董
sha-chou tsung-chü 沙州總局
sha-kun 沙棍
sha-tung 沙董
shan-t'ang 善堂
shang-hsia 上下
shang-hsia i-t'i 上下一體
shang-hu 上户
shang-k'ung 上控
shao-hsiang hui 燒香會
she-hsueh 社學
she-mu 社木
shen 紳
shen-chin 紳搢
Shen Pao 申報
shen-tung 紳董
sheng 生
sheng-chien 生監
Sheng-yü kuang-hsun 聖諭廣訓
shih 識
shih-k'uei 市儈
shih-lun 時論
shih-min 士民
shih-nien sheng-chü 十年生聚

shih-shen 士紳
shih-yung 試用
shou-liu tzu-sung hui-chi chü 收留資送回籍局
shu 恕
shu-yuan 書院
shui-ying 水影
shui-ying kuang-t'an 水影光灘
shun-chuang 順莊
ssu-she pan-kuan 私設班館
ssu-tsui 私罪
sui-k'ao 歲考
sung-kun 訟棍

ta-chi 大計
ta-hu 大户
t'ai-ch'iang 擡槍
tai-li 代理
t'an-chüan 攤捐
t'an-ch'üan 貪泉
t'ao-yu 謟諛
ti-hsiao 抵銷
ti-pao 地保
ti-ting 地丁
tien-wan 墊完
ts'ao-liang 漕糧
ts'ao-shu 漕書
tso-ch'ai 坐差
tso-erh 佐貳
tso-tsa 佐雜
tsu 阻
ts'ui-k'o 催科
ts'un 村
ts'un-tung 村董
tu 都
t'u 圖
t'u-cheng 圖正
t'u-hao 土豪
t'u-tung 土董
t'uan-lien 團練
t'ung 通
tzu-hsin 自新
tzu-li tz'u-sung 自理詞訟
tzu-ming ho-teng 自命何等
tzu-shou mien-tsui chih-li 自首免罪之例

wai-chien 外監
wai-huan 外患
wang-shui sheng-k'o 望水升科
wei-che chang-shih shih-cho; mi-che chieh-chih shih hsuan 微者彰之使,祕者揭之使宣
wei-yuan 委員
wen-chiao 文教

ya-i 衙役
ya-so 押所
yang-ch'i yuan 養齊院
yang-huo kung-so 洋貨公所
yang-lien 養廉
yang-wu 洋務

yao-chan 腰站
yen-an jen-tu 晏安酖毒
yin-chu 淫祝
yin-hsun 因循
yin-ssu 淫詞
ying-i 嬰醫
ying-shen sai-hui 迎神賽會
yu chih-jen wu chih-fa 有治人無治法
yu-i tzu-hsin chih-lu 予以自新之路
yu-min 莠民
yu-yü 寓於
yu-yung 游勇
yü 圩
yü-chia 圩甲
Yü-lin ts'e 魚鱗冊
yü-tung 圩董
yü-ying t'ang 育嬰堂
yuan-fu 怨府
yueh-k'ung 越控
yueh-su 越訴
yueh-sung 越訟

Personal Names

Chang Chin 張溍
Chang Na-t'ai 張那泰
Chang Yao-tung 張兆棟
Chu Chih-chen 朱之榛
Ho Kuang-lun 何光綸
Huang Shou-ch'en 黄守臣
Ko Sheng-hsiao 葛繩孝
Kuo Po-yin 郭柏蔭
Li Chang-yü 李璋煜
Lin Ta-ch'üan 林大泉
Shen Hsi-hua 沈錫華
Sung T'ing 松亭
Ting Chi-tsu 丁繼祖
Ting Hsien-pa 丁賢拔
Ting Hui-heng 丁惠衡
Ting Pin 丁炳
Tu Wen-lan 杜文瀾
Wang K'ai-t'ai 王凱泰
Wang Ta-ching 王大經
Wang Tsung-lien 王宗濂
Yen Tuan-shu 宴端書
Ying Pao-shih 應寶時
Yuan Shou-ting 袁保定

Index

Harvard East Asian Monographs

1. Liang Fang-chung, *The Single-Whip Method of Taxation in China*
2. Harold C. Hinton, *The Grain Tribute System of China, 1845–1911*
3. Ellsworth C. Carlson, *The Kaiping Mines, 1877–1912*
4. Chao Kuo-chün, *Agrarian Policies of Mainland China: A Documentary Study, 1949–1956*
5. Edgar Snow, *Random Notes on Red China, 1936–1945*
6. Edwin George Beal, Jr., *The Origin of Likin, 1835–1864*
7. Chao Kuo-chün, *Economic Planning and Organization in Mainland China: A Documentary Study, 1949–1957*
8. John K. Fairbank, *Ch'ing Documents: An Introductory Syllabus*
9. Helen Yin and Yi-chang Yin, *Economic Statistics of Mainland China, 1949–1957*
10. Wolfgang Franke, *The Reform and Abolition of the Traditional Chinese Examination System*
11. Albert Feuerwerker and S. Cheng, *Chinese Communist Studies of Modern Chinese History*
12. C. John Stanley, *Late Ch'ing Finance: Hu Kuang-yung as an Innovator*
13. S. M. Meng, *The Tsungli Yamen: Its Organization and Functions*
14. Ssu-yü Teng, *Historiography of the Taiping Rebellion*
15. Chun-Jo Liu, *Controversies in Modern Chinese Intellectual History: An Analytic Bibliography of Periodical Articles, Mainly of the May Fourth and Post-May Fourth Era*
16. Edward J. M. Rhoads, *The Chinese Red Army, 1927–1963: An Annotated Bibliography*
17. Andrew J. Nathan, *A History of the China International Famine Relief Commission*
18. Frank H. H. King (ed.) and Prescott Clarke, *A Research Guide to China-Coast Newspapers, 1822–1911*
19. Ellis Joffe, *Party and Army: Professionalism and Political Control in the Chinese Officer Corps, 1949–1964*
20. Toshio G. Tsukahira, *Feudal Control in Tokugawa Japan: The Sankin Kōtai System*

21. Kwang-Ching Liu, ed., *American Missionaries in China: Papers from Harvard Seminars*
22. George Moseley, *A Sino-Soviet Cultural Frontier: The Ili Kazakh Autonomous Chou*
23. Carl F. Nathan, *Plague Prevention and Politics in Manchuria, 1910–1931*
24. Adrian Arthur Bennett, *John Fryer: The Introduction of Western Science and Technology into Nineteenth-Century China*
25. Donald J. Friedman, *The Road from Isolation: The Campaign of the American Committee for Non-Participation in Japanese Aggression, 1938–1941*
26. Edward Le Fevour, *Western Enterprise in Late Ch'ing China: A Selective Survey of Jardine, Matheson and Company's Operations, 1842–1895*
27. Charles Neuhauser, *Third World Politics: China and the Afro-Asian People's Solidarity Organization, 1957–1967*
28. Kungtu C. Sun, assisted by Ralph W. Huenemann, *The Economic Development of Manchuria in the First Half of the Twentieth Century*
29. Shahid Javed Burki, *A Study of Chinese Communes, 1965*
30. John Carter Vincent, *The Extraterritorial System in China: Final Phase*
31. Madeleine Chi, *China Diplomacy, 1914–1918*
32. Clifton Jackson Phillips, *Protestant America and the Pagan World: The First Half Century of the American Board of Commissioners for Foreign Missions, 1810–1860*
33. James Pusey, *Wu Han: Attacking the Present through the Past*
34. Ying-wan Cheng, *Postal Communication in China and Its Modernization, 1860–1896*
35. Tuvia Blumenthal, *Saving in Postwar Japan*
36. Peter Frost, *The Bakumatsu Currency Crisis*
37. Stephen C. Lockwood, *Augustine Heard and Company, 1858–1862*
38. Robert R. Campbell, *James Duncan Campbell: A Memoir by His Son*
39. Jerome Alan Cohen, ed., *The Dynamics of China's Foreign Relations*
40. V. V. Vishnyakova-Akimova, *Two Years in Revolutionary China, 1925–1927*, tr. Steven I. Levine
41. Meron Medzini, *French Policy in Japan during the Closing Years of the Tokugawa Regime*
42. *The Cultural Revolution in the Provinces*
43. Sidney A. Forsythe, *An American Missionary Community in China, 1895–1905*
44. Benjamin I. Schwartz, ed., *Reflections on the May Fourth Movement: A Symposium*
45. Ching Young Choe, *The Rule of the Taewŏn'gun, 1864–1873: Restoration in Yi Korea*

46. W. P. J. Hall, *A Bibliographical Guide to Japanese Research on the Chinese Economy, 1958–1970*
47. Jack J. Gerson, *Horatio Nelson Lay and Sino-British Relations, 1854–1864*
48. Paul Richard Bohr, *Famine and the Missionary: Timothy Richard as Relief Administrator and Advocate of National Reform*
49. Endymion Wilkinson, *The History of Imperial China: A Research Guide*
50. Britten Dean, *China and Great Britain: The Diplomacy of Commerical Relations, 1860–1864*
51. Ellsworth C. Carlson, *The Foochow Missionaries, 1847–1880*
52. Yeh-chien Wang, *An Estimate of the Land-Tax Collection in China, 1753 and 1908*
53. Richard M. Pfeffer, *Understanding Business Contracts in China, 1949–1963*
54. Han-sheng Chuan and Richard Kraus, *Mid-Ch'ing Rice Markets and Trade, An Essay in Price History*
55. Ranbir Vohra, *Lao She and the Chinese Revolution*
56. Liang-lin Hsiao, *China's Foreign Trade Statistics, 1864–1949*
57. Lee-hsia Hsu Ting, *Government Control of the Press in Modern China, 1900–1949*
58. Edward W. Wagner, *The Literati Purges: Political Conflict in Early Yi Korea*
59. Joungwon A. Kim, *Divided Korea: The Politics of Development, 1945–1972*
60. Noriko Kamachi, John K. Fairbank, and Chūzō Ichiko, *Japanese Studies of Modern China Since 1953: A Bibliographical Guide to Historical and Social-Science Research on the Nineteenth and Twentieth Centuries, Supplementary Volume for 1953–1969*
61. Donald A. Gibbs and Yun-chen Li, *A Bibliography of Studies and Translations of Modern Chinese Literature, 1918–1942*
62. Robert H. Silin, *Leadership and Values: The Organization of Large-Scale Taiwanese Enterprises*
63. David Pong, *A Critical Guide to the Kwangtung Provincial Archives Deposited at the Public Record Office of London*
64. Fred W. Drake, *China Charts the World: Hsu Chi-yü and His Geography of 1848*
65. William A. Brown and Urgunge Onon, translators and annotators, *History of the Mongolian People's Republic*
66. Edward L. Farmer, *Early Ming Government: The Evolution of Dual Capitals*
67. Ralph C. Croizier, *Koxinga and Chinese Nationalism: History, Myth, and the Hero*
68. William J. Tyler, tr., *The Psychological World of Natsumi Sōseki*, by Doi Takeo

69. Eric Widmer, *The Russian Ecclesiastical Mission in Peking during the Eighteenth Century*
70. Charlton M. Lewis, *Prologue to the Chinese Revolution: The Transformation of Ideas and Institutions in Hunan Province, 1891–1907*
71. Preston Torbert, *The Ch'ing Imperial Household Department: A Study of its Organization and Principal Functions, 1662–1796*
72. Paul A. Cohen and John E. Schrecker, eds., *Reform in Nineteenth-Century China*
73. Jon Sigurdson, *Rural Industrialization in China*
74. Kang Chao, *The Development of Cotton Textile Production in China*
75. Valentin Rabe, *The Home Base of American China Missions, 1880–1920*
76. Sarasin Viraphol, *Tribute and Profit: Sino-Siamese Trade, 1652–1853*
77. Ch'i-ch'ing Hsiao, *The Military Establishment of the Yuan Dynasty*
78. Meishi Tsai, *Contemporary Chinese Novels and Short Stories, 1949–1974: An Annotated Bibliography*
79. Wellington K. K. Chan, *Merchants, Mandarins, and Modern Enterprise in Late Ch'ing China*
80. Endymion Wilkinson, *Landlord and Labor in Late Imperial China: Case Studies from Shandong by Jing Su and Luo Lun*
81. Barry Keenan, *The Dewey Experiment in China: Educational Reform and Political Power in the Early Republic*
82. George A. Hayden, *Crime and Punishment in Medieval Chinese Drama: Three Judge Pao Plays*
83. Sang-Chul Suh, *Growth and Structural Changes in the Korean Economy, 1910–1940*
84. J. W. Dower, *Empire and Aftermath: Yoshida Shigeru and the Japanese Experience, 1878–1954*
85. Martin Collcutt, *Five Mountains: The Rinzai Zen Monastic Institution in Medieval Japan*

STUDIES IN THE MODERNIZATION OF THE REPUBLIC OF KOREA: 1945–1975

86. Kwang Suk Kim and Michael Roemer, *Growth and Structural Transformation*
87. Anne O. Krueger, *The Developmental Role of the Foreign Sector and Aid*
88. Edwin S. Mills and Byung-Nak Song, *Urbanization and Urban Problems*
89. Sung Hwan Ban, Pal Yong Moon, and Dwight H. Perkins, *Rural Development*

90. Noel F. McGinn, Donald R. Snodgrass, Yung Bong Kim, Shin-Bok Kim, and Quee-Young Kim, *Education and Development in Korea*
91. Leroy P. Jones and Il SaKong, *Government, Business, and Entrepreneurship in Economic Development: The Korean Case*
92. Edward S. Mason, Dwight H. Perkins, Kwang Suk Kim, David C. Cole, Mahn Je Kim, et al., *The Economic and Social Modernization of the Republic of Korea*
93. Robert Repetto, Tai Hwan Kwon, Son-Ung Kim, Dae Young Kim, John E. Sloboda, and Peter J. Donaldson, *Economic Development, Population Policy, and Demographic Transition in the Republic of Korea*
94. Parks M. Coble, *The Shanghai Capitalists and the Nationalist Government, 1927–1937*
95. Noriko Kamachi, *Reform in China: Huang Tsun-hsien and the Japanese Model*
96. Richard Wich, *Sino-Soviet Crisis Politics: A Study of Political Change and Communication*
97. Lillian M. Li, *China's Silk Trade: Traditional Industry in the Modern World, 1842–1937*
98. R. David Arkush, *Fei Xiaotong and Sociology in Revolutionary China*
99. Kenneth Alan Grossberg, *Japan's Renaissance: The Politics of the Muromachi Bakufu*
101. Hoyt Cleveland Tillman, *Utilitarian Confucianism: Ch'en Liang's Challenge to Chu Hsi*
102. Thomas A. Stanley, *Ōsugi Sakae, Anarchist in Taishō Japan: The Creativity of the Ego*
103. Jonathan K. Ocko, *Bureaucratic Reform in Provincial China: Ting Jih-ch'ang in Restoration Kiangsu, 1867–1870*
104. James Reed, *The Missionary Mind and American East Asia Policy, 1911–1915*